Psychology for the Fighting Man

Prepared for the Fighting Man Himself
By a Committee of the
NATIONAL RESEARCH COUNCIL
with the Collaboration of
SCIENCE SERVICE
as a Contribution to the War Effort

Martino Fine Books
Eastford, CT
2019

Martino Fine Books
P.O. Box 913,
Eastford, CT 06242 USA

ISBN   978-1-68422-364-0

Copyright 2019
Martino Fine Books

Cover Design Tiziana Matarazzo

Printed in the United States of America On 100% Acid-Free Paper

Psychology for the Fighting Man

Prepared for the Fighting Man Himself
By a Committee of the
NATIONAL RESEARCH COUNCIL
with the Collaboration of
SCIENCE SERVICE
as a Contribution to the War Effort

WASHINGTON

THE INFANTRY JOURNAL

Collaborators

G. W. Allport, Harvard University

T. G. Alper, Harvard University

J. W. Appel, M.D., Pennsylvania Hospital

Kenneth Appel, M.D., Pennsylvania Hospital

H. P. Bechtoldt, Personnel Procedures Section, War Department

J. G. Beebe-Center, Harvard University

W. V. Bingham, Personnel Procedures Section, War Department

C. S. Bird, University of Minnesota

E. G. Boring, Harvard University

R. D. Churchill, Personnel Procedures Section, War Department

B. J. Covner, University of Pennsylvania

A. L. Edwards, Office of War Information

R. N. Faulkner, Personnel Procedures Section, War Department

C. A. Federer Jr., Harvard College Observatory

J. E. Finesinger, M.D., Massachusetts General Hospital

Lt. Col. Verne C. Fryklund, Teacher Training Department, Armored Force School

John Gorsuch, University of Pennsylvania

C. H. Graham, Brown University

Colonel Joseph I. Greene, Infantry Journal

E. R. Guthrie, University of Washington

Roscoe Hall, M.D., St. Elizabeth's Hospital, Washington, D.C.

J. S. Harding, Office of Public Opinion Research

Major T. W. Harrell, Personnel Procedures Section, War Department

R. R. Holt, Harvard University

Colonel George H. Horkan, Quartermaster School, Camp Lee, Va.

J. McV. Hunt, Brown University

L. M. Hurvich, Harvard University

Captain E. L. Jacques, M.D., Department of National Defense, Canada

Ben Karpman, M.D., St. Elizabeth's Hospital, Washington, D.C.

R. H. Knapp, Office of Strategic Services

A. W. Kornhauser, University of Chicago

H. S. Langfeld, Princeton University

D. W. MacKinnon, Bryn Mawr College

W. R. Miles, Yale University

C. T. Morgan, Harvard University

O. H. Mowrer, Harvard University

R. A. H. Mueller, University of Pennsylvania

Colonel E. L. Munson Jr., Special Services Division, War Department

H. A. Murray, Harvard University

H. S. Odbert, National Research Council

Lieut. Carl Pfaffman, U. S. Naval Reserve

S. T. Possony, Princeton University

Brig. Gen. Guy I. Rowe, Quartermaster Replacement Training Center, Camp Lee, Va.

G. R. Schmeidler, Harvard University

C. F. Scofield, Office of Strategic Services

6

R. R. Sears, State University of Iowa

Harold Silverstein, M.D., Military Training Division, Quartermaster Corps

Colonel Elam L. Stewart, Quartermaster Replacement Training Center, Camp Lee, Va.

S. A. Stouffer, Special Services Division, War Department

Lieut. F. W. Swift, Psychological Research Unit 1, Army Air Forces

F. V. Taylor, Princeton University

A. S. Thompson, University of Pennsylvania

Marjorie Van de Water, Science Service

M. S. Viteles, University of Pennsylvania

Corporal J. L. Wallen, Psychological Research Unit 1, Army Air Forces

C. H. Wedell, Princeton University

G. R. Wendt, Wesleyan University

E. G. Wever, Princeton University

Kimball Young, Queens College.

The opinions and assertions contained in this book are the private ones of the collaborators and editors and are not to be construed as official or reflecting the views of the U. S. Army or the U. S. Navy or any of the armed or government services at large.

Responsibility for the text in its final form is assumed by E. G. Boring, Harvard University, and M. Van de Water, Science Service.

Contents

Chapter		Page
I:	Psychology and Combat	11
II:	Sight as a Weapon	24
III:	Seeing in the Dark	60
IV:	Color and Camouflage	76
V:	Hearing as a Tool in Warfare	114
VI:	Smell—A Sentry	142
VII:	The Sense of Position and the Sense of Direction	151
VIII:	The Right Soldier in the Right Job	175
IX:	Training Makes the Soldier	200
X:	How the Army Teaches	227
XI:	Efficiency in the Army	244
XII:	Heat, Cold, Oxygen and Stimulants	268
XIII:	Morale	285
XIV:	Food and Sex as Military Problems	333
XV:	The Soldier's Personal Adjustment	343
XVI:	Leadership	366
XVII:	Mobs and Panic	385
XVIII:	Differences Among Races and Peoples	397
XIX:	Rumor	413
XX:	Psychological Warfare	431
	Index	448

NOTE TO THE READER

This book tells all about military psychology. It is prepared from manuscripts written by experts, but it has been rewritten in popular form without sacrifice of its scientific accuracy. What it says is as true as scientists can make it today.

Military psychology is, however, a very broad field. This book starts in with the psychology of the proper uses of your sense-organs in war—your eyes, your ears, your nose, your organs of balance. It tells about the aptitudes and abilities of soldiers for the many jobs to which the Army may assign them, and how soldiers actually are assigned to different jobs. It discusses efficiency, both physical and psychological. It tells about morale and emotion, about the effects and control of fear and anger, about how men's motives help them or hurt them as soldiers. It discusses leadership, panic, rumor, propaganda, psychological warware.

YOU DO NOT HAVE TO READ THE CHAPTERS IN THE ORDER IN WHICH THEY ARE PRINTED. Almost every chapter makes sense by itself. Look at the table of contents and turn to the chapter that interests you most. Try it out on yourself. Then try another chapter. Perhaps you will want to read all the chapters if you start in that way. Or perhaps you will keep the book with you, and read the chapter on Seeing in the Dark, for instance, when you are first assigned to night patrol duty.

I: PSYCHOLOGY AND COMBAT

WHEN THE BRITISH EIGHTH ARMY pursued the retreating Axis forces from Egypt through Libya, they found along the route great quantities of abandoned equipment—some tanks and guns in perfect condition, and gasoline for the tanks and ammunition for the guns. The physical matériel of a large Axis force was there, but it was useless to the Axis. There were no men left to operate it.

You keep hearing it said that men cannot fight without weapons, but it is just as true that weapons cannot fight without men. An army *is* men. Not any men at all, for a crowd of men may be only a mob. But trained and equipped men.

What sort of equipment do the men of an army need? Planes, tanks, guns, and jeeps. Mortars, grenades, rifles, and bayonets. Camouflage and mess-kits. Above all food and water. Everything that the Ordnance and the Q.M. can supply. But that is not all.

No, the men need morale. They need courage. They must have confidence in each other and the belief in ultimate victory. Who is the Q.M. who can issue stocks of courage and confidence? Yet these are essential weapons.

And the Army must have leaders, too. Plenty of them. CO's and NCO's. Who supplies them?

Besides leaders it must have all sorts of special abilities and skills. Mechanical ability in particular is needed in this new mechanized war. Ability to drive trucks. Pilot ability. Mathematical ability. Cooking ability. Clerks' skills. Lots and lots of abilities. You can't fight a war without them.

The Army needs efficiency, too, and efficiency means not only effective organization. There is also the basic efficiency of the individual man—his strength and health, his resistance to hardship and fatigue, his alertness even when fatigued and despite freezing cold or exhausting heat. Toughness of body is a weapon indispensable to victory.

Are there still other essential weapons? Yes. The eye is a basic weapon. Good eyes are essential, though soldiers must learn how to use them to the best advantage, how to get the most out of them. Good ears are necessary, too. Could a totally deaf army ever win a battle? Good noses help sometimes too when war gases are around, and all the other senses also play their parts in fighting. A pilot needs to know when he is right side up, and that depends on an organ in his inner ear. The enemy and our own men are born with just about the same equipment in sense organs. But the victory will probably go to those who know how to make use of them best.

In other words, the Army has a perpetual problem of psychological logistics, a problem of the supply of motives and emotions, of aptitudes and abilities, of habits and wisdom, of trained eyes and educated ears. How does it get this mental matériel to the right places at the right time? That is what this book is about.

It gets them, of course, by selection and by training. It selects the best men for every job first. If the Army cannot find a man with needed ability, an

12

effort is made to find one with an aptitude for being trained in that ability. And then it trains them all —in part by teaching them the rules and the techniques, in part by giving them practice. No troops are ready to go into combat until their training period is over, and even then they are still green troops. The training is still going on in combat until finally the men are seasoned troops, have learned how to meet the unexpected emergencies of war, have acquired that competence and confidence that is the basis of their courage.

It is this human matériel that determines more than any other one thing whether an army will win or lose. Guns and chow are essential too, but, given equality of supply, victory goes to the better troops, troops composed of men who know their jobs and do them willingly and well, men with initiative to act by themselves, the trained troops which make up the seasoned army.

There are, moreover, fundamental differences between peoples that affect their ways of fighting and their abilities to fight. These differences are not, however, due to "blood," as the Nazis teach, but mostly to training, tradition, home life and other things that have a powerful effect on the character of men. War is waged best by choosing methods of warfare best adapted to the nature of our own people and opposed to the natures of the enemy peoples.

American men have no particular love of killing. For the most part they hate killing—they think it is wrong, sinful, ordinarily punishable by death. They do not look upon death as a beautiful and glorious experience, and most of them do not consider the military life as being a suitable life work.

War, to American men, is a dirty, disagreeable business, to be gotten over as soon as possible so that we, as a nation, can get along with what we were happily engrossed in—inventing, producing, growing, making life more useful and satisfying.

Well, German soldiers would like to see the war over quickly, too, but for a different reason. A blitzkrieg is to the great advantage of the Axis for the same reason that a long war is to the advantage of the United Nations. It takes time for a citizen army to get mobilized up to full strength and to be adequately trained. It takes more time for industries, built for producing the goods of peace and good living, to convert and be tooled up for mass production of the tools of war in the American way. It takes time to get men and matériel to the scattered places where the enemy has attacked.

And it takes time, too, for a peace-loving nation, a nation brought up in the tradition of treating other peoples as friends, not rivals—as business associates, not gangsters—to build up the mighty wave of indignation that is required to wipe out an attacking enemy.

But Americans can stand a long, hard pull. They look forward, not back. They are slow to accept war, will not go all out for one until they are attacked or are sure their ideals are in grave danger. But once they have started, they do not stop or spare themselves until the goal of victory seems to them to be secure. Perhaps in 1919 they made a mistake about having already made the world safe for democracy, but they would not have stopped had they

14

not thought themselves safe. Nor will they stop now.

They are not demoralized by temporary adversity or single defeats.

It has been said that war is inevitable, that men are so made that they just have to fight. That is true if you mean they have to be aggressive, that they need to have power and to use it, that they are forever wanting to change things that are hard to change so as to get on with better living. But the fact is that they do not have to fight each other, and not many Americans agree with Hitler in thinking fighting other nations a good thing for any nation—even when the ugly business ends in victory.

There are other things than men and nations to fight. Men can fight calamity and disaster—flood, fire and famine—with anger and zest, can even fight nature to prevent disasters happening. They fight disease, having for a century been waging effective war upon it with the innumerable conquests which history now records. They fight for freedom—freedom to worship as they wish, freedom to think and speak as they please, freedom from want and poverty, freedom from fear. This kind of fighting goes on between wars as well as in war. You've got to fight if you are going to have the kind of life you want, but you do not have to fight to keep other nations from having the kind of life they want—you don't unless they won't do as well by you as you are ready to do by them.

That's the American and the democratic philosophy, the reason why America is now at war. Every American ought to understand this, to know why a nation that wants peace has to go to war.

15

Because nobody likes murder, you have to kill murderers. You cannot get along without police and this war is a policing job. It's a large-scale job because it is a total war.

TOTAL WAR

Total war is just what its name implies—war on all fronts with all possible weapons. There's the home front as well as all the battle fronts. There are also the military front, the economic front, and the psychological front. Military, economic, and psychological warfare make up total war. The Germans had that big idea first, but the Americans can fight the devil with his own fire and a hotter one—and are doing it.

The three kinds of warfare are all related. A military success may also be an economic victory, if it results in the capture of great quantities of enemy matériel or blocks important supply routes to the enemy nation. Or it can be a psychological victory if it lowers enemy morale, helps to make soldiers expect defeat, leads the enemy people to be ready to submit.

An economic success of our own can lead to a military defeat of the enemy if it robs him of essential supplies. It can become a psychological victory if it disheartens him, makes him readier to give in.

On the other hand, of course, a military victory is useless if it leads to a psychological defeat. The Japanese may have done great military damage at Pearl Harbor, but it resulted in net loss to them because of the effect of uniting the Americans in anger.

Real defeats, other than death, are psychological

16

in the end. The enemy gives up, surrenders. You have to kill the enemy or make him surrender; there isn't any other kind of victory. If he is fanatical, you may just have to kill him. Americans would rather get him to surrender.

Psychological warfare is the newest arm in war. It is directed at opinion, belief, confidence, courage, and the will to fight. It is both defensive and offensive, for it tries to build up morale in our people and troops and to break down morale in the enemy.

The chief weapon of psychological warfare is propaganda. The radio and the press are used to bolster the home front. The enemy is reached by newspapers and leaflets dropped from airplanes, and by short-wave radio—for in spite of penalties there are always some in Axis countries who listen to and repeat the foreign broadcasts. At the front loud speakers can bombard the enemy lines. And then there is always rumor which can be started intentionally—insidious rumor, which, unverifiable by nature, spreads unverified by word of mouth.

Propaganda, in spite of what many people think, is not necessarily dishonest. The truth is often the best propaganda, especially when it is fed to persons who are starving for it. The most effective propaganda must be founded on fact, must start from some important event that actually happened and is known to be true. Then the propagandist interprets the event, much as a good lawyer interprets evidence in favor of his client, or as the honest advertiser makes a claim for his product.

You cannot, however, undertake to change opinion and feeling unless you know first the state of the opinions and feelings which you wish to change. There are various ways of making this necessary assessment of public opinion. The best is the public opinion poll which is used in the democracies. Since its results are published, both the United Nations and the Axis learn the facts. For knowledge of public opinion in Axis countries the democracies have to rely on the reports of neutral travellers, espionage, the expert interpretation of Axis propaganda, and similar indirect means. For the home front the propagandist studies newspaper circulations, crowds at public addresses, the popularity of radio commentators, applause at speeches, and at news reels. At the fighting front prisoners are questioned, not only about military matters but also about conditions at their homes.

MILITARY PSYCHOLOGY

Psychological warfare is not, however, the only way in which psychology contributes to success in combat. There are hundreds of others, and soldiers and officers need to know what psychologists know and what psychological methods can find out.

For instance, soldiers need to understand men in order to understand themselves and their comrades, and officers must learn how to interpret and influence the conduct of those for whom they are responsible. The soldier must know about human needs, motives, and emotions—about fear, when it comes, what to do about it—about anger, when it is useful, when it makes trouble—about zest which is the core of good morale in a unit—about anxiety and the sense of insecurity—about indignation

18

against the enemy and irritation against comrades —about the relation of food and of sex to the military life. He should know also the relation of all these things to morale and thus learn how to avoid bad morale and to build up good morale.

Every soldier ought to understand further the problems of the mental adjustment of men, first to the army, later to combat. Why men feel insecure. What makes for courage. The signs of approaching breakdown. How to prevent breakdown, and what to do about it when it happens.

The selection and training of leaders for the Army has become one of the most important problems in the psychology of war. Not enough is known about it, but what is known to some should be known to all. The good leader is the man who builds up good morale. How does he do it? What kind of man must he be? If he is a poor leader can he become a better one?

And there are mobs and panics to be understood too. Civilian mobs and panics may be the concern of the soldier when the populace gets mixed up with fighting, or when the enemy's home front begins to break. Panics may, moreover, occur even in well disciplined troops, if all the conditions for panic are present. What are these conditions? Why are seasoned troops panicked less than green troops?

An understanding of how individuals differ from one another, and how to measure or assay human resources, enables the Army to put men where they will be of greatest usefulness.

The Army wants radio operators and tank mechanics, pilots and weather observers, clerks and officers. It has hundreds of jobs and needs, therefore, hundreds of special abilities. Many of these army jobs are counterparts of civilian jobs. Others depend upon civilian skills but require special additional training. A civilian truck driver has still to learn how to drive army trucks—through mud, in the dark, under fire, in convoy. So what does the Army do?

It has to pick out the men with the necessary skills. Of them there are, however, never enough. Men must, therefore, be trained to new skills, and for that the Army selects the men who will learn most quickly, the men who have aptitude for learning and performing the job in which there is a shortage.

So individual abilities are determined by tests, interviews, and records of previous performance. Those who have none of the needed abilities have their aptitudes tested, so that the most apt can be trained. This work constitutes a huge program of classification and selection of the Army's manpower, of brains and muscle, of knowledges and dexterities. It requires also the establishment of innumerable training schools.

When the right man is in the right job, everybody benefits. The Army benefits, because it gets its work done efficiently. The soldier benefits because he is happier when using a special ability, filling a special place, knowing that the Army counts upon him. The soldier accepts responsibility and his morale goes up. Then the Army benefits again because, more than any special skill, it needs morale—the loyalty and enthusiasms that inoculate it against defeat.

Not only must the Army place each man where his talents will be used to best advantage, but each individual must know how to get the most out of his talents.

To help him use every sense effectively the soldier can draw upon a huge body of scientific knowledge accumulated throughout the years and being enlarged by innumerable researches in progress during this war. Perception is a basic tool of warfare.

The well-informed soldier will want to know how his eyes work, how easily they get fatigued; how fatigue can be prevented or overcome. He will want to know how distance is perceived by sight, what advantage that perception has for pilots, for bombardiers, for range-finders, for camouflage penetrators. He will want to know how to make his eyes more sensitive for seeing in the dark and how to keep the enemy from seeing him. He may be a night flyer, or he may have to do patrol duty at night. Does it matter much if a soldier is color blind? And what makes camouflage work? How can objects be obscured? Can you see objects even though they are obscured? An army relies on its eyes.

And the soldier wants to know about hearing too, which provides almost the only means of communication. When the din of mechanized battle is on—under a barrage, in a tank, in an airplane—the ability to hear speech may fail. How does it fail? What makes it fail? How can auditory communication be maintained in spite of tremendous racket? How much is a man deafened by airplane noise, by gun-fire, and how long does such deafness last? What other kinds of deafness are there?

Even smell has its place in war. It does sentry duty. A soldier must learn to detect war gases. How does he learn? When, having learned, is he likely to fail? How good a detector is the nose and what makes it inefficient?

Balance is important, especially in pilots. The organs of the inner ear play an important role in telling the pilot when he is flying crooked on blind flight, when he is upside down. How do they work? What conditions make them give false information?

And then there is efficiency. What are the effects of general fatigue? Of hunger? Do drugs increase efficiency? Are they good things to use? What happens when a man does not get enough oxygen because he is up too high in an airplane? Lots. And usually it happens before the flyer realizes it is beginning to happen.

This book is written about all these matters of psychological warfare and military psychology. It shows for the field of psychology how complicated combat has become. The primitive fact of combat is that man pushes when he encounters an obstacle to the achievement of his desire,, pushes more if blocked, gets angry if still thwarted, and then fights. But to this fighting he eventually brings all of the knowledge and skill that has made him supreme among the animals. He fights by learning how to use his eyes at night and learning how to arrange a system that will let him hear inside an airplane. He fights by selecting good leaders and good truck drivers. He fights by understanding human nature in order to build up good morale that will overcome fear. He fights by saying the right thing in the right

22

way to the right people at the right time, and sometimes that is propaganda. He uses every resource of science and intelligence, including psychology. He has to, for this is total war.

II: SIGHT AS A WEAPON

THE HUMAN EYE is one of the most important military instruments that the armed forces possess. The human brain and its nervous system are, of course, even more important. But an army had better be deaf than blind. The use of airplanes, tanks, trucks, jeeps, guns, rifles and most military matériel depends on fairly good eyes to make them work.

So the soldier who wants to understand his tools must understand his own eyes. What they are. How they work. How well they can see small objects and fine marks on instrument scales. How good they are at discriminating colors and when they fail. How well they can see in the dark. What tires them. How one eye and two eyes perceive distance. How the eyes control precise movement, enable the soldier to handle tools, drive a car, point a gun.

Because vision is so important in combat, every soldier is given a test of his ability to see sharply, clearly, and accurately. A common way to test eyesight is to show the soldier a chart printed in different sizes of type in order to discover the smallest size he can read without making mistakes.

A better test uses a series of broken circles. (Fig. 1.) This test is better, because there is less guessing. The examiner spins the circle around and when it stops has the soldier say where the break is. If he sees the break, the examiner tries him out with a smaller circle, and then with a still smaller one, until the break is so tiny that he just can't see where it is.

These tests are not just for reading. They measure the soldier's ability to see at a distance, too. That is because all objects look small in the distance. A

FIG. 1.

B-19 bomber with a 200-foot wing-spread is about as hard to see, at an altitude of 6000 feet, as the word airplane in the type on this page held 15 inches from your eyes.

Unless a soldier has sharp vision for small details, it is hard to distinguish shapes in the distance, hard to count the number of objects, especially if they are close together, hard to recognize ships or airplanes or tanks.

At 100 feet, many men cannot count the gold stripes on the sleeve of a naval officer. At 5000 feet it may be difficult to tell whether an airplane has two engines or four.

There are ways in which you can aid your vision —help your eyes to see their best.

For any seeing that requires attention to fine detail, have plenty of light—on the work, not in your eyes. Don't allow shadows to fall across the page you are reading or the instrument you are watching. The finer the type or the instrument markings, the brighter your light should be. There is a limit though. No one should try to read the type on microfilm, not even with the brightest sunlight. Use an enlarger.

For distant objects, use binoculars—if you can get them.

Contrast helps in seeing. Black type on a white or buff paper is easily read. Yellow print on the same paper is very hard to read. Shapes with sharp, well defined outlines are easily identified; those with smeary, fuzzy edges are hard to make out. Dark objects are best seen against a light background, light objects against a dark ground.

Space between objects makes them much easier to see. Putting extra white space between lines of type actually makes the printed letters look larger.

Contrasting colors do not make objects stand out unless they also differ in brightness. Nothing is harder to read than red letters printed on a green background, because a good red and a good green are generally about equally bright. But you can easily see yellow on blue, or blue on yellow, because yellow is light and blue is dark. One state made the mistake of making license plates with red letters on a green ground. They couldn't be read more than a few feet away.

The direction from which the light comes is important for seeing. When you want to see texture or a raised pattern, the light should be nearly on a level with the object, so that it shines almost along the surface you are trying to see.

You can see how this works if you go into a dark room and look at the letters on your dog tag by flashlight. Hold the light so that it shines directly down on the letters and they will be difficult to make out. Hold the light almost on a level with the tag so that it shines across the letters from one side and they will stand out much more clearly.

Airplane observers who want to look for such details as low hills, shell holes, buildings, can make their observations best in the early morning or late afternoon when the sun is low and shadows are long. A high sun makes the ground look level.

When light falls from directly behind you on the object you are looking at, that is what photographers call a "flat lighting." It makes everything look smooth. It is fine for reading a book or looking at any flat object. But when you want to see the shape of things or estimate height or thickness, have the light come from the right or left—at right angles to the direction in which you are looking.

Thus, have the light behind you when you are looking at a map; have it at one side (not in your eyes) when you are looking at a sand-table model or a piece of terrain (if the battle situation makes this possible).

When you are trying to see through something— a windshield, window, observation blister—have as little light as possible on your side of the glass, as much as possible on the outside. A dial that is visible because of light shining through it is best seen when viewed in complete darkness.

The angle at which you look at things is as important as the angle of the lighting. Letters painted on a road surface so that a driver must read them by looking down at them obliquely are so distorted that they are very hard to read. They are made very

27

tall to allow for this. If you try to read a book or a map laid flat on a table top, you have the same trouble. It should be tilted up at an angle if you are sitting in usual reading position—pinned on the wall if you don't want to hold it. It should always be at right angles to the direction in which you are looking.

Since, in warfare, the object is to see the enemy and keep unseen yourself, many of these hints may be applied in reverse for making it difficult for the enemy to see you.

The enemy should be approached, when other things permit this, so that the light is in his eyes, but behind your back. Avoid positions in which you form a contrast against the background. Never stand on a hilltop or ridge so that you can be seen silhouetted against the sky. Place buildings if possible where they will not cast long conspicuous shadows in the morning or afternoon sun. The way they are faced may help in this—the longer sides should be away from the low sun, toward the north and south. Or they may be placed so that the shadow of a hillside or trees will mask the shadow of the building. Or arrange to have the building's shadows fall on trees or shrubs which, when in leaf and seen from the air, look very dark all the time.

GLARE

Without light you can't see anything, but with too much light you can't see very much either. You can't look directly at the sun even for an instant without being blinded by its great light. You can't see an airplane when the sun is in your eyes. You can't even keep a truck on the road if the lights of another truck shine directly at you. Instead of vision you get only confusion and sometimes pain.

One reason that light shining into your eyes is blinding is that the lens and other parts of your eyes are not perfectly clear, but have in them imperfections which reflect the light and scatter it in all directions. Seeing is made possible only when a clear image is thrown onto the retina of your eye. When the light rays are broken up and scattered, this image is distorted and blurred, or is dimmed out. That's what's called glare.

Smoke and haze also produce glare. So do dirty eye-glasses or a dirty windshield.

Men's eyes are not all alike in this regard, are not all equally clear. Some are less able to see distinctly with bright light in their eyes than others are.

There are two things you can do to avoid the blinding effect of glare. You can use a mask or screen to cover the light, or you can throw an even brighter light on the object you are trying to see.

Spotters trying to see airplanes in a bright sky can use a screen to mask the sun itself. A driver sometimes puts a colored celluloid screen on his windshield at a height which prevents approaching headlights from shining directly into his eyes.

A few years ago, drivers used to try to overcome the blinding effect of approaching lights by having even brighter lights of their own to turn on. This was not, however, a very good system, for only the man with the brighter lights could see clearly, and it takes only one blinded man to make an accident. It was much better when headlights were arranged to shine on the road instead of in the other fellow's eyes.

Bright light, like the sun, reflected from shiny surfaces like water, metal, glass or a smooth roadway, can be very troublesome, but fortunately there is a good way of overcoming this blinding annoyance.

A shiny surface makes the light waves reflected from it vibrate in only one direction—parallel to the surface. Polaroid sun glasses cut out the light that vibrates horizontally, letting all other light through. By wearing this kind of sun glasses, you can see what you want to look at by means of the other light, while the bright light reflected from the shiny surfaces is much reduced.

The only other thing to do about glare is to be ingenious enough to keep the sun at your back when you are making observations and also when you are attacking, if the battle situation otherwise permits. Then you can see what you want and where you are going, and the man you are approaching cannot see you. That is why airplanes fly out of the sun at dawn or sunset, hiding successfully behind the glare.

How the Eyes Work

To use any precision instrument most effectively, it helps to understand something about how it is constructed and how it works. Your eyes are very fine precision instruments.

They are in many ways like a camera—the very expensive kind that is small but beautifully contrived to do fine work. If you look at Fig. 2, you can see what the similarities are.

Your eye is a tough-walled ball filled full with a

gelatin-like substance except in the front part where there is a watery fluid.

Like the expensive camera, it has a good lens. Also like the camera it has an opening which opens

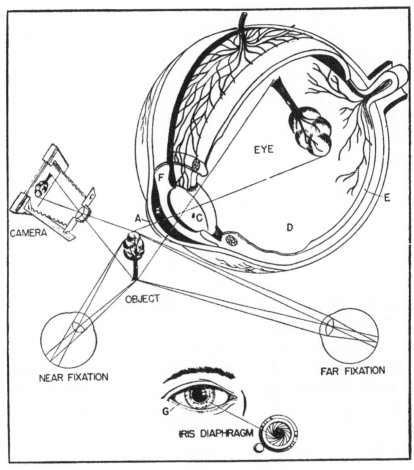

FIG. 2.

up wide to let in light when you are using it in dim illumination. That is the pupil. It automatically closes down to a pin-head opening when the light is bright.

In a camera, the image is recorded on a film. You have a film in your eye, too. It is called the retina and is at the back of your eye.

You can focus your eye, as you can the more expensive cameras, but you don't do it the same way. There are no knobs to turn or settings to make for "portrait," "20 feet" or "infinity." Automatically, without your even giving it a thought, your eye instantly adjusts itself so that you can see sharply and clearly the type on this page or a distant mountain peak or a ship miles away at sea. Seldom do you fail and get a blurred out-of-focus picture on your retina.

In a camera you focus by moving the lens back and forth, farther from the film or closer to it.

In your eye, the focus is adjusted by muscles attached to the lens which actually change its shape. When the muscles are relaxed, your eye is at rest and is focussed on objects far away. When the muscles contract they make the lens bulge more, changing the focus to "near fixation," which is like the portrait setting on the camera.

You can see why it is more of a strain to keep looking at close objects than to look into the distance. The lens muscle has to keep contracted when you are reading a book held in your hand or when you are looking at an instrument or doing close work. It rests your eyes if you occasionally look up and away from your work.

In normal young eyes, the changing of focus is done instantly and with no trouble at all. You can look back and forth from a distant ship to a map or instrument close to your eyes with no difficulty, except that your eye muscles may get tired if you shift your gaze back and forth too frequently.

As a man grows older, the lens of his eye does change, however. It becomes less elastic and focussing on close work gets more difficult. This change with age is so continuous, in fact, that you can usually make a pretty good guess at how old a man is by using this little experiment.

Have him hold a book and bring it closer and closer to his eyes (with his glasses off if he wears them) until he reaches the closest place where he can read the type without its blurring. Measure this distance. And then use this table to guess his age.

Years	Distance
10	Under 3 inches
20	4 inches
30	5½ inches
40	8½ inches
50	15¾ inches
60	Over 39 inches

You don't ordinarily notice this ageing of your eyes until you have to hold your work ten inches or more away in order to see it clearly. That usually happens between the ages of 40 and 50.

Unless you have very long arms, you will probably have to put an extra "portrait lens" on your eyes when you are getting on toward fifty in order to overcome this "old-sightedness." You will have to wear glasses. If your eyes are normal, you will not have to use these eye-glasses except for close work, such as reading.

Seeing, so far as the eye's part is concerned, is a chemical process, just as photography is. Light rays, reflected into your eye from the object you are looking at, shine on the retina and instantly make there a chemical change which affects the nerve endings in the retina.

But from that point on the process is electrical. Impulses travel along the fibers of the optic nerve from those nerve endings at a rate of 140 miles an hour. They consist of a series of little electrical "explosions" which pass along the nerve fiber. The brighter the light, the more closely do these "explosions," these bursts of energy, follow each other.

The end of the road for this train of impulses is the brain. There, all sorts of connections are made which enable you to take the proper action as a result of what you see—to reach out and pick up your rifle, or to blink when something falls close to your face.

The visual center of your brain, which is the terminal for most of the nervous connections to your eyes, is located in the back of your head. If you get hurt badly in this part of your head, you may be blind in part of your field of vision, or even totally blind.

TIRED EYES

Your eyes are hardy organs. They can move and focus, focus and move, all day and still be doing a pretty good job. Yet they do get tired if there is too much focussing required of them, if they have to strain constantly to see small things, tiny differences.

Close work is more tiring than distant looking. Constant shifting of the gaze from far to near and back again is always fatiguing. Yet your eyes keep working as long as you are awake and have them open.

When eyes tire, first they smart or burn, or else feel dry or as if something were in them. Then the eyelids get inflamed and sore, and the eyes water. All that happens outside the eyeball. From inside there are strains, aches, and even pain that come with too much use—especially from too much focussing.

Vision may be blurred in a tired eye, because the focus is bad. Or you may see double. And you may get headaches, become nervous. Fatigue of the eyes is not a simple affair.

The best way to cure eye fatigue is rest. Enough rest. Shut the eyes so that they do not have to keep adjusting to changes in illumination, so that they do not have to keep moving to look at objects which come under attention. Give them darkness and no work to do, so that they can relax and cure themselves.

In extreme fatigue they may need hot or ice cold compresses on them. Eye-washes help lubricate hot dry eyes, being a substitute for the secretions which normally do this job.

There are plenty of muscles about the eye to get tired. Each eye moves in its socket under the action of six muscles attached to the eye-ball (Fig. 3). The action of these muscles is very finely adjusted and coordinated. You can instantly look at anything you want to. If it is far away, the lines of sight of the two eyes are almost parallel; if it is near, the two eyes draw together—always just the right amount. The lens muscle changes the shape of the lens for near and far vision (Fig. 2). The pupil muscles change the pupil's size when illumination changes, when your gaze shifts from far to near.

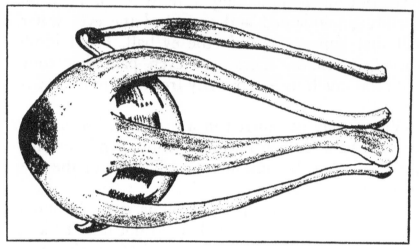

FIG. 3.

The eyelids blink constantly to keep the eye clean and lubricated; and that means more muscles working. Also the muscles of your face come into use, when you squint from a light that is too bright, when you lower your brows to peer into the distance. No wonder that prolonged use of the eyes produces fatigue.

The most general cause of eye fatigue is, therefore, use—use of the elaborate system of muscles that come into play for keeping the eyes moving in coordination with each other, for getting both eyes to focus on near and far objects as they move together, for adjusting the eyes to varying amounts of light.

A very frequent cause of fatigue is glare and unequal illumination of the visual field. If the pages of your book are brightly lighted and the rest of the room is quite dark, then the light that gets into your eyes as you move them over the lines of print keeps changing. The change is greater if sometimes you look away from the book into the dark room. And every time there is a change in illumination the pupil starts to change size. If this is kept up too long, the eyes get tired.

A constant change of focus is particularly fatiguing. Looking back and fourth between near and far objects tires the muscles of the lens. This is an airplane pilot's difficulty. He looks at the ground, back at his instrument board, ahead into space, back at the instruments. A rifleman, too, looks back and forth at his sights and his distant target. Especially does changing distance fatigue the eyes of older men, men over thirty, whose lens-mechanisms are beginning to stiffen up. But even the young fliers get tired in time—some of them after an hour's flight, most of them after four hours' flight.

Fatigue of the eyes is bad. It ought to be avoided. Here are the rules for preventing it, or, when it cannot be prevented, for lessening it.

(1) *Avoid looking at small objects.* That is not always possible on reconnaissance, but sometimes it is. You can sometimes go nearer the things you want to examine. If you can't choose the size print you want, you may be able to use a reading-glass. If you need glasses, get them; and, if you get them, use them. Often the job of the glasses is magnification.

(2) *Use good illumination,* not too much nor too

little. If you use too much, it is likely to be uneven and you get strain from glare. If it is evenly distributed, still you may have to strain by contracting the pupil and squinting the brows to keep out the extra light that adaptation cannot take care of. If you use too little light, then there are the other strains from moving the eyes, blinking, refocussing as the image fades out, peering into the dark. Common sense tells you when the light is about right. It isn't the same for everybody.

(3) *Don't look back and forth between light and dark objects* if you can help it. In night flying, the crew should not keep shifting vision back and forth from lighted instruments or charts to the darkness outside.

(4) *Don't look back and forth between far and near objects too frequently.* If there is nothing to look at for the moment, your eyes will of themselves look off into the distance. That is the resting situation, when the lens muscles are relaxed.

(5) *Don't try to see too much at once.* Pay attention briefly to a part of the whole area you want to observe. If you try to spread your attention all at once over too large an expanse, then your eyes will shift back and forth over it. But also—

(6) *Learn to scan.* Frequently shift your attention from one part of the area to be observed to another, shifting systematically in accordance with rule 5. This habit not only keeps the field of attention small enough for clear vision, but it counteracts the tendency for details to fade out when you have stared at them too long. Dark objects show up darker when you have been looking at something

light. And light objects look lighter when you have been looking at something dark. As you keep looking at them, they begin to fade out. It pays to look away occasionally and back again.

(7) *Blink often.* Generally your eyes will automatically blink for you. But if they don't, blink voluntarily. Build up the habit of blinking. Blinking lubricates the eye-ball. It helps circulation in the eye. It gives vision a fresh start, preventing the strains of staring. It helps you—the reason is not plain—to see objects clearly when they are quite close to the eye. Almost everyone knows these facts, blinks when vision gets blurred, finds that blinking helps clear it up. Especially are the less adjustable eyes of older people helped by blinking.

(8) *Avoid general fatigue when you can.* To a certain extent the whole body gets tired together. The eyes are not isolated. Waste products in the blood or reduced oxygen affect the eye muscles as well as other muscles.

(9) *Avoid headaches, indigestion, nausea, dizziness.* That is no simple prescription. It may be that the eyes are responsible for the nausea or headache. But, in general, remember that the body is a single machine, that its parts are all connected for action together, that visual defects may come from the stomach or sea-sickness from the eyes.

The Eyes as a Range Finder

There is one way in which your eyes are far better than the most expensive camera. With your eyes you can take better account of distance and solidity. You can tell that one tree or one hill is

39

farther off than another. You can tell a flat wall from a round tower. Even from the air it may be possible to tell a ridge from a ravine.

In other words, the world you see has three dimensions—up-down and right-left, but also near-far. Seeing the third dimension is a pretty complicated business and there are plenty of chances of going wrong in it—of letting your eyes deceive you. But it is, in general, fairly accurate and is extremely important in warfare.

You need to know, and know instantly, whether an enemy soldier is within range of your weapon. You need to know how distant a tank is or an airplane, and you may have to know this without knowing beforehand how large they are. It pays, whenever possible, to learn beforehand the relative distance of some landmarks in the scene, such as telegraph poles or trees and to use these as a sort of scale for getting your range.

Your eyes give you this information, but not directly. What happens is that you use a variety of different clues to distance, as if you were collecting all the evidence and reasoning out which of two objects must be further away, or whether you are looking down on a mound or a shell hole. You do not really reason about it, not often; your nervous system does it for you, and does it instantaneously and irresistably. Still the nervous system must have clues. It will help you to know what these clues are, so that you can use them to see in three dimensions more readily, and also that you can prevent, if possible, your enemy from having this kind of vision of you.

40

THREE-DIMENSION SEEING WITH ONE EYE

As compared with a man with two eyes, a one-eyed man is at a great disadvantage in perceiving distance and solidity. He has clues to these things, and he uses them. But there are some that he doesn't have. Suppose we list first what he can do, and then note later what a second eye adds to one-eyed vision.

The one-eyed man has seven clues for seeing in the third dimension:

(1) When you know the *size* of an object, that may be an important clue to its distance. If you see a man a quarter of a mile away down a straight stretch of road he looks small and therefore fairly far away. As he approaches you, he seems to get larger—and so nearer. The size of his image on your retina tells you how far he is away, because you know how big men are and can make that judgment instantly without thinking about it.

This rule holds only for big changes in the size of the image in the eye. Small changes of familiar objects you do not notice at all. A man 40 feet away looks just about as big as a man 20 feet away, not half as big. But a man a mile away does look much smaller than a man at 20 or 40 feet.

It is the same with familiar objects of definite size—horses, automobiles, railroad cars. Airplanes may fool you though, because there are big planes and little planes, and you may think that a big bomber far away is just a training plane quite near.

Unfamiliar objects that have no definitely known size fool you most. Visitors in Washington, D. C., often think they are only a short walk from the

Washington Monument when they are really several miles off. They do not know that it is 555 feet high. Perhaps they thought it was like the obelisk in Central Park in New York City, which has the same shape but is only 68 feet high.

(2) *Perspective* is a second clue to distance and solidity. Railroad tracks seem to get closer together in the distance. The far end of a book lying on the table looks farther away than the near end, because the far corners appear closer together. Thus perspective really uses size as a clue.

(3) *Hazy objects look farther away.* You can tell which hills are nearer by their color and the clearness with which you see them. Those that are more distant look blue from the haze and are blurred. This fact fools you when you are in a climate that is drier than you are used to. In Arizona, where the air is very clear, you may walk all morning to get to a hill that looks to you only a little distance off.

(4) Near objects may *cover up* part of those farther away. This clue can tell you about hills and mountains and also about trees and houses and many other objects. You may not know from size, perspective, or haze whether tree or house is more distant, but if the tree blots out one corner of the house, then you know.

(5) *Motion* is another clue. If you are looking with one eye at a tree and a pole and can't tell which is nearer, try moving your head or take a step or two and watch them as you walk. Very distant objects seem to move with you. Close objects go the other way.

If you fix your eyes on some object as you move and keep your gaze there, it will seem to stand still. But things the other side of it will move with you, and the farther off they are the faster they seem to move. Things nearer to you go backwards —the nearer, the faster.

Suppose you are riding on a train. You look at a tree half a mile off. The hills beyond it move steadily ahead. The moon rising behind them moves ahead more rapidly. But the fence a hundred yards off moves backward and the telegraph poles close to the track snap by.

(6) *Shadows* are another clue for seeing solidity and depth. If the shadow is on the side toward the sun, it's hollow—perhaps a shell-hole. If it's on the side away from the sun, it's a hill or a gun with camouflage over it. If it's all shadow, it's just low bushes or something else that absorbs light. If there's no shadow, it's something flat on the ground.

(7) Finally, *focussing* helps. The camera fan who owns a camera equipped with a range finder knows that he could use his camera as a yardstick. He just focusses the camera until the tree or house he is interested in is clear and then reads the focussing scale. This would tell him whether the object is 20 feet distant or only 10.

You do something similar with your eyes without realizing it. When you look at an object, your eyes automatically put it in focus. But it takes an effort of your eye muscles to focus on a near object, and relaxation to focus on a far object. It is the action of these muscles that tells you, in part, how far away you are looking.

From these seven clues a one-eyed man can see a lot of depth and distance. If he moves, he can see even more. If he has used only one eye from childhood, or for a long time, he probably gets along very well. A one-eyed man can learn to land a plane safely. Nevertheless, a second eye would give him much better perception.

THREE-DIMENSION SEEING WITH TWO EYES

In addition to the seven clues provided by one eye alone, all of which are true of two eyes, there are two more, available only when your two eyes are working together.

(1) The first is *convergence*. When you look at anything close to your face, your eyes roll toward your nose as they both look directly toward the object—they converge, or "toe in." (Fig. 4.) They converge less when you look at objects farther away from your face. Their lines of sight become parallel for very distant objects.

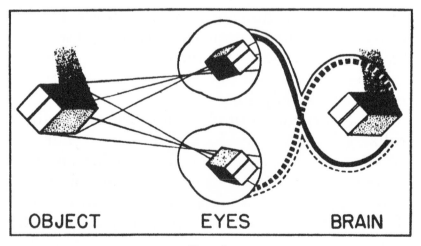

OBJECT   EYES   BRAIN

FIG. 4.

It is easy to find out just how your eye muscles tell you about distance in this way. Just hold up a pencil and look at the point. Keep looking at it and bring it gradually closer to your eyes. You will soon reach the point where it is painful to keep on looking at it. You can surely feel the strain on your eye muscles now. But without your realizing it, your eye muscles have been signaling you right along. That is one of the best ways to see distance.

It is like the triangulation method that surveyors use to find distances. Your eyes are always the same distance apart—about 2½ inches. They converge so that each looks directly at the object and the amount of convergence tells you how far away the object is. You don't have to do any figuring, however. From experience with distances all your life you know, and know immediately, whether the object is five feet away or ten or fifty.

(2) The other clue furnished by your two eyes working together is the *disparity* between what your right eye sees and what your left eye sees. Your two eyes generally get slightly different views of the same object because they see it from different angles.

Try it yourself. Look at some object near you with both eyes. Close the right eye first. Then open it and close the left. You will notice that the object seems to jump back and forth. If you hold your finger up and look at it, this is very noticeable. But look closer. You will notice that the finger itself looks different. The left eye sees more of the left side, the right eye more of the right side.

Now look at Fig. 5. There two eyes are shown

looking at a solid cube. The left eye sees the image B. It sees a little of the left side of the cube, none of the right. The right eye sees the image C, a little of the right wall, none of the left. You can bring the two views back together again and see the cube standing out from the paper as a solid, if

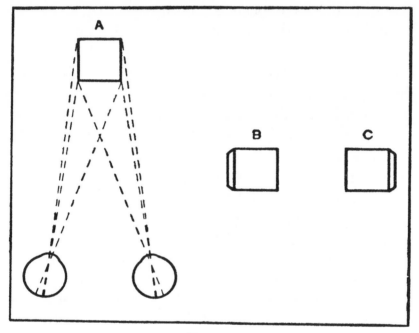

FIG. 5.

you will put the edge of a sheet of paper between the two drawings and hold it up to your face so that your left eye can see only B and your right eye can see only C.

Twin photographs made to give right-eyed views and left-eyed views of the same landscape are of great military importance. They are called stereoscopic photographs—from two Greek words which

46

mean "solid view." The two cameras (or two lenses) used in making the photographs are just as far apart as are your eyes—about 2½ inches. The photographs are placed in a machine that enables you to look at the left picture with your left eye only— the right picture with your right eye (Fig. 6). This

FIG. 6.

allows you to see the landscape exactly as it would look to your two eyes.

The instrument through which these military stereoscopic photographs are viewed is equipped with a gadget that enables the observer to measure as well as see the height of hills, trees, buildings, or even curb stones. Such photographs are of ex-

47

treme value in reconnaissance and in the penetration of camouflage.

RANGE-FINDING INSTRUMENTS

Your two eyes make a good range finder for distances that are not very far away. You can nearly always tell which of two objects is the nearer one, and if you know the distance of one, you can make a pretty good guess at the distance of the other.

But with more distant objects your eyes do not do so well. As in the camera, all long distances are just "infinity." Your eyes would have a longer range, however, if they were farther apart. One of the range finders used by the Army, a *telestereoscope,* actually gets this effect.

The range finder (Fig. 7) is an extremely com-

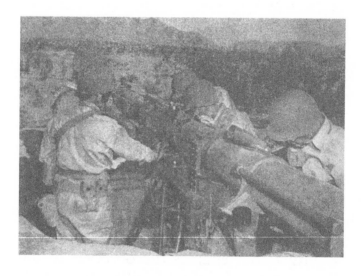

FIG. 7.

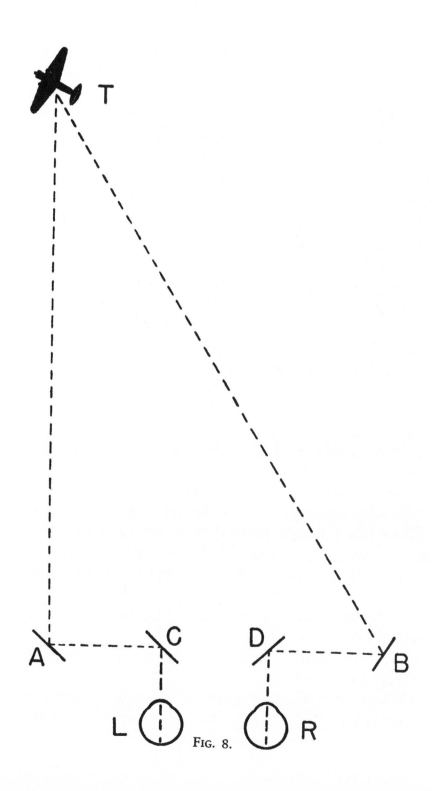

Fig. 8.

plicated instrument. However, the principle on which it works is fairly simple. The following simplified description is right in principle, but it is not an account of the range finder itself.

Instead of looking directly at the airplane, you look at reflections of it in two pairs of mirrors (Fig. 8). Your right eye looks at mirror D which picks up the image of the airplane as reflected from mirror B. Your left eye sees another view of the plane. It sees the reflection in C of the reflection in mirror A. The two views fuse, however, so that you see just one plane. The effect is the same as it would be if you could put your right eye at B and your left eye at A, much farther apart than nature would permit.

So when A and B are 10 feet apart, your vision for distance is as good at 1,000 feet distance as it is without mirrors at 20 feet. In addition, telescopes are provided with the range finder so that distance vision is given further aid. The telescopes, when they are used as eyepieces of the instrument, magnify small objects so that they may be seen clearly. Besides, the telescopes increase the depth effect.

Besides the mirrors and the telescopes, the range finder has a dozen vertical lines between A and C and between B and D. These lines are so arranged that when you look into the instrument, they fuse and seem to be lines which are suspended in thin air at different distances in space. The fused lines are called a reticle.

The operation of the range finder may be summarized this way:

When an airplane is spotted, you must depend on two men to help you get the plane in view. These men are called trackers. One tracker mans a telescope at one end of the range finder (beyond mirror A) and the other man looks through a telescope at the other end of the range finder (beyond mirror B). One man moves the instrument along the horizontal line until the plane appears centered in his telescope; the other man moves the instrument in an up-and-down direction so that the plane appears centered in his telescope. When the plane is centered in both the trackers' telescopes, you can then look into the eyepieces of the range finder and see the plane in space, either in front of or beyond the reticle.

Then you adjust the angle of mirror B until the fused image of the plane is seen directly over the reticle. At the time when the mirror B is adjusted until the plane is seen directly over the reticle, the reading is sent, by electrical and mechanical devices, into elaborate instruments which control the position of the guns. Thus, from the time that a reading is made of the plane's position nearly all of the firing of the guns may be done, at least in a great number of batteries, automatically.

The airplane's distance is really determined by triangulation, because your setting of mirror B serves to measure the angle between the base line from mirror A to mirror B and a line directly to the airplane. But the range finder is so constructed that you don't have to work out any calculations. That is all taken care of automatically.

There is another type of range finder—the contour-break kind—that depends upon the adjustment of mirrors or prisms, but does not separate the views of your two eyes. It merely enables you to read from a

51

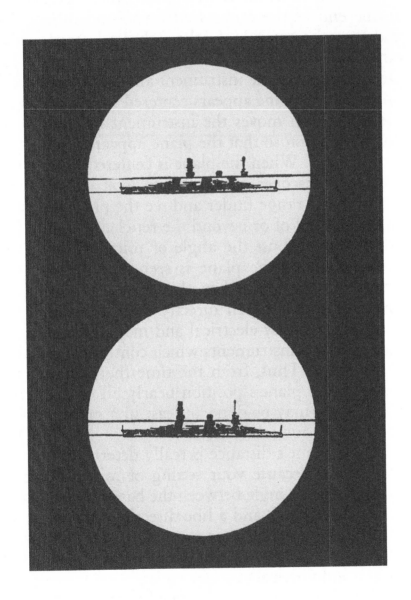

FIG. 9.

scale the exact distance of the object—in feet or meters.

It has two openings—"eyes"—through which the rays of light from the battleship or other object come. One "eye" of the machine sees the top of the object that has been spotted—a battleship, perhaps—and the other sees the bottom. If the object is far enough away the rays of light to the two "eyes" of the instrument are parallel and the views of the top and bottom match. They fit together properly. But when the target is nearer, the two views do not match and the observer sees something that looks like the upper view in Fig. 9. By adjusting a mirror, however, you can bring the two views together so that they exactly fit. The amount of the adjustment shows how far away the object is.

Although the use of such range finders supplements your own unaided eyes and makes them ever so much more useful as military instruments, they also put increased demands upon them. It takes young eyes and good ones to look through these instruments and use them accurately.

The airplane pilot in landing needs to do some rapid range finding with his own unaided eyes if he is to make a smooth three-point landing. Aloft, two-eyed seeing is not so important, but in landing the pilot needs to know just how far it is to the ground. Two eyes are lots better than one for this.

On the other hand, there are some good one-eyed pilots, and an experienced pilot can land pretty well with one eye covered. A pilot who loses an eye can eventually learn to make a good landing, even if he cannot do it when he first tries.

At present there is no agreement as to whether prospective pilots should be tested for accuracy of two-eyed distance vision, should be rejected if they do poorly in such tests. It would be well for them to be able to perceive distances accurately, but there are so many other requirements for a good pilot that the Air Forces quite naturally does not wish to insist on more requirements than necessary. The stiffer the requirements, the harder it becomes to get enough pilots.

If you see something that looks suspicious on a starry night, there is a trick way of finding the distance to it. Suppose you can see this object, some distance off, and you are in a car on a straight stretch of road. Drive along until a line from you to the object to a particular star which you have picked out seems to you to make a right angle with the road you are on. If the object is off at the left of the road, pick a star to the left of the object, and drive ahead. The star will move with you, pass behind the object, and emerge when the line from it to the object and to you is at right angles to the road—if you have picked the right star. If you have not, pick another star.

Now look at your speedometer. Then drive ahead until the star, which still moves along with you, is separated from the edge of the object by a distance that is just exactly filled by the width of your four fingers, when your arm is stretched out in front of you as far as it can reach. Then see how far you have travelled along the road by consulting your speedometer again.

The distance of the object from the road is about 8 times the distance you have travelled.

That magic number 8 is exactly right if your four fingers, close together, measure 3 inches across and if they, when your arm is stretched out, are just 24 inches from your eyes. 24 divided by 3 is 8. The average number for men is about 7.7. The figure varies in men, however, from 6 to 9, and is higher in women. If you want to be accurate, measure your own fingers and your own stretch, and then find and remember your own figure.

If you have to drive a mile, then the object is 8 miles or 7.7 miles away. But you must drive, not walk, because the stars themselves are moving and the observation must be made within 5 or 10 minutes.

If the object is nearer, you can pace the distance fast enough. One hundred paces along the road means that the object is 800 or 770 paces away. Not exactly though, for you have had to guess about the line from the star to the object being at right angles to the road.

Seeing Speed

Movement attracts attention. Especially when the world is still, any sort of movement is conspicuous and a warning signal. That is why you freeze when you don't want the enemy to see you.

Very slow and very fast movements are not, however, noticed. You cannot see the hour hand on a clock move, although you may be just able to see the minute hand move.

And an object that falls from a great height past the window is just a streak or a blur.

The nearer the object to you, the slower are the

speeds at which it can be seen clearly as moving. If you are in a plane going at the rate of 200 miles an hour and another plane going at the same speed and in the opposite direction passes you a hundred yards away, then you do not see a moving plane. You see only a blur. But if the other plane is a mile off, then you see it flying rapidly along.

The slowest speed you can perceive as movement is about a tenth of an inch a second for a moving object 10 feet away, or 10 inches a second for an object 1,000 feet away.

Defense against low-flying planes is difficult because they come over so "fast." Actually they fly no faster when low than when high, but the image of a plane 100 feet up moves across the retina 100 times as fast as the image of a plane 10,000 feet up does. So the low plane does go much faster across the eye's retina.

An antiaircraft gunner has not only to perceive movement but has also to estimate its speed. He aims ahead of his target, "leads" it. If his estimate of its speed is good, then he makes a hit, for then the bullets or shell and the plane will arrive at the same spot together.

Nearly always the background is important in seeing movement and estimating speed. The distant airplane does not appear to move except in relation to the ground or clouds or some other objects in sight at the same time. If you see the airplane against low clouds that are themselves blowing along rapidly, it is very hard to judge its speed. The moon sometimes appears to sail along at a rapid clip—just because of clouds scudding over it.

56

You judge your own speed, when you are on a train, by the apparent movement of the landscape that is disappearing behind you. But, if another train passes you, going faster in the same direction, you may suddenly feel that you are going backwards. In this case the eyes determine both what you see and what you feel about your own movement.

While everyone who is not blind can see movement —when it occurs, and sometimes when it does not exactly occur, as in the movies—there are nevertheless great differences in men's ability to estimate speed correctly. Truck drivers are tested for this capacity. They need to know which truck is going to reach the intersection first, whether to slow up or speed up to avoid a collision.

Vision Helps Action

The hand may be faster than the eye—under some circumstances—but nevertheless the hand needs the eye in order to do its work well.

"Look before you leap." You have to, to avoid disaster. But, having once looked, you can leap with surprising accuracy.

As you walk along a sidewalk and approach a curb, one glance is enough to let you adjust your steps so that you don't come out with one foot on the edge of the curb. Only when fatigue or alcohol interferes with your coordination are you likely to make a mistake. But you need that one glance. Vision is always coaching action in this way.

Reaching is an action in which you can make remarkably precise adjustments. It starts with looking.

Generally one look is enough. You can look, shut

57

your eyes and then reach out and grasp the desired object accurately.

You can even look, shut your eyes, and then walk across the room and put your hand right on the object that you wanted.

Of course, you can generally move more accurately when you have seeing to help you. The man, who cannot touch his nose with his forefinger at the first try when his eyes are closed, can certainly do it with his eyes open. And if he practices with his eyes open, he will learn the sooner to do it accurately than if, like a blind man, he has to practice without the aid of vision. Nevertheless, seeing merely speeds the learning, for the blind man can learn remarkably precise movements without seeing at all.

Driving nails isn't hard to learn for an adult, provided he can see clearly what he is doing. Otherwise he is likely to hit his thumb more often than the nail. It would take lots of practice and many sore thumbs to learn to drive nails in the dark.

All use of tools requires coordination—smooth teamwork between eyes and hands. So does landing an airplane or shooting a rifle or driving a truck. In a mechanized army eye-muscle coordination is at a premium, and some men are much better at it than others. Nearly every soldier is given a test of mechanical aptitude which measures, among other things, his coordination ability. Tests of coordination are also given all those who want to become airplane pilots or bombardiers.

Although men do differ in the smoothness and accuracy of their coordination, that does not mean that they were born that way. Any soldier knows how to reach. Seldom does any adult over-reach or fail to reach far enough. But a young baby can't reach accurately. He will reach confidently for the moon or miss in an attempt to grab his own fist.

So the main thing to remember about any sort of eye-muscle coordination is that exceedingly complex actions can be learned, and also that they do have to be learned. The expert rifleman has had to work hard to acquire his skill. The man who can shoot accurately "from the hip" has acquired mastery of an even more complex coordination, for he is working by eye and muscle without lining up sights. He is making an adjustment much more difficult than reaching for an object in the dark after glancing at it once in the light.

Every pilot has learned a very complex series of coordinations when he has learned to land his plane.

Many other military tasks are just as difficult, but don't be discouraged by that fact. The Army does more learning than fighting, because it does a lot of learning without fighting, and no fighting without learning. Give your nervous system a chance. Its capacity for learning is remarkable. And that's the sort of thing it is for—to help the eye learn to direct the muscle.

III: SEEING IN THE DARK

MODERN WAR is often war at night. That means that men must learn to see in the dark and to use their eyes in new and unfamiliar ways.

So the fighting man needs to know how to make the best use of his eyes at night—whether his job puts him in an airplane or a tank, on a ship, driving a truck, or just getting about on his own feet.

You can't make a man into an owl or a cat, but you can let him have rules and aids that will give him just enough edge on the enemy so that he can get in the first shot.

Everyone knows that when you go into a dark room from a bright one it is hard to see until your eyes have become used to the gloom. At a movie it takes a minute or two to see the vacant seat. It may take a couple of minutes more before you can recognize a friend. During these minutes your eyes are steadily becoming more sensitive to the faint light.

There are two ways in which your eyes adjust for seeing in the dark. They can open up to let in more light, and they can shift over to a more sensitive set of light-detectors. They do both.

It's the pupil of the eye that opens up in the dark to let more light in—and closes down in bright light to a pin-head opening so as to keep out too much light (Fig. 10). The pupil works like the diaphragm in a camera, which you open wide for taking pictures in dim light.

But the important change is this shift to the more sensitive set of detectors.

The retinas of your eyes (Fig. 11) have two batteries of light-detectors called *cones* and *rods*. The nerve fibers run from them to the brain. The cones

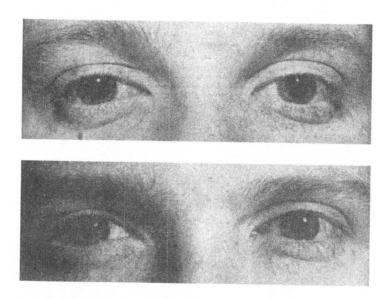

FIG. 10. The pupils of the eyes expand (top) to let in more light in darkness, but are normally smaller in daylight (bottom).

do the seeing in bright light, the rods at night. In twilight and bright moonlight both are working together.

The cones—there are millions of them in each eye —are packed together most closely in the very center of the retina, the part that does the most accurate seeing in daylight. That's why in daylight you always have to look directly at something in order to see it

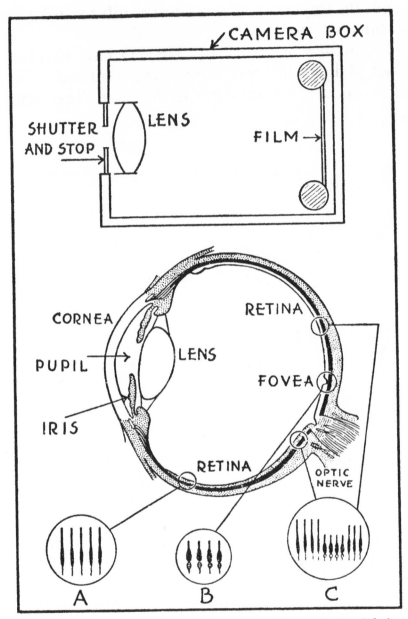

FIG. 11. The eye and the camera. In this much simplified diagram the principal parts of a camera and the corresponding parts of the eye are shown. The three circles beneath the eye are enlargements of the spots at which rods and cones appear on the retina—*A*, only rods present; *B*, only cones present; and *C*, rods and cones together.

best. The cones also see colors.

The rods—and there are millions of them too—are color blind. That is why "all cats look gray at night." Cats really do—and so do trees and flowers, provided the night is dark enough. But a red or green signal-light is seen as colored at night because it is bright enough to get the cones working.

The rods are packed most closely together at the outside edges of your retinas, and there aren't any rods at all in the very center. The part of your eye that is most sensitive in daylight is actually blind at night. So don't look directly at a thing to see it in the dark. Look alongside of it. That faint object out there in the dark. It caught your attention because it moved a little. What is it? It disappears when you look at it closely, but it's there again when you look to one side. Keep looking to one side or the other and you may be able to tell whether it's a man, or simply a bush that moved in the wind.

Both the rods and the cones are differently sensitive to different colors of light. The cones are most sensitive to yellow light. That's why yellows in daylight are brighter than reds, greens and blues. The rods are most sensitive to yellow-green light, but they differ most from the cones in seeing blue light. To blue light they are one thousand times as sensitive as the cones. So don't use blue lights in black-outs. The enemy's eyes, like your own, can see blues easily in the dark. Use red lights instead, for the rods see pure red light as black. But don't use intense ordinary red light, because that is not pure and will affect the rods.

Night-eyes lack the sharp vision for detail that

your day-eyes have. You can't read, or study an instrument dial, or examine a map, a road sign or your watch, by using your rods. For that you must put your cones to work by having more light, of course, shielding it carefully from the enemy if he is not to know where you are.

FIG. 12.

But night-eyes are extraordinarily sensitive to faint light. An ordinary candle flame or a lighted match (Fig. 12) could be seen ten miles away if the night were completely black, if there were no haze at all in the air. Even with haze and starlight, a match can be seen for many miles. So don't strike matches in a blackout or when the enemy may be watching.

64

It takes time—half an hour or more—for the rods to get completely into action after you have been in the light. When you first go from a brightly lighted room into a blacked-out night, you are at first completely blind. Neither the cones nor the rods work.

Then three things happen. First the pupils of your eyes dilate, letting more light into your eyes. That helps a little.

Next the cones get more sensitive. They divide up the blacks into blacks, dark grays and light grays. That takes about five minutes.

More slowly the rods get adjusted. You begin to see shapes and outlines in the gloom where there were not even vague bulking shadows when you first came in. This is due to a slow chemical change, which is rapid at first but not fully completed for half an hour.

The soldier, who at a command or an alert signal leaves a lighted room to run on duty without having prepared his eyes, is completely at the mercy of the enemy as far as his vision is concerned. By the time he gains the use of his night eyes the emergency may be all over.

And even when your eyes are adapted to the dark, flashing on a light, though only for a short time, may ruin your night vision for another half hour. You can lose by a few minutes of light all you gained by a half hour in the dark. The brighter the light and the longer you look at it, the more you lose.

Getting Ready to See in the Dark

Complete darkness is the best preparation for night fighting. Protect your eyes from light before you start and while you are out. If you can't stay in darkness, keep the lights around you as low as possible and never look straight at them. And if you have to look at a lighted object, be quick about it. Looking at an instrument dial lighted only by radium paint can cut down the distance at which you can see a friendly or an enemy plane by fifty per cent. So don't look at the dial any longer than you must.

Experienced gun pointers and spotters know that they must not watch the flashes of their own guns as they fire. The flash of a six-inch gun can dull the eyes for more than a minute. Under continuous fire at dawn or dusk it is impossible to aim some rapid-fire guns accurately at a target when the gunners let themselves watch the flash. At night the effect is even greater. Luckily the flashes of rifles and small-caliber guns have much less effect on the eyes.

There are several ways in which you can become adapted to the dark even though you must work in fairly bright light. Each way is suitable only for certain kinds of jobs.

Ship pilots and bridge officers have long known a clever but simple trick. When they have to work their way among dark islands with the beacons un-lit, or to move in company with other blacked-out ships, these men often have to go back and forth from a lookout post to a lighted bridge or chartroom.

When they go into the light, they cover one eye and use the other.

Then, when they come out into the night, they uncover this eye and use it.

To cover the eye an ordinary black eye-patch is sometimes used. This trick should not be used, however, to prepare for night duty except in an emergency. Experienced men know they must stay out of the light for 15 minutes to half an hour before they go on night duty. With the patch over but one eye, only that eye becomes prepared, and two eyes are always better than one.

A better way to get the eyes dark adapted is to work in deep *red light*. Remember that pure red has almost no effect on the rod cells of your night-eyes. So, if deep red light is available, you can read or work—if you have to—and still be dark-adapting your night-eyes so that you will be ready for nearly instant action in the dark. If you can't get bulbs of deep red, you may get by with a red cellophane covering for a light or an instrument. But the red cellophane is pretty poor because it lets through some orange and some white light that tend to desensitize your rods. Even the red bulb is not perfect and it ought not to be any brighter than is absolutely necessary.

The very best arrangement is tight-fitting *goggles* with red filters in them. They can be made so that only red light gets through, so that the rods are not affected at all. Put them on half an hour before your night duty begins. And take them off, of course, when you are outside in the dark or you will be quite blind.

The trouble with the use of red light and the goggles is that they keep you from distinguishing colors properly. Red lines on a white chart disappear in red light. Red and white signal lights look alike. All red objects become white or gray or some other color. Be careful about color if you have red goggles on.

It isn't enough to get your night-eyes working at full capacity by staying in the dark or using red light, red goggles, or patches. You have to learn to use night-eyes after you get them.

First try an experiment to show you how your eyes work in the dark. You must have a room that can be completely blacked out into which you can let just a little light, shutting the light out gradually. If the windows are dark, you can close the door slowly.

Take a sheet of typewriter paper. Cut it in two. Then cut one half in two, then one of these quarters in two, and keep on until you have a piece not more than a quarter of an inch across. You now have almost a dozen pieces of white paper ranging in size from a tiny scrap up to a piece about 8 by 5 inches. Lay them out on a black table or other dark surface.

Now shut the door and let your eyes get used to the dark. Wait ten minutes at the least—half an hour if you can spare the time.

Now open the door a crack until you can just see the smallest piece. The bigger pieces will be brighter than the smaller. The biggest piece will almost glow. The more light a piece reflects, the brighter it appears.

Now watch the big piece. You are seeing it with your cones. Gradually it will fade out until you cannot see it at all. That is the cones getting fatigued.

Now pay attention to the other pieces while trying to keep your eyes fixed on the place where the big piece disappeared. They are still visible—to the rods. In fact viewed this way, out of the corner of your eye, they seem to glow as though phosphorescent.

If you look directly at one though, it disappears— because there are no rods in the center of the retina. Move your eyes away, however, and the little piece that disappeared pops back again into view. You can make them come and go. A piece is there when you don't look at it, gone when you fix your eyes on the spot where it was.

That's one alarming thing about being in a strange area in the dark. The object that might possibly be a sniper isn't there when you look at it, comes back when it thinks you aren't noticing.

You may not in the dark be able to spot an airplane if you look directly at it. Yet you can pick it up again out of the corner of your eye if you will look away. It disappears again if you look straight at it. The same thing is true if you try to see a distant ship, an unlighted car or tank, or even a faint star.

Always remember, therefore, that you must look a little to one side (Fig. 13) in order to see best on a very dark night. Learn to pay attention to things which are just a little off the center of your field of vision. Learn to keep from looking directly at any object in the dark. As you feel your eyes drawn almost irrestibly toward what you want to see, just let them slide on over to the other side of it and look again with the tail of your eye. It takes practice to learn to do this without fail, but it is worth the trouble to learn the trick.

And don't keep looking steadily to the same side of the object, because then it will disappear too. Use first one side and then the other.

Try this out.

When you are in a darkened room or outdoors on a dark night, hold up your finger and look steadily at it. It will disappear. Look a little to one side and make it appear again. Keep staring and it will go again. Then look to the other side of it and let it come back.

This means that in searching the sea or sky for a dark object, you must look first at one area and then

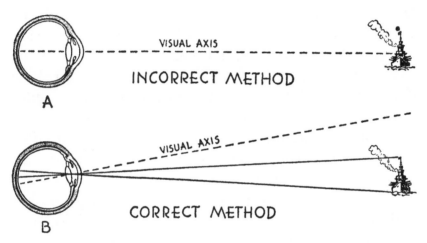

Fig. 13. Night lookout technique. Practice the use of the "corners of the eyes." Night targets are better seen by not looking directly at them. This is because the edges of the retina are more sensitive to dim light than is the very center of the retina.

at another. When you think you have spotted something, look first to one side of it and then to the other—then above it, below it.

But don't ever try sweeping your eyes over the sky or horizon. You can't see well when the eyes are moving. Scan the sky, don't sweep it. Look here, then there, then at the next place.

Night-eyes are slow in responding except to bright

objects and moving objects. You may have to look several times before you can be sure you have spotted something. But don't stare. Keep looking again and again, always just alongside of the dark still object.

Small objects are much harder to see at night than in daytime. The average airplane becomes too small to be seen beyond 1000 feet on a clear starry night. But the plane is smaller when seen on edge from ahead, behind, or at the side. Then you may not spot it more than 400 or 500 feet away. So, if you are pursuing a plane, try to keep above or below it until you are close in.

The same thing should be done in chasing a boat. Keep off to one side when far away, if you can, so that the boat will be seen more nearly broadside on.

Night glasses are useful because they magnify an object without much loss of light. Binoculars magnify too, but they cut down the light so much that a very faint object disappears. The night glasses do not give so clear a view as the binoculars, but your night-eyes cannot see sharp outlines anyhow.

Darkness may make things look smaller. A tree in the dark in winter looks smaller because you cannot see the twigs and the ends of the branches at all. A plane at night seems to get larger when a search-light falls upon it, because the light brings out so many details that could not be seen before.

The best you can do at night is to see dark fuzzy silhouettes of objects. That makes it hard to recognize objects, but you can learn recognition.

Even in daytime *recognition* is largely a matter of jumping to conclusions from slight hints. You can recognize a friend long before you can see the color

71

of his eyes, even before you can tell whether he has his nose on this morning. His general shape or his style of walk may be enough.

At night the clues are still fewer, and so it pays to study the silhouettes of ships and planes, to study them at all possible angles and positions. Then you may learn to tell one plane from another, one ship from another, even though you never do know just what clues you are using.

A lookout or scout at night can't afford to wait to be sure just what he has seen before reporting it, or taking cover. Follow your hunches. Trust vague impressions. Those are the best rules for night seeing. The cautious man who waits to be sure may not live that long.

Sometimes you may be able to detect a moving airplane in the sky by its motion alone. Or by what you don't see, more than by what you do see. If a star blinks out and then on again, something may have passed between you and it.

CONTRAST

Contrast helps vision. If the thing observed is much lighter or darker than its background, it is much more easily seen. Even at night the sky is so much lighter than the ground or the water, that the chances of seeing an airplane from below against the sky are ever so much better than of seeing it from above against the ground—especially if it is painted dark on top to match the ground. A ship is easily seen against a dimly lighted sky. It is very clear against a coast not properly dimmed out. It may be invisible against the dark sea, or to an airplane flying over it.

72

But, if the white underside of a plane is illuminated by moonlight reflected from clouds beneath the plane, then the plane as seen from below may almost match the moonlit haze of the sky and disappear. That's in moonlight. You can't get the shaded underside of a plane light enough in daylight to match the daytime sky.

But contrast helps vision only when outlines are clear. For this reason the windshields of night fighters must be kept clear and free of scratches or fog. These scatter the light, make contours fuzzy, and reduce contrast. Careless night fighters have been known to tolerate enough dirt on their windshields to double the time it takes them to see a plane moving along near by. And sailors on ships sometimes let the salt from the spray pile up in blotches on the glass. That is courting death.

For the same reason it is important to keep down the light on your own side of the windshield. It produces glare, spoils outlines, reduces contrast, makes faint objects invisible. That is why you push up close to the window when you try to look out at night. By coming up close you shade part of the glass and reduce the glare. If there has to be any light on your side of the glass, screen it from the glass.

Good Food and Good Health

There has been a great deal of talk about the effect of shortages of vitamins A and C on ability to see at night. These are the vitamins in fresh vegetables, cheese, and fruit. People who don't get enough of these vitamins do become poor in night vision, but the regular Army and Navy rations supply plenty

73

of them. Occasionally when ships are on long trips or when fighting lasts until fresh foods are all gone, a shortage of vitamins may occur. Then medical officers supply men who are likely to be on night duty with vitamin capsules. Extra vitamins don't improve night vision when your diet and your night vision are already normal.

Night vision is affected by fatigue. Anything that reduces your physical well-being has a greater effect on night vision than on day vision. Hangovers, slight illnesses, or excessive fatigue may double or even triple the amount of light needed to see a faint object in the dark.

So the night fighter must train for his job as a boxer trains for the big match. The boxer who is not at the peak of training is likely to be knocked out. The night fighter whose eyes are not at the peak of efficiency is likely to be killed.

RULES FOR SEEING IN THE DARK

1. *Protect your eyes from light* before you go on night duty and while you are out.

2. *Stay in the dark* beforehand, or use *red light* or red goggles. The goggles are best, when you can get them.

3. *Never look directly at any light,* nor at any illuminated object except in red light. If you must break this rule, be quick with your looking.

4. *Use the corners of your eyes* when you are out on duty. Keep looking alongside of what you think is there, until you have made up your mind about it.

5. *Keep your eyes moving.* Look and move, look and move. Don't sweep them over large regions, and

don't stare continuously at one spot.

6. *Keep your windshield spotless,* free of dirt, salt, fog, and scratches.

7. *Keep down the light on your own side of the windshield,* and screen it from the windshield.

8. *Keep yourself wide awake and on the alert.* Don't break training. Use good sense about eating, drinking and smoking. Keep rested, if you can.

9. *Practice recognition.* Learn by experience to recognize from slight clues the objects you need to recognize.

10. *Practice all the rules* for seeing at night until they become second nature to you. And use every possible device to aid you.

It is the night fighter with the best eyes who wins his part of the war.

IV: COLOR AND CAMOUFLAGE

A MAN DOES NOT SEE with his eyes alone. It takes his brain and his mind to sort out the confusion of colors and forms that continually assault his eyes and to see them as trees, grass, men, tanks, guns, airplanes, birds, clouds, and water.

Because his brain has so very much to do with what he observes, it is possible to camouflage an object without making it exactly invisible—merely by disguising it in such a way that it will fool the enemy because it does not look like a separate thing but as part of something else.

People can be fooled if you know how. As a matter of fact everyone is being fooled all the time for his own good. A man forty feet away is only half as tall to the eye as a man twenty feet away, but not to the brain, which does not see him as shrinking rapidly when he walks away. That's the brain correcting the eye, telling how things really are, not how the eye sees them.

But you can take advantage of another man's brain, use its own rules to deceive it, to make it perceive something that is not real.

One reason the brain makes such mistakes is due to its habit of building up familiar objects on the basis of a fleeting glance, a quick vague impression. It takes a look at what the eye sends it and then fills in all the wealth of detail that it knows—or believes —belongs in that object.

76

You get a glimpse of a friend disappearing into a doorway. Your eye actually sees only one familiar shoulder, an ear, the back of his head and a flying coat tail. But your brain immediately knows "That is Jack." It fills out the picture, puts a name on it, makes it into a familiar object—all on the basis of a few clues, a hasty general impression provided by your eyes. It's a good brain. It saves you time and work.

As a matter of fact your brain is really your secretary. It's got everything on file, and digs the important data out in a moment when the eyes telegraph a few scanty facts into it.

You seldom notice the unimportant details anyway. To convince yourself of this you have only to list on a sheet of paper the names of six people you know moderately well. After each name try to write down a description telling the exact color of his eyes, the shape of his nose, how he parts his hair (if he does), how his ears are shaped, and whether he has big feet. You won't be able to fill in all these details, not if you are an ordinary observer; yet you would not have the slightest difficulty in recognizing any of these friends.

Many a man cannot tell you what sort of numbers are on the face of his own watch, whether roman or arabic, whether the maker's name appears on it, or whether all twelve numbers are there.

Although airplane recognition is often taught by a system of looking for certain details, such as the shape of the tail or wing, one school in the Navy has found that split-second recognition is easier if you learn to depend on the same sort of general instant recognition that you use in recognizing a friend. You recognize planes by making friends with them. In a fraction of a second you get an impression and seldom more. Yet if you can learn to tell an airplane friend from an airplane enemy in that first fleeting glance, it may spell the difference between life and death—victory or defeat.

But while this ability of the mind to do without detail is a great help when you want to recognize a familiar object, it can be a weakness when the enemy is trying to fool you. It means that often, just by making the general impression of the scene right, he can make all sorts of minor changes in details without being caught at it.

If you recognize an airplane as a particular type of bomber, for example, you "see" the guns on it, even when you are close enough for them to be visible, just where you expect them to be. You might never notice a new one on the tail where there has been no gun before.

And if you, aloft, recognize a bomber on the ground, you will see all its guns on it in the right places even though it hasn't any guns—because it is a dummy plane put there for the express purpose of getting your brain's habits to fool you.

It is easy for you to see what you expect to see, and very hard for you to recognize anything you are not prepared to encounter. If you think a friend of yours is in Africa, you might walk right by him in camp without recognizing him—just because you never expected to see him there.

And if you see a camel lying down in a field near Pittsburgh, you might instantly recognize him as a pile of stones. "Why," you'd say, when you got up close, "it's really a camel!"

But if you knew the circus had lost a camel that morning, then perhaps he wouldn't be a pile of stones at all. Or if you were near Cairo instead of Pittsburgh.

COLOR

A chief aid in making the Army's camels and guns and other objects look like a natural part of the scenery is through the use of color. But it has to be a very intelligent use. Because the enemy knows about camouflage, too.

You must not only paint or drape a military object so that it will look to enemy eyes like a natural part of the woods or fields or city streets. You must also make it look the same when the enemy uses his various tricks to expose the deception. It must look the same in daylight and by searchlight at night. It must look the same when seen through the eye of the camera. It must stand the test of various filters and of special films such as the infra-red sensitive films used with or without filters.

This requires a thorough knowledge of how the eye perceives colors, how colors can be mixed and how they can be "unmixed" by filters or other devices, and what happens when mixtures of colors are themselves mixed.

Light itself is an electric wave, similar to radio waves and moving at tremendous speed. It becomes visible when it strikes the retina of your eye either directly, or when it is reflected from some object. You can't see light at all if you look at it sideways.

79

A beam of light passing through a hole in one wall of a dark room and out a hole at the other side would be invisible to a man in the room, if it did not light up dust or haze in the air—as it almost always does. You see light only when it enters your eye and falls head on on your retina, and it is then that you recognize its color. Then orange light looks orange, and green light green.

A scrap of white paper reflecting the light looks orange if the light is orange, but that is not the whole story. You could shine pure red and pure yellow light on it simultaneously and it would still look orange with no orange light there at all. Red and yellow lights mix to make orange. You could shine red and yellow light on a "white" wall—a wall that would look white in daylight—and it too will look orange.

But if you looked at this orange-colored "white" wall through a red filter, it would look red, because this would screen out the yellow light. If you used a blue filter it would look black because neither the red nor the yellow would get through.

You very seldom see anything by light of a single color. Practically all light is a mixture of colors. And there really isn't any such thing as white light, in spite of all you hear said about it. There are only the colors—the colors of the rainbow from red to yellow to green to blue to violet—and mixtures of these colors.

The colors differ from each other because the electric waves that make them are of different lengths. In the rainbow or, as it is called, the *spectrum,* there are actually thousands or millions of different kinds of light. There are a few which are called by different names—red, orange, yellow, green, blue, violet. But everyone knows there are a great many more—the red-oranges, the yellow-oranges, blue-greens, the blue-violets. Some of these colors have special names, like *brown* (it's a dark orange), *olive, peacock,* and *lavender.* Altogether, if you have normal color vision, you can see about 130 different colors in the whole range of wave-lengths that are visible—from red, with the longest wave-length, to violet with the shortest.

Like white, purple and carmine are never seen for pure lights. They are gotten only by mixing. Purple is seen when red and blue lights are mixed, or red and violet—in the right amounts. If you have too much red to get a violet, then you may get a carmine.

Besides differing in wave-length from other colors, a colored light or a colored object may vary in strength, or *saturation*—from the best possible red, for example, to one less intense, to a still poorer red, to a grayish red, to a reddish gray, to a gray just tinged with red and finally at the extreme to gray with no red visible in it at all.

When you mix two or more colors, you not only get a new color resulting from the mixture, but you also lessen the saturation—you get a color that is not as rich as either of the original colors. The more different the colors mixed, the greater the loss in saturation is likely to be.

That is why colored pictures never show up as vividly as the colors of nature—because the pictures depend on the use of a few very different colors, sometimes of only three. Technicolor movies use

81

only three fundamental colors. To paint objects to look like nature you need many more than three colors of paint.

Figure 14 was designed as an aid in figuring out what will happen when you mix colors. This is how it works:

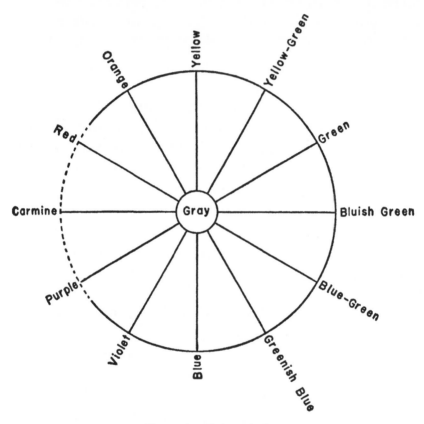

FIG. 14. Color circle.

When two colors, with the right amounts of each, mix together to produce gray, they are called *complementary* colors. Red and bluish green are complementary colors. You will notice that these two

82

colors are directly opposite each other on the color circle in Figure 14. Every color has its complementary. Figure 14 is drawn so that every pair of points opposite each other on the circle are complementary, will give the gray in the center if mixed in the right proportions.

So there are many different ways of getting exactly the same gray by mixing only two colors. You can mix red and bluish green, orange and a blue-green, yellow-green and violet, green and purple. In every case you get the same gray. They all look exactly alike to the normal eye in daylight, but to the reconnaissance observer they could look very different. They are not at all the same in appearance when examined through properly colored goggles.

Each spoke in the color wheel of Figure 14 is drawn to represent a scale of saturation from the richest at the edge of the circle down to the gray at the hub. It is also so drawn that, if you connect any two colors that you want to mix by a straight line, the distance of that line from the center of the circle will indicate the strength, or saturation, of the resulting mixture. When a strong yellow is mixed with a strong orange, for example, the result is also a strong color—the line that would connect these two colors in Figure 14 would cut across near the outer edge of the circle. A line connecting any two complementary colors would, on the other hand, cut right through the center of the circle. That tells you that the resulting mixture would have poor saturation, somewhere well inside of the big circle, or might even have no saturation at all and be the gray in the small center circle.

You can work out for yourself, if you are a camouflage man, how three colors, ten colors, a hundred colors would mix and with what results. You start with two and see what they would give. Then you see what would happen by adding a third to the mixture of the first two. And so on. The more you mix them, the poorer their saturations are bound to be, because they tend to cancel each other out.

Color mixtures in nature are very complicated. Nearly all objects reflect some of every color in the spectrum. Grass reflects a lot of green light, but also some yellow light, a little orange light, and some blue light. But it is a peculiar thing about grass and leaves that they do not reflect any of the red light at the very end of the spectrum. Green paint, however, although it may exactly match grass to the eye, nearly always does reflect a great deal of red light.

You don't see this red as red, because it is cancelled out by some of its blue-green complementary color. But that means that green paint and grass look very different through red goggles, even when they match perfectly to the eye.

Another way to show up the deceits of camouflage is to observe them in dim light—at dawn or dusk. A purple gets bluer as twilight comes on because your night eyes see blue as brighter than your day eyes do, and red as darker. Sometimes mixed colors that match at noon do not match just after sunset, because the change-over from your day eyes to your night eyes affects the colors differently. The camouflage man must not forget that.

And if you change the color of the light, then the colors of objects are apt to change too and they may

84

not change to the same extent. Colors that match in daylight often will not match under yellowish artificial light. Ask any woman shopper or her husband.

Any object that looks colored does so because it is particular about the wave-lengths of the light it reflects. It reflects some better than others, or it may refuse altogether to reflect some wave-lengths. However, it can never reflect any color that it does not receive.

A white object is one that reflects any and every color it receives. But in yellowish light, it will look yellowish, too. An orange will reflect some of all the lights in the spectrum, but more of orange than of other colors. Under light that is only green, the orange will look green. On the other hand, you can't make grass look deep red by using only deep red light on it. It looks black then, because grass does not ever reflect deep red light.

CAMOUFLAGE

In camouflage, it is easy to put over a deceit, provided the enemy does not become suspicious. A factory can get by unseen with relatively poor camouflage when the enemy has no information or suspicion that a factory exists in that region. Enemy observers might pass right overhead without spotting it, because it matches its surroundings more or less. But, once they start looking for it there, then the camouflage had better be pretty good.

Look at Figure 15. If you have not seen this pattern before, you may think it looks suspicious. You may look for some kind of military weapon—a gun or a tank or a locomotive. But the chances are that you will not see it as anything at all unless you have a pretty definite hint of what to look for. Once you have that hint, however, the whole thing is obvious

FIG. 15. What is this a picture of?

and you feel like kicking yourself because you didn't see it before.

Too often, the enemy is suspicious. He is on the lookout for airplanes around an airfield. But that makes him easy to fool with dummy planes placed just where he is looking for real ones. The imitation doesn't have to be very close. If he is sure there are planes there, he will see planes. Only when something like the absence of shadows makes him suspicious again, is he likely to avoid being deceived.

If the fragmentary pattern of Figure 15 fooled you, look back at it again now. Look for a general on a spirited horse. With this hint you probably will have no trouble in filling in the details. You can see the horse's daintily lifted forefoot, his tail, and the way his ears are perked up. You may even be able to see how tightly the general is holding the reins.

It is this ability of your brain to see what you are looking for, even when the clues from your eyes are meager and confused, that makes it possible to penetrate the enemy's camouflage.

Your best hope of hiding from the enemy is to keep him in the dark about your presence. Don't give away your position by any careless slip. For once he knows where to look for you, your chances of surprising him are much smaller.

But, even when the enemy is on the lookout for you, when he knows about where to look, it is still possible to make his seeing pretty difficult. This, in fact, is the purpose of most camouflage.

To make things hard for the enemy to see, you merely have to reverse the principles by which you make it easy to see objects yourself.

To see, you want to have good light. You want to have the object you are trying to see large enough. And the nearer, the larger—in general. If necessary you use eye-glasses, a reading glass, or a telescope to make it bigger. It must stand out from its background and from other objects by being different from them. In the distance, you want considerable space between objects to make them look like separate forms. To see heights and the texture of surfaces, you want low lighting or lighting from the side rather than overhead or front lighting. Shadows help a lot. Especially do you want clear, well-defined contours, or outlines—not fuzzy blurred edges. And you get the best contours when the object and its surroundings are different in brightness, when they give a light-dark contrast.

All these are the rules for good seeing. For good hiding, the rules are about as follows:

(1) *Avoid lights.* Move under cover of darkness if possible. No-light-at-all is perfect camouflage. When you must take your chances in broad daylight, take advantage of deep shadow wherever you can. Use dark clothing except when it would contrast with your background, as it would on snow or desert sand. Avoid bright brasswork or shiny objects that catch the sunlight. Keep away from white walls or any surfaces that would reflect bright light on you.

(2) *Make yourself small.* Men flattened on the earth or crouching make a smaller target. Small objects are harder to see than larger ones. But remember that when you mass many guns or tanks or tents close together, they form a large pattern regardless of how small the separate items may look. A squad of men marching in close order can be seen six times as far away as the same men widely separated.

(3) *Avoid brightness contrasts.* Don't stand on a

ridge where you will be silhouetted against the bright sky. Don't place a gun in such a position. Ski troopers dress in white so that they will not show up against the snow. Soldiers wear drab when they fight on sand or dusty soil. They wear dark green in the woods. Because your background is behind you and also because during your whole life you have been in the habit of ignoring backgrounds, you must be constantly reminding yourself how you must look against it. To be inconspicuous you always try to stand where your uniform will resemble other things around you.

But, even when the soldier and his equipment are carefully matched with his background, some small detail that is particularly dark or bright may give him away. Helmets reflecting sunlight stand out conspicuously from the background as in Figure 16, giving away the presence of troops. Similarly, dark

Fig. 16. Brightness contrast. The presence of troops is revealed because the light on the helmets makes them contrast with their background.

tracks leading over white concrete to a gun emplacement, are a give-away of the position.

(4) *Avoid differences in texture*—differences in roughness, smoothness, or depth of surface. Because different surfaces reflect light differently, they look lighter or darker. Water reflects the most light, a pine forest least. A pine forest seen from an airplane is blacker than the blackest black paint. In the same way, black velvet is blacker than any smooth black cloth, for the light gets trapped between the threads of the pile. A river, by contrast, looks like a bright streak, even by starlight. By moonlight, it is a silvery ribbon—a perfect guide for the enemy plane.

So these differences of texture are really differences in brightness and this rule is really a special case of rule 3.

The following surfaces are arranged in order of light-reflecting texture: The surface of a quiet pool, an unpainted tin roof, a painted tin roof, a stretch of smooth gravel, a lawn with the grass cut, a field of hay, the top of a hardwood forest, the top of a pine forest. Much of camouflage consists of changing surfaces to alter their texture—putting gravel over rooftops, foliage over helmets, feathers over guns.

A man walking once through long grass to a gun emplacement leaves behind him a trail that is visible from a plane, because the grass bent over has a different texture from the upright grass. He should go backwards and try to pull the grass up to obscure his trail. No gun, no matter how well camouflaged at the emplacement, is obscured if it has a lot of visible paths leading directly to it.

In Figure 17 the antiaircraft gun and its emplacement are covered with sugarcane and match the background in looks and especially in texture. Figure 18 shows guns under camouflage netting with strips of cloth woven into it to make the surface texture similar to that of the neighboring terrain.

(5) *Avoid shadows.* A soldier may well be afraid of his own shadow—it is a dead give-away. A shadow

FIG. 17. Antiaircraft gun camouflaged with cut sugarcane. The sugarcane makes the gun match its background in texture and general appearance. Photo from U. S. Army Signal Corps.

not only betrays the location of an object which may otherwise be perfectly hidden by camouflage; it is also a clue to the height and distance of the object.

No, you can't paint your shadow in. The shadow has got to move with the sun. Moreover, black paint in sunlight reflects more light and looks brighter than white paint in shadow—even the blackest black

91

FIG. 18. Guns under camouflage netting. The netting with its cloth strips provides a texture that matches the surroundings. Photo from U. S. Army Signal Corps.

paint and the whitest white paint. In other words, you simply can't buy black and white in cans. You get them only by controlling the light and the eye.

But there are ways of getting rid of shadow. The first way is—*flatten out*. Get down yourself, and keep everything you have low. Make roofs or tents sloping so that the shadows will be inconspicuous. If a building one story high could have walls making an angle of only 15 degrees with the ground, the shadow problem would disappear—except for a building on a plain during the hour after sunrise and the hour before sunset.

Mask your shadow with the shadows of nature—hills, trees, boulders, ravines. Even if the camouflage shadow does not block out your shadow, it may change its shape so that it no longer betrays you.

Remember that the morning sun and the afternoon sun are the shadow makers. A sun high in the sky casts small shadows. Winter brings more shadows than summer because the sun is lower then. Even at noon, it does not climb very high in the winter sky.

In Figure 19 the embossing is brought out prominently by the shadows formed when the light is at the side.

When a hut or other structure is put up, it is possible to place it so that the long side is to the north and south and the ends point east and west. Then the early-morning and late-afternoon sun casts the smallest possible shadows.

Although you can't paint your shadows, you can paint the ground where they will fall, or, better, cover it with dark foliage. A shadow is conspicuous if it falls on white concrete or light colored sand or gravel. It shows up hardly at all on dark shrubbery. A lone tall pine left standing in a forest of younger pines casts scarcely any shadow at all, because its shadow falls on the dark tops of the shorter trees.

(6) *Break up contours.* Whenever a structure has straight, smooth, clearly defined outlines, it is easily picked out from other objects or the background. Make the outlines fuzzy, irregular, and rough, so

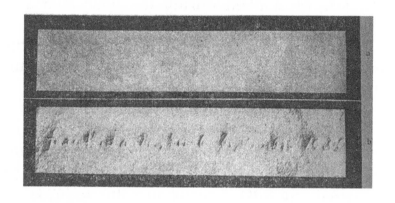

FIG. 19. Shadows give relief. With the light from overhead (upper picture) the embossing does not show. With the light from the side (below) it does.

that in the distance it will be hard to see where the structure leaves off and the background begins. False projections and shelves are sometimes attached to buildings merely to distort the regular outline of the roof and also of the shadow.

Dazzle painting—those peculiar irregular shapes in contrasting brightnesses that are sometimes painted on ships—is intended to break up contours in this way. It certainly does not make a ship or a

94

building invisible. Far from it. But it does make it hard to decide just where the bow is, which way the ship points, what kind of a ship it is.

In Figure 20 try to count the men. One man you can make out easily because of the pronounced shadow of his left arm and the straight edge of the

FIG. 20. Sniper outfits. The men blend into the background. The contours formed by the shadows and the straight lines of the rifles give them away. Photo from U. S. Marine Corps.

bottom of his blouse. A soldier would not want to wear a scalloped flounce on his blouse, but it would be good camouflage, as you can see. A second man is allowing his right arm to cast a shadow that gives him away. But these students at the Marine Camouflage School at Quantico, Virginia, wearing sniper outfits, blend into their background pretty well, because their contours are broken up and you do not easily see the men as separate objects. It is the long straight lines of the rifles which show most.

(7) *Avoid conspicuous patterns.* Tents, tanks, barracks, or even men arranged in neat rows and all facing the same way make patterns that are easily seen at a great distance. If they are broken up and dispersed, with contours broken by trees the same objects would be hard to spot.

A straight line, provided it runs along with other straight lines, is inconspicuous. But, if it cuts across them diagonally, it is the first thing you see. That's what makes the roads in the aerial photograph of Figure 21 stand out so clearly.

Circles, especially if they appear among straight forms or irregular lines, stand out boldly. It is easy to locate a silo, a gasoline tank, a stadium, or a traffic circle from the air. A large wheel catches the attention at once. Break up its outline with bushes.

(8) *Make the object fit into the background.* The soldier and his equipment must match the background in brightness (Fig. 16), in color and in general pattern (Figures 17 and 20). Look at the Marine sniper in the spider trap of Figure 22. He is almost invisible now, and when the lid is down the area looks like a plain plot of land. Or see the snow camouflage in Figure 23. Even in this position the soldier may look like a mound of snow with a dark rock poking through.

The soldiers deployed at the left of Figure 24 are easily seen. They do not fit in with the pattern of the terrain. In the right half of the picture they al-

96

Fig. 21. A telephoto from Wright Field. The straight diagonal lines of the roads stand out with especial clarity. Photo from U. S. Army Air Corps.

most disappear, looking like additional bushes in the gulley.

A column marching down a road with trees on either side should divide, if it wishes to escape observation, and march near the trees in two columns. Even though the trees are spaced too far apart to hide all the men, the columns will be less visible if the lines of men merge with the lines of the trees.

(9) *Avoid uniqueness.* It is the object that is different from everything else that gets attention. One tree in a forest isn't noticed. One tree in a big field

Fig. 22. Spider trap. The sniper fits in with his background, is almost invisible. Photo from U. S. Marine Corps.

FIG. 23. Snow camouflage. The soldier is on patrol in a slit trench and uses the cloth to make himself match his background. Photo from U. S. Army Signal Corps.

FIG. 24. Soldiers should go when possible where they will match the pattern of the terrain. The men deployed at the left are fully visible because they do not fit into the pattern of the terrain. At the right they almost disappear because they become objects in line with other objects.

of short grass is conspicuous. You could hide even the Washington Monument by erecting fifty duplicates all around it.

Thus the false tree of Figure 25 is not noticed. An old dead standing trunk is nothing unusual in

FIG. 25. Camouflage tree trunk. The tree trunk is good camouflage in wooded land, but it would not work in the middle of a desert. There it would be unique. Photo from U. S. Marine Corps.

wooded land. Nor is a rubbish heap anything unusual back of the lines. So the camouflages in Figure 26 have concealed the tents of a company of Engineers by rubbish supported on netting.

The field piece of Figure 27 is certainly excellently camouflaged by foliage against observation from a distance. In the picture, however, the round wheel and the straight barrel stand out. They are unique. Bushes don't have wheels or anything like them.

(10) *Avoid movement.* Movement, especially

FIG. 26. Rubbish-heap camouflage. The rubbish, supported by netting, covers the tents of a company of Engineers. The rubbish is easily visible but it is not unique. Photo from U. S. Army Signal Corps.

when everything around is still, seldom fails to catch attention. But a particular movement is not conspicuous, if other things around it are in violent motion. You won't be noticed if you scratch your nose when your company is charging up a hill, but try scratching it when the company is at parade rest. And you can afford to move, even when the enemy is close, if you are surrounded by small trees being whipped around by a gale.

Very slow movement does not attract attention, and the farther you are from the enemy, the faster you dare move. It's not how fast you really move

FIG. 27. Field piece camouflaged with foliage. The concealment does not work at close range because the wheel and gun barrel stand out as unique against the woods. Photo from U. S. Army Signal Corps.

that matters, but how fast the image of you moves on the enemy's retina.

(11) *Beware of the camera.* Things do not always look the same to the eye of the camera as they do to the human eye. When camouflage is applied to any object, the camera of the enemy must be considered as well as his eyes. Human eyes, for example, are not sensitive to infra-red light—the invisible light beyond the red in the spectrum. But by using film that is sensitive to infra-red light, it is possible to pick up with the camera things that no retina can see.

When green paint is used to camouflage a military objective, the match may be perfect to the eye. Ordinary green paint, however, reflects a good deal of red light, though hardly any infra-red light. Chlorophyl, the green coloring matter of plants, on the other hand, reflects almost no red light but lots of

Fig. 28. Infra-red camouflage. Left: spherical tank with aluminum paint is obvious in any photograph. Middle: tank with infra-red paint is less obvious in ordinary photograph. Right: tank with infra-red paint disappears in infra-red photograph because it and foliage appear white, due to fact that foliage reflects infra-red light.

103

invisible infra-red light. So with infra-red sensitive film, photographs show up foliage or grass as snowy white and the green paint as dark gray. Paint is now available, however, which does reflect enough infra-red light to fool infra-red sensitive film.

In Figure 28 the spherical structure at the left is painted with aluminum paint and is the most conspicuous object in the landscape, even though it is well surrounded by trees. In the center picture camouflage paint makes the structure blend better with the foliage around it. The picture at the right shows how it looks when photographed with infra-red sensitive film—just as white as the leaves.

Counter-Camouflage

To penetrate camouflage the Army needs trained alert observers, with intelligence and insight, with knowledge of what to look for and of the principles of camouflage. Back at the air bases it needs the same sort of men to examine the photographs taken on reconnaissance flights. The observers examine objects and shadows, compare photographs to find new objects that have appeared since the last observation flight, try to interpret what they see. Intelligence and experience count for much, and success depends on more than the application of simple rules.

There are, however, some special techniques:

(1) *Depth Photography.* Your two eyes are good for seeing depth in a landscape only when the objects are close to you. When you look down on the earth from several thousand feet up, the whole world is pretty well flattened out. It is hard to tell a mountain from a molehill—a forest from a field of cabbages.

But the camera can restore depth perception to you. If, in a stereoscope, you look with your left eye at one photograph of the terrain and with your right eye at another photograph of the same terrain taken a suitable distance away, you can see the mountains rise to their proper heights again, the trees tower over the bushes, and buildings are no longer flat roofs laid on the ground.

Such photographs can show that dummy airplanes are not real ones, that their fuselages are flat pieces of wood instead of solid bodies. They may also show that scenery painted on the roof of a war factory is just make-believe with a grim purpose and not what it pretends to be.

A photographic reconnaissance plane takes these photographs continuously as it flies along. The views of the successive photographs overlap, but, being successive, they are taken from different angles. Any two successive views can be matched up and viewed through a stereoscope, the instrument which combines them to bring out the depth.

The time which must elapse between successive photographs to give the proper depth effect depends on the height and speed of the plane and the focal length of the camera. With a camera of 25-cm. focal length, the plane ought to fly a distance equal to a quarter of its height from the ground to give the best results. If the distance is greater, the heights or depths in the picture appear exaggerated.

(2) *New Objects.* A clever device that astronomers use to spot new stars has gone to war for the purpose of spotting new objects in a scene that has been observed and photographed before.

The old photograph of an area is viewed in an observation instrument; then a new photograph of the same area is instantaneously flicked into its place. If the two photographs are exactly the same, you don't notice any change—think you are still looking at the same picture. But, if something has been altered between the times of taking two pictures, then there is a flicker of movement at the spot where the alteration has occurred. Since movement always catches your attention, you notice the spot immediately and can study it to see just what new thing is there.

(3) *Long Shadows.* Photographs of observations made just after sunrise or just before sunset show up tall structures by the long shadows they cast. Painted scenery shows up for the fake it is, when repeated observation reveals that the shadows do not move with the sun. Even an object, built purposely with sides sloping enough so that it does not ordinarily cast a shadow, will be betrayed by a shadow when the sun is close to the horizon. (See Figure 19.)

(4) *Filters.* An observer can wear goggles with colored filters in them. These let through some colors of light more than others, and objects that match in ordinary daylight may not match when seen through the goggles. Every one knows that it is never safe to try to match colors in yellow artificial light when a daylight match is wanted. It is the same with the goggles.

Suppose you have a common green paint that exactly matches some green leaves in full daylight, and you look at both the paint and the leaves through deep red goggles. You may be able to see the paint, because ordinary green paint reflects so much red light, but the leaves may be almost black because they do not reflect much red light. The green, of course, won't get through the goggles.

And other kinds of filters will penetrate other daylight color matches. An observer on reconnaissance cannot, however, carry a battery of colored goggles with him and use them all on everything.

(5) *Special Photographic Methods.* The camera can be used to penetrate the trickery arranged to deceive human eyes. If color is used to fool your eyes —distract you from what you are not supposed to see—then an ordinary photograph which shows only dark and light but no color may see through the deceit.

Filters can be used on a camera to increase the contrast between an object and its background in just the same way that the amateur photographer uses them to heighten artistic effects, to make clouds show up better. This makes some objects easier to spot.

Infra-red sensitive film can be used to penetrate the blanket camouflage of a blackout. The heat from a factory chimney or an airplane exhaust will photograph on this film even when there is no visible light. And, of course, the infra-red photographs can be used to expose the differences between the colors of nature and imperfect imitations from the paint bucket.

Color Blindness

Color is important in war because many a military objective can be identified by its color, or show its identity because it differs in color from the background.

For camouflage you may spread over a gun a net on which are tied green strips of cloth. Then the observer in an airplane sees, instead of a black gun surrounded by green grass, a batch of green things that look like the leaves of bushes.

You never allow brown paths to get trod through the grass to the gun, for then the observer will surely see them. He will see them unless he is color-blind, but he had better not be color-blind if he is to go on aerial reconnaissance. Color is too important in observation.

Army Air Forces has even developed a practical method for taking colored photographs from the air for reconnaisance. They take them from altitudes as high as 15,000 feet, and sometimes at great heights the camera can get colors which the human eye fails to see. Colors of ordinary objects don't get through the air above 10,000 feet enough for the eyes to see them.

Men vary greatly in sensitivity to colors. Some are good, and some are poor, and some cannot see some of the colors at all.

Although the armed forces often bar men known to be color-blind, especially from flying and other kinds of work where color is considered particularly important, many of the men in the services are actually pretty poor in color vision.

For, out of every 20 men, about one man has weak color vision and another is partially color-blind. Color-blindness is not nearly so common among women—only about one in a thousand. It is mainly a male defect, but the men inherit it from their mothers. A mother can pass on color blindness to her son

108

from her father or her mother's father without being color-blind herself.

Complete color blindness is very rare, however. Men who are completely color-blind see objects only as blacks, grays and whites, as in an ordinary photograph. They see no color at all. They are not likely to be in the armed services, because they are usually completely blind in the center of the eye and often have other difficulties in vision. They may, however, be good night observers.

The most common form of color blindness is the inability to distinguish red from green. Men with this defect of color vision find it difficult to pick out ripe strawberries from green ones or a rotten apple from a barrel of red apples. They can't see red ripe cherries on a green cherry tree, but they usually can —though not always—tell a red traffic light from a green one. That's because the traffic lights are so bright.

An observer who is red-green blind would not notice a mound of red clay in a green field, unless one were lighter or darker than the other, or bluer or yellower. He might miss the fact that a trench had been dug there.

Once in a while—not often—the color-blind man has the edge on the man with normal vision.

To the normal eye most country landscape in summer appears as a variegated pattern of patches of reddish brown dirt, yellowish brown dirt, and yellowish green leaves and grass. It looks quite varied. But take out all the reds and greens, and you have a much more uniform expanse of dirty yellows, differing a little from each other, but not so much.

Now suppose that in such an expanse of landscape there is a gun position that has been camouflaged with branches, so that the greens of the camouflage would match their surroundings even to the infrared camera. And suppose, as so often happens, that the artillerymen had been careless and allowed the cut foliage to wither until it got pale. The normal eye might not notice this pale patch. It would be only one drab spot in a confusing field. But the color-blind man could see it as a conspicuous pale spot in a sea of darker yellows. To him it would stand out at once in contrast to its background. (So keep remembering daily not to let camouflage get withered, and to replace it.)

Yet no one would choose color-blind men for reconnaissance, just because once in a great while they might notice something that a man with normal vision would miss. The color-blind are definitely defective and handicapped. They cannot see nearly so much as other men. For instance, a man with normal color vision can discriminate 150 different hues from red to orange to yellow to green to blue to violet to purple and so back to red again. (Figure 14. It's only 130 if you don't include the nonspectral purples and carmines.) A color-blind man can discriminate, perhaps, only thirty hues in this series, or sometimes only twenty. The rainbow is to him blue, gray and yellow, with perhaps an edge of black where red should be. Blue and yellow, yellow and blue, black, gray and white, that's what his world is like.

Except for very bright colors like traffic lights and signal lights. Then he may see a little red and green—not much. It all depends on how color-blind he is. Nevertheless, it's a good thing that it was finally decided, years ago, always to have the green traffic signal on top and the red below it. There's no sense in taking a chance on whether one man in twenty is going to start his car up when the red light goes on; and now the color-blind man can remember that Top means Go, and Bottom means Stop.

Since the color-blind person has never seen the wealth of colors visible to other men, he is not aware of what he misses. He may even be able to name the colors of objects correctly. He says that the grass is green because he has learned early in life that grass is green. He knows that the flag on the golf course is red, even though he wonders privately why they use for the flag a color so much like the color of green grass.

But he doesn't talk about color much because he has been laughed at for things he said as a child, and has learned to keep quiet. And he's especially good at remembering the colors of common red and green objects because he does not like to make mistakes. He'd never call a cow green. He knows better.

Such a man may be very useful in the armed services, but there are many jobs to which he should not be assigned. For that reason, tests of color vision are important in assignment of men to jobs.

Most of the many tests in use require a man to discriminate among colors or to match them—especially the various tints and shades of red and green The number of errors he makes is an index of his color weakness. The man to be tested can be asked to match colored wools, colored papers or enamelled chips to some sample or series of samples. The wools do not work very well because the differences in appearance are so great, and because the wool used is likely to fade slightly or change color as it becomes soiled. But the metal chips do a good job. They are made in weak carmines, reds and orangish reds, or in yellowish greens, greens, and bluish greens. You have to be a color expert to get a perfect score on such a test, but you are not counted as color-blind unless you have done pretty poorly.

Another type of test commonly used consists of a series of charts filled with small spots of different shapes, sizes and brightnesses. The background is formed by spots all of the same hue or hues very much alike. In among these background spots, a pattern is formed by another set of spots, which also vary irregularly in shape, size and brightness, but which are of a different hue. For instance, on a background of gray spots, the number 32 might appear in reds or carmines. The color-blind man sees the reds as gray and so cannot read the number.

The simplest test of all is one which merely duplicates the conditions that the man must be ready to meet. A naval officer must be able to distinguish a green light from a red under varying degrees of intensity and when fog or haze obscures the light. So he can be tried out directly on the lights themselves, but that test may not show what he can do with the weaker colors of signal flags or those that appear on a mariner's chart.

The tests are, however, misleading when they classify some men as color-blind and all the rest as normal. Actually men vary all the way from great sensitiveness to color down to none at all. It would be better if there were time to rate soldiers from 0 to 10 on a scale of color sensitivity. Most of the men would turn up near the middle of this scale, and only very rarely indeed would the Army get a 0-man or a 10-man.

V: HEARING AS A TOOL IN WARFARE

How Sounds Differ

IN CLOSE GROUND COMBAT particularly, but also in many other military situations, it is extremely important to distinguish different sounds and identify them. You want to be able to know the noise of a human footstep, if you can, from the pad of a four-footed beast. You want to tell the click of a rifle being loaded from the snap of a breaking twig.

One way sounds are distinguished is by their highness or lowness—their *pitch*. The whistle of a rifle bullet, like the squeak of a shoe, has a high pitch. Thunder or gun fire has a low pitch. Human voices are in between. Pitch depends for the most part on the frequency of the vibrations that make up the sound.

Loudness helps in identifying or in judging the distance of familiar sounds. Loudness is governed by the amount of energy behind the noise. The roar of a cannon or the blast of a bomb has more energy than the bang of a rifle. The engines of a tank or a plane have more than those of a jeep.

More important than mere pitch or loudness for identifying sounds is what is known as the *quality* of a sound. It is the quality rather than the pitch that permits you to know one man's voice from another's, even if both use exactly the same words in speaking or giving a command. The bandmaster can tell the sound of one instrument from another by their qual-

114

ities. He may even be able to tell one cornet from another.

The quality of a sound or a noise depends on the mixture of tones that make it up, just as the flavor of a cocktail depends on how the various liquors and seasonings are proportioned. A perfectly pure tone is hardly ever heard. Nearly always it has other tones mixed up with it, put in by the individual instrument that makes it or by the individual ear that picks up the sound.

It is this mixture of pitches that determines whether the sound is musical or just a noise. When the complexity becomes too great, the result is noise. Noises do not have as definite pitches as musical tones do, because they are really mixtures of many pitches. There is even a "swish" sound that actually combines all the audible pitches.

A sound is a vibration or series of waves set up in the air or other material through which the sound travels. Sound can travel through the earth. That is why it sometimes helps to hear a distant sound if you put your ear to the ground. Sound can also travel through the water, actually better than through air. That helps a lot in the detection of submarines and the propeller noise of surface vessels. Sound can travel through any sort of solid, liquid, or gas—through almost anything except a soft inelastic solid, like felt or a cushion.

The waves travel from the source of the sound in much the same way that the ripples spread out in a widening circle when you drop a pebble into water. The longer the waves, the slower they come by, the lower their frequency, and the deeper in pitch is the sound. The shorter the waves, the higher the frequency and the higher pitched the sound.

There are many sounds that human ears cannot pick up. The best ears cannot generally hear sounds with frequencies below fifteen waves a second. A frequency of twenty does not sound like a tone, but just a low fluttering sound. And at the other end of the scale people can seldom hear tones much above 20,000 waves per second. That is just about the pitch of the chirp of a cricket. Notes too low to be heard are sometimes felt as vibrations on the body and may be annoying, especially if they are very intense. Notes too high to be audible—sometimes called the "death ray" —are damaging to small organisms such as germs but, so far as is known, have no appreciable effect on human beings.

Some animals, however, can hear noises much too high in pitch to be heard by human ears. So there are "silent" whistles made for dogs, whistles which dogs can hear but people cannot.

Bats, it has recently been found, guide themselves around in dark caves by these inaudible sounds. Their own cries, too high in pitch for human ears to hear, echo against the walls of the caves and warn them of the obstacles. Oddly enough, ships sailing the seas in the darkness of wartime night make use of the same principle to detect their foe, the submarine. High-pitched super-frequencies of sound are sent out by the ship in a beam like an under-water searchlight of inaudible noise. When this beam strikes the hull of an undersea boat, an echo is returned and is picked up on the ship, warning it of the danger of attack.

As people grow older they generally lose the ability

to hear sound at the highest pitches that young people easily hear. This may be due to a natural aging process or, some scientists believe, it may be due to the colds and other nose and ear infections that occur during the course of a lifetime. Whatever the reason, a young man of twenty with exceptionally good hearing may be able to detect a frequency of 24,000 waves a second, but by the time he is thirty it is likely that his limit will have dropped to 18,000 or 16,000, which is still far above the upper end of the musical scale. At fifty he may be down to an upper limit of 10,000. He may begin to have difficulty with hearing even lower sounds and in understanding speech. For instance, he may not be able to distinguish a word from its plural, because the s-sound requires frequencies near 4,000.

The loudness of a sound depends upon its energy, but it takes more energy to make the highest or the lowest frequencies audible than it does for the medium range where musical notes and the sounds of speech are contained.

Believe it or not, most of the noise made by the firing of a big gun is below the range which can be heard at all by human ears. But the rest of it, since the energy is very high, is nevertheless very well heard.

Physicists and engineers measure the energy of sound in *decibels* (db). This is a scale, the steps of which are so planned that when you double the energy of a sound you increase the noise by about three decibels, no matter whether it is a faint or loud sound that you are doubling in volume. The ear also works in just about this same way—by ratios instead of even steps. A difference of one decibel is, at every

117

intensity, just about the smallest difference in loudness that the ear can sense.

Figure 29 shows the frequencies and decibels at which audible sounds occur. The lower curve represents the threshold of hearing—the faintest sound

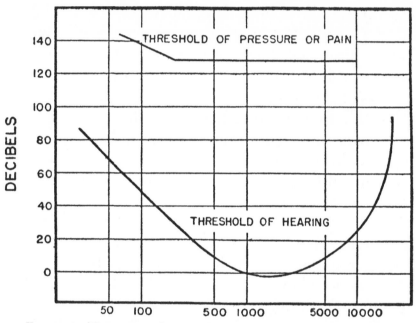

FIG. 29. The curve shows what intensity of sound is just audible (the threshold) at different frequencies. It also shows the high intensity at which pressure or pain begins to be felt in the ear.

that can be heard at each frequency. At any frequency a sound can be heard only if it has at least as many decibels as is necessary to bring it up to or above the threshold. The upper curve shows the threshold at which uncomfortable pressure or pain comes. Sounds with more decibels than shown by this line hurt, nor are they much louder. At 140 decibels, a sound is pretty close to the ceiling of hear-

118

ing. You can have more energy and more pain, but not much louder sounds.

It is astonishing how sensitive your ears are to sounds in the frequency range of 1,000-4,000. If you could hear sounds only ten decibels fainter than you are now able to pick up, you would actually begin to hear the incredibly tiny movements of the molecules of the air. At a frequency of 3,600 your eardrum has to move only one one-thousandth of a millionth of an inch to make a sound just audible.

High frequency sounds do not carry so well as do lower toned noises. For that reason, the sound of an airplane, which includes a great many different pitches, is only a low rumble or roar when it is in the distance, a higher pitched shooshing noise when very close. Thunder is a low rumble in the distance, but is a crack or crash close by.

It is for that reason that noises of this sort are not unpleasant when heard at a considerable distance— for it is the high frequencies, in general, that are so distressing.

How We Hear

The sound vibrations have to travel through a good many different changes before they get to the place in the inner ear where the auditory nerve begins. See Figure 30.

First they go through the air in the auditory canal and make the eardrum at the end of it vibrate.

The eardrum sets in motion a set of three small bones which bridge the middle ear to the inner ear. The middle ear is full of air and connects by a tube to the back of the mouth. That is why you have to

119

swallow as you go up or down in an airplane or under a river in a railway tunnel. Maybe you chew gum to help you keep swallowing. Your swallowing opens this tube to the middle ear and allows the air in the middle ear to change to the same pressure as the air outside. Opening your mouth when you expect a bomb to burst similarly helps to keep the pressures equal on the two sides of the eardrum. It feels un-

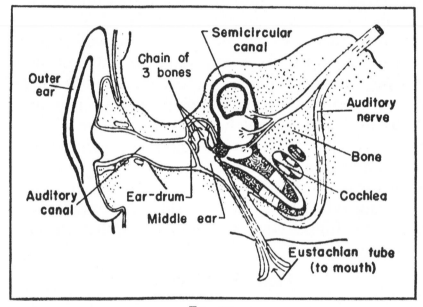

FIG. 30.

comfortable to have the pressures unequal—and it also deafens you.

In the inner ear are the semicircular canals. These canals have nothing at all to do with hearing. The sense-organs in them, however, help a man to keep his balance, tell him when he is rotating, when speeding up or slowing down.

In the inner ear also is the *cochlea*. This is a longish

tube, curled up like a snail-shell, filled with liquid, and divided through its length by a partition. Part of this partition is a long strip of membrane, narrow at the broad base of the cochlea, wide at its tip. The auditory nerve-fibers begin in cells that rest on this membrane. When this membrane vibrates you hear sound.

This membrane vibrates differently for different frequencies of sound. Probably the part of the membrane near the base of the cochlea is most important for hearing high pitches. Old people who have become deaf to high pitches are likely to have defects in this part of the membrane. We do not know about the low pitches. People sensitive to high pitches are seldom deaf to low.

Deafness of different kinds may occur as a result of injury in military service.

If the eardrum is lost there is a general deafness for all frequencies, but it is not very great—not more than twenty decibels. If the bones of the middle ear are injured, as well as the eardrum, then the loss becomes serious, but loud speech can still be heard.

When the inner ear is damaged, there may be a hearing loss for one range of pitches and not for others—especially if the injury lies at the base of the cochlea.

Figure 31 shows just what an airplane noise can do to hearing. If the intensity of the noise is 100 decibels and it lasts for half an hour, then there is a slight deafening effect of a few decibels for frequencies in the region of 1,000-5,000. The effect is much greater for a half hour with a noise of 110 decibels, still greater for 120 decibels—which is a

121

very loud noise indeed. The man, after the noise is over, is badly deafened, has trouble in understanding speech correctly unless the speaker shouts. Unfortunately, he is deafened most for faint and moderate sounds. Loud noises are just as loud as ever. But he

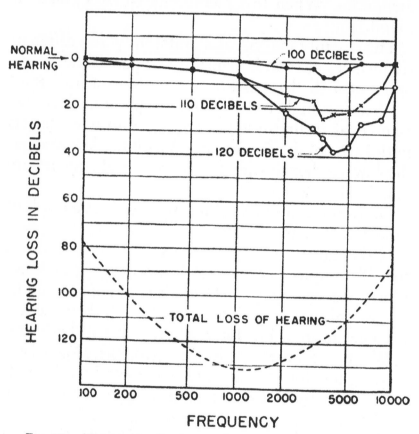

FIG. 31. The curves showing hearing losses for three different intensities of airplane noise after a half hour's exposure.

recovers about half of his normal hearing in a half hour of quiet, all of it in the course of a day.

On the other hand, flyers repeatedly subjected to these deafening noises for long periods may suffer permanent injury of the inner ear, permanent difficulty in perceiving the high frequencies. Boiler makers and others continuously exposed to loud continued racket show the same kind of effect.

A big gun may be even more damaging to hearing. It makes two sounds, a boom and a crack. If you are half a mile away from a big gun when it is fired you hear the crack first. It is produced by the projectile going through the air and comes to you about when the projectile does. You won't hear it if you're going to be hit, because the crack will arrive with the shell. The boom comes after the crack and the projectile, for the projectile may travel at a speed of about half a mile a second, whereas the boom, which is a sound produced by the explosion at the muzzle of the gun, travels to you from the gun at the ordinary speed of sound, about a fifth of a mile in a second.

You can tell the distance a gun is away if you can see its flash and then count, "One dead Jap, two dead Japs, three dead Japs," until you hear the boom. If it takes one second to say "One dead Jap," then the distance of the gun in miles is about the number of dead Japs divided by five.

The boom of the gun, if you are half a mile off, is just a boom. But if you are near the muzzle, a little in advance of it, it is the end of your hearing. Your eardrum would be ruptured, the bones in your middle ear wrecked, and your inner ear permanently injured. The pressure of this sound on the ear is tremendous, as much as forty-five times the normal pressure of the atmosphere.

If you are farther away, off to the side but in advance of the muzzle, you may only have your ear-

123

drum ruptured and acquire temporary deafness of your inner ear. Still farther off the effect may be like that of too loud an airplane noise—only temporary deafness to high frequencies.

The man behind the gun is in a more advantageous position. The sound-pressure is not so great there, and the gun-shield may protect him a little too. His expectation of the noise also helps, for it leads him to adjust muscles attached to the bones of his middle ear in such a way that they resist the impact of the sound. But he will do well to wear ear-plugs or at least to put cotton in his ears if he does not want to have his hearing interfered with for a time afterwards.

Putting cotton in his ears may be a great advantage to a soldier exposed to much less intense noise, also. On a pistol or rifle range, for example, such protection to the hearing has been found to improve marksmanship. Another man's shot, or even the anticipation of your own next one, may make you jerk just enough to spoil your precision. This does not happen when the noise is dulled.

Ear-plugs are a great aid, not only for gunners but also for men in airplanes. But all the men in the gun crew or the airplane crew must wear them at the same time. Otherwise the man with the plugs will miss the commands of the man without them, because the man without the plugs will forget to shout. But a man with plugs in his ear never forgets to shout because he always wants to hear himself talking, and he has to shout to hear himself.

In an airplane you can hear shouting better with the plugs in your ear than without, strange as that may seem. With no plugs the noise may be so near the pain threshold that men do not shout loud enough to be heard. No one likes to hurt himself by his own shouting. It is, moreover, hard to get the ear to hear an increase in loudness that is above the pain threshold. But with the plugs in your own ears and another man outshouting the noise, you may hear his words perfectly, for then the extra energy in the shouting can have its full effect.

If, therefore, you want to hear speech above a loud continuous noise, you had better plug your ears—stick your fingers in them. That sounds crazy, but men who have tried it know that it works.

Sometimes soldiers fake deafness in order to avoid assuming responsibilities. The man who feigns deafness can, however, usually be detected. The examiner tests his sensitivity for each ear separately and then for both together. If the soldier is just pretending deafness his thresholds (the loudness at which he says he can just hear) will be inconsistent—one threshold at one trial, another later. His thresholds should, moreover, be only half as large for the two ears together as for one alone, since the ears reënforce each other; yet the malingerer, even if he knows this fact, is unable correctly to fake these measurements.

There is also a psychological kind of deafness which is called hysterical. Because of great fear or emotional shock, a man may become genuinely unable to hear although his ears are still normally sensitive. This trouble lies in the brain. The man is not faking. He cannot cure his deafness by an act of will. He is a neurotic case and should receive medical attention as soon as possible.

Loud sounds, especially when they are sudden and strange, are natural causes of fear. Many sounds are terrifying.

A sudden loud noise, like the discharge of a pistol, will make anyone blink and jump—it will startle him. This is true even of well trained men who pride themselves on their familiarity with firearms. It is an instantaneous response that may be all over before the eye can see it. It shows up, however, in slow motion pictures.

Loud noises are also distracting. You pay attention to a sudden infernal racket or din; you have to. The enemy often takes advantage of this fact, so beware. One of the effects of the dive bomber or strafing plane lies in the noise it makes. When one of them shrieks down over the heads of troops they are impelled, almost irresistibly, to look up. Thus they may disregard for dangerous moments tanks or other ground forces which may be their greatest danger at the time. Experienced combat soldiers know that they must usually ignore the great noises of planes and shells and keep their attention on the job of killing a more dangerous ground enemy.

Seasoned troops get so that they don't appear to pay any particular attention to the din of battle. Even horses will stand still under the rising roar of a diving bomber—will only toss a head impatiently.

The inexperienced soldier, on the other hand, needs first to become adapted to the noises of war. He must be exposed to them in training as much as possible. After the noise has become familiar, its

126

loudness will not affect him so greatly in combat.

Control over a noise makes it less fearful. You don't mind the noise of gun fire so much if you are doing the shooting. Even in London in the Battle of Britain, the people came to welcome the noise of the antiaircraft guns. It became for them a pleasant sound.

But men subjected to the excessive noises of war over a long period sometimes build up a sensitiveness to any sort of loud, sharp report. They are in the state of a man with a hang-over. The bang of a door will make them jump. A loud shout is painful. The noise of a truck exhaust is frightening.

In the hospital where men are convalescing from bad cases of these war nerves, the dropping of a pan will startle a ward full of sleeping men so violently that the jerk will bring them out of their sleep and even out of their beds on to the floor.

But this state of nerves, though linked in their minds with the noise, and produced by the noise, is due mainly to more disturbing things that have become associated with the noise.

Noises just as loud and originally just as distressing as the noises of war, if they are just a part of everyday work or fun, are tolerated. Men become used to the din of a boiler factory or a pneumatic drill. It may deafen them, but it does not demoralize them.

It is when a particular noise is always linked with the threat of personal injury or death, or with the injury to friends and damage to vital objects, that noise in general comes to have a particular horror in addition to its natural disturbing quality.

This sort of emotionally charged noise can shock

the mind and may possibly cause it serious injury.

The noise of battle is stimulating—exciting—to the soldier who is prepared for it. It makes his heart beat faster, sends the blood coursing through his veins. He is stirred to work faster, fight better, yell louder. It is hard to sit still under this powerful excitement, but often men must—both soldiers and civilians. When there is something urgent to be done, however, the noise of war comes as an appropriate and helpful accompaniment to action.

Although noise keeps men alert for immediate activity, it may hinder the work of a soldier if he must be responsible for some deliberate task like the careful plotting of a plane's course or artillery fire, or the movement of troops for an attack. For men who have to do these things, advance training in doing them under conditions of loud and distracting noise is especially important.

It is because noise stimulates activity that it is eventually fatiguing. That is why most adults do not like noise. Their muscles get tense and they get tired. If they are not taking active part in the crashing drama, this tenseness is translated into irritability and jumpiness. But young men, like children, usually enjoy noise, especially when they know its source or are creating it themselves.

BEATS

The pilot of a bimotored plane keeps his motors operating at the same speed by listening for beats and adjusting the speed of one motor until the beats disappear. It has also been reported that the Germans purposely keep the motors of their planes at different speeds so as to create beats which make the use of sound-detection apparatus more difficult. What are beats?

If two tones of the same frequency sound together, they simply add up to a louder tone.

But if they differ slightly in frequency, then they beat. You hear OOOooooooOOOooooooOOO. A frequency of 1,000, sounding along with a frequency of 1,004, will give four beats per second. That is because the two sound waves get out of step and partially cancel each other four times every second, getting in step and reënforcing each other in between the cancellations. You get one beat a second from 1,000 and 1,001; one beat every two seconds from 1,000 and 1,000.5. Musical instruments can be tuned by beats, in the same way that a pilot "tunes" the motor of his plane.

COMMUNICATION

Loud sounds drown out faint. It is hard to talk inside a moving tank. Low sounds drown out high more than high drown low. That is another reason why the low-pitched noise of a tank, or a plane, makes conversation impossible. But it would take a tremendous number of crickets to mask a conversation by their chirpings.

The masking of speech sounds by the loud low-pitched noises of mechanized warfare creates a serious problem. It is impossible to give an oral command to a man in the field unless you can shout into his ear. Inside tanks, airplanes and gun turrets it may be entirely impossible. Hence resort has to be made to other means.

Figure 32 shows what the noise in an airplane does to the understanding of speech. For speech in quiet surroundings all the frequencies are available at all the intensities, from the threshold of hearing in quiet, up to the threshold where pressure of pain begins to be felt in the ears. The airplane noise masks

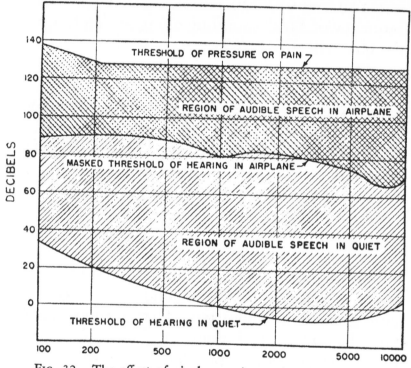

FIG. 32. The effect of airplane noise on hearing speech.

all the low intensities, moving the threshold up toward the top of the diagram and leaving only a small region available for communication. For you to hear under these conditions, the speaker has to speak at 80 or 90 decibels above a whisper. That means that he is shouting at the very top of his voice.

Visual signals can sometimes be substituted for auditory. A man can wig-wag a message with flags,

130

can flash code by using a flashlight, can raise his arm and point. A gunner in a tank can tell the driver something by different pressures with his foot. But none of these substitutes is so good as speech, for speech is quick, easy, and specific. It does not have to be learned after the soldier has come into the Army. Every recruit can speak and understand speech—at least in some language—almost as readily as he can walk.

Thus the telephone, including the Walkie-Talkie, becomes an extremely important military instrument, because it can be used to make speech carry over great distances, or to make it carry over a few feet in the presence of deafening noise. In this latter case the noise is shut out—at least partially—by padding on the receivers of the head-set which the listener has to wear—in a tank, in an airplane.

Fortunately, it is easier to hear speech than many other sounds, because the pitch range used in speech is in the region for which human ears are most sensitive.

The fundamental pitch of the human voice may be a frequency as low as 90 in a man with a bass voice and as high as 300 in a woman's shrill voice. But there are also higher frequencies that come in. High component tones around 3,000 are common. The characteristic pitches for some vowels and consonants go as high as 4,000.

In fact it is the higher frequencies that are most important. If all the frequencies below 500 are cut out, voices sound strange but are still intelligible. Understanding of speech is reduced by only two per cent. But if all the frequencies above 1,500 are eliminated, then the intelligibility of speech is reduced by about thirty-five per cent. It is important, therefore, to preserve these higher frequencies in any telephonic system of communication. A single order misunderstood may lose a battle.

There are all sorts of ways of testing communication systems, but they all boil down to the same thing You speak and then measure the intelligibility of your speech to a listener. In this way you can find out how a masking noise works, as in Figure 32. You can discover how good a telephone system is—and that is important because telephones distort speech and cut down its intelligibility. Some phones are, moreover, worse than others.

A simple practical method is to ask questions and to see how often you get the right answers, but that does not tell you why the mistakes occur. A more precise method is to study how particular consonants and vowels are communicated. For instance, if the sound is faint, *three* may be heard as *free,* because *th* and *f* are hard to understand in faint sounds, but *ee* is likely to remain clear. So, to measure intelligibility of speech, you simply count up the errors for each consonant, each vowel, or, perhaps, for a set of questions taken as a whole.

When there are no masking noises, speech remains intelligible at great varieties of intensity. Intelligibility stays above ninety per cent for loudness between 50 and 120 decibels above the threshold of hearing, for everything between a quiet voice and shout. The sound *z* gets into difficulties at very weak intensities.

In general *th, f,* and *v* give the most trouble at every degree of loudness. On the other hand, the sounds *i* (as in t*i*me), *ou* (as in t*ou*n), *er* (as in t*er*m), and *o* (as in t*o*ne) are easy to understand. Even in a faint whisper they generally come through correctly.

The telephone, however, tends to distort speech by cutting out high frequencies and leaving in the low, whereas it is these high frequencies that are the most important for intelligibility. The sound *s* suffers most since it depends almost entirely on high frequencies. Often you cannot hear *s* over a poor telephone, although you may put in the *s*'s in the right places if you know the sense of the message. Similar to *s* is *th*, which needs some high frequencies in order to be clear; and similar to *th* are *z, t,* and *f* which depend only a little less on the high frequencies. Vowels like *u* (as in t*u*ne) and *o* (as in t*o*ne) are characterized almost entirely by low pitches and do not get into trouble on the phone. There is trouble for *u* though when a soprano singer tries to sing it on a high note, a note above its natural pitch.

You can hear the pitches of the different vowels if you say over and over to yourself *oo-oh-ah-ay-ee.* The pitch goes up, even if you sing the series with your voice going down. Say *ee-ay-ah-oh-oo,* and you hear the vowel-pitch go down. That is why the telephone lets *ee* by less frequently than the other vowels, why the telephone operator trills the *r* in th*r*ee so that the listener will not think she said *two.*

LOCATING OBJECTS BY SOUND

The ear is not so good as the eye for locating the position of objects. Edgar Bergen talks without moving his lips, while Charlie McCarthy on Bergen's lap

133

makes the mouth movements. It is Charlie who seems to be talking, because the eyes of the audience locate the speaking mouth exactly, whereas the ears cannot give such accurate information.

Nevertheless the ears can do a very good job in telling whether a sound is from the right or the left or from some intermediate position, although they make mistakes about the difference between front and back, or up and down, and in estimating distances.

It is true that you can sometimes know something about distance with only the sound to go by. If the sound is familiar so that you know how loud it really is, then, if it appears faint, you judge it to be far away. If it has the low and high pitches in it, you will think it must be near, because you can hear only the middle pitches—those for which the ear is most sensitive—for sounds that come from far away.

It is also true that the pitch of a rapidly approaching sound gets higher, because the speed of the object that makes the sound speeds up the frequency of the sound. You notice this in hearing the whistle of an approaching locomotive.

The whistle of a bomb goes up in pitch as the bomb falls, sometimes because the bomb is speeding up, sometimes because it is getting nearer to you so that you hear more and more high components in its sound. High pitched sounds do not travel as far as low.

But the best localization of sounds by human ears is for their direction. That capacity depends on the fact that people have two ears, one on each side of the head. The sound gets to a far ear after it ar-

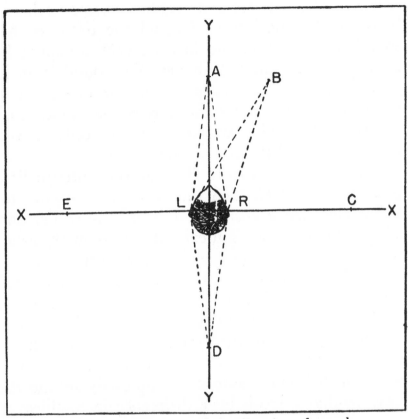

FIG. 33.   Localization of the direction of sound.

rives at the near ear, and it is louder at an ear that it reaches directly than at an ear that is screened by the head.

Look at Figure 33. A sound at *E* is loud in the left ear, faint in the right; and it gets to the left ear first. Either or both of these differences thus make it appear to come from the left. The opposite relation is true for a sound starting at *C*.

If the sound comes from *A*, it gets to both ears at the same time and with the same intensity, a relationship which leads the hearer to localize the sound

135

halfway between left and right. The same relation holds for a sound from *D,* and the result is that sounds in front (*A*) and in back (*D*) are apt to be confused, although not always. The sound from in back may be a little fainter than the one from in front because the outer ears screen the sound from the rear. That clue works, however, only if you know how loud the sound ought to be.

If a sound comes from *B,* a position intermediate between *A* and *C,* then the two ears, working together, localize it correctly. It is a little earlier and a little louder at the right ear, but not so much earlier nor so much louder as it would have been at *C.*

The low frequencies (as in gunfire) are localized mostly by the difference in time of their arrival at the two ears. Since these sound waves are long, there is a good chance for the time difference between the arrivals of the same wave at the two ears to be effective. For the same reason, they slip easily around the head so that there is little difference in loudness at the two ears.

On the other hand, the high frequencies (as in a whistle) are localized almost entirely by the intensity-difference. The waves are very short and do not leave much chance for differences in time to operate, but, being short, they cannot easily get around the head. Thus the ear that is wholly or partly screened by the head hears only a faint sound.

Localization is worse for the middle frequencies in the neighborhood of 2,000, because this frequency is too high for time-difference to be very effective, too low for intensity-difference to be very effective.

Both principles operate together for most sounds,

because most sounds are complex. They have in them both low and high frequencies.

A source of sound is localized best if the head is free to move. You settle the question of the direction of a sound by moving your head from side to side until the stimulation is alike in both your ears. Then your nose is pointing toward the sound—unless you have made the unlikely mistake of pointing your nose directly away from it.

There is an experiment in which a man has his head surrounded by a horizontal circle of telephone receivers, and in which a mechanical device always turns on the sound in the receiver that the man, as he turns his head, is facing at the moment. Where does he then think the sound to be? Why, right above his head. That is the only position in which a single sound would continue to be alike at both ears, no matter how much he turned his head around horizontally.

The Army uses, when better devices are not available, auditory direction-finders (Fig. 34). This instrument has large receiving horns, widely separated and connected up by telephones to the ears of the observer. It is like giving the observer bigger ears further apart, so as to increase the differences of intensity. The device can be used for determining either horizontal or vertical directions, and works pretty well with the high frequencies where difference in loudness is the important factor. It does not work so well for lower frequencies where time-difference becomes important, because exaggerating the time-difference by having a large distance between the horns confuses the observation more than

FIG. 34.

it helps. This trouble arises because the time-differences between the two ears get to be as large as the time-differences between successive waves of the same sound.

The observer in this apparatus has a means for rotating himself along with his artificial ears, so that he can aim himself at the sound. That is the natural way in which a man localizes the direction of a sound, and the natural method is usually the most accurate.

SOUND CAMOUFLAGE

It isn't always wise to shoot your rifle when you get a chance for a shot at one of the enemy. If you shoot, you give away your position. But you can shoot when others are shooting, shoot when the enemy starts making the noise. In the confusion of sounds, nothing may be localized.

Sometimes one man, safe behind a tree, can break sticks to draw enemy fire, while his comrades off in

138

another place are ready to shoot where he drew the fire from. There are all sorts of simple ruses with rifle fire that are really sound camouflage.

The chief principles of sound camouflage are three —all quite simple. (1) The actual occurrence of one sound is masked by another sound. An artillery barrage masks rifle fire. Low airplanes sometimes mask the sound of approaching tanks. (2) Localization becomes indefinite if there are too many simultaneous sounds, unless one sound stands out clearly from the others. It is easier to locate a single machine gun than one of three when they are all letting go together. (3) False sounds may deceive as to the nature or location of an actually threatening military weapon or activity. Jericho was taken by a few men with lots of trumpets.

Hearing Rules

Here are a few simple rules to help you to get the most out of your ears.

(1) Keep the wax cleaned out of your ears. Otherwise it may deafen you. Especially in hot weather and hot climates is it likely to make trouble. You had better not take it out yourself. You ought to get help from a medical officer.

(2) Keep well. Avoid colds. If you have a cold, it may be dangerous to subject your ears to great changes of pressure, as you do in going up in a plane and coming down. The cold is likely to have closed the tube from your mouth to your middle ear, so that the pressure on the inside of the eardrum cannot be equalized to the outside pressure. Unequal pressures deafen you.

139

(3) Avoid exposure to loud sounds, heavy gun fire, airplane noise, if right afterwards you are going to need to listen for faint sounds. The effects of the loud sounds may easily last for half an hour, sometimes even for a day. Protect your hearing with cotton as you protect your eyes with goggles.

(4) If you do not want to be temporarily deafened by your own rifle fire, plug your left ear with cotton. It's the one that gets the explosion pulse from the muzzle of your own gun.

(5) If you are in the midst of loud noise and want to hear speech, plug your ears with ear-plugs or cotton, or even your own fingers, if you have them free. Then you can hear the shouts of other men better. And if all of a gun crew have their ears plugged, then no one of them will forget that he has to shout to make the others hear, for he will inevitably shout in order to hear his own voice.

(6) Listen, especially when you know what kind of a sound to expect. On patrol and reconnaisance, keep quiet and listen. The strain you feel in your ears when you listen is your middle-ear muscles adjusting themselves to the most sensitive hearing.

(7) Get interested in sounds. You can learn to recognize all sorts of objects when you have trained yourself by practice. Some men can, under certain conditions, distinguish between two different airplanes by the sounds of their motors. They could not describe the difference to you, but they recognize it. Trained woods and jungle fighters learn the differences between the sounds of human and animal movements in the undergrowth.

And here are some rules to help you from being

deafened, temporarily or permanently, by very loud sounds.

(1) Protect your ears from loud sounds. Use earplugs or cotton when they will not interfere with your hearing commands—when the men who give commands are using them too. Put your fingers in your ears and open your mouth when a gun is about to discharge close by. The new helmets protect your ears from blasts but not from loud sounds—except the special padded helmets with phones inside them. Some helmets actually distort localization sound.

(2) Keep your ears away from the places where the sounds from gun-discharges are greatest. Keep away from any position ahead of the muzzle of a gun. Face the direction from which the sound will come, turning neither ear directly toward it. The head itself is an excellent screen for the ear behind it, but when it shields one ear well it is generally exposing the other ear unless you put your finger in it.

(3) Hunt for objects to screen the ear. Keep behind walls when an explosion's coming. Lie down in hollows. The explosion pulse generally rises from the ground anyhow, so you are better off when prone.

(4) Open your mouth when an explosion is coming. It helps the pressures on the two sides of the eardrum to become equal, and may even save you from having the drum ruptured.

(5) Expect the explosion. If you are prepared for it, your middle-ear muscles are set to resist violent movement of the bones in the middle ear. They are very differently adjusted in listening for a faint sound and in expecting a loud one.

VI: SMELL—A SENTRY

IN MAN SMELL DOES GUARD DUTY—mostly. A dog uses smell for all sorts of purposes—for recognizing friends, enemies, and his master, for identifying cats and other dogs, for finding persons and animals by tracking them, for a great variety of purposes. A dog's nose is about as useful as his eyes and his ears. That is partly because he keeps his nose near the ground where the odors collect, whereas man, with his nose five feet or more up in the air, misses most of what is going on in the world of odors.

It is true that smell, although a sentry, has also some pleasant duties for man. It is the most important contributor to the flavor of foods, for taste in the mouth contributes only sweet, sour, salt, and bitters to flavors. The rest of the flavor of food depends on the nose, the odors that come directly from the dining table or those others that get to the nose inside from the back of the mouth.

But the odors that matter most are the warning odors—the foul and the burnt odors that mean, more often than not, Look out! there is something unpleasant here.

There are really three senses working together here at the entrance to the body where food goes in. In the tongue are the nerve-endings for taste. They respond simply to sweet, sour, salt, and bitter. The nerve-endings for smell lie high up in a recess at the top of each nostril. They provide information about the fragrant, ethereal, spicy, resinous, putrid and burnt qualities of food and other objects.

Then there is a third sense, also a chemical sense, located in the cavities of the nose and mouth that adds the cold of peppermint, the prickle of carbonated drinks, the sting of ammonia, the irritation of chlorine gas.

All three combine when food is in the mouth. Smell and the chemical sense join to give information about outside objects. Food tastes flat when you have a bad cold because then the nose is out of use and you get only the combinations of the four simple tastes. They are not enough to provide the variety you expect from a good dinner.

NAMING AND RECOGNIZING ODORS

Don't rely on any spoken or written description of a dangerous odor like that of a war gas. Smell it for yourself. For it isn't easy to describe an odor. That is because people do not have special names for smell sensations and because they do not think of odors in relation to each other, but rather as quite independent of each other.

Other sensations for the most part have names which people know and use—red, bitter, cold, rough, loud, painful. Everyone knows what those six sensations are like, but the smells are merely named after the objects that give rise to them—the smell of roses, of oranges, of turpentine, of toast, of rotten eggs. There just isn't a good set of smell words in the dictionary.

But the reason there isn't a good vocabulary for smell is that we have no habits of describing smells

143

by relating them to one another. You can describe a new color, because you can think of where it lies in the rainbow of colors. If you do not know what color *fuchsia* is, you can be told. It is a red with a good deal of blue in it, a very strong color, neither very dark nor very light.

What does magnesium chloride taste like? If you don't know, you can be told that too. It is bitterish-salty, more salty than bitter.

Tones don't have names that everyone can recognize. They cannot whistle middle-C-sharp and be sure it isn't middle-C; but you can describe C-sharp as a little higher than C.

For the smells, however, there is no such sure system. The best attempt at one specifies six principal classes of odors, as follows:

Fragrant—like the smell of violets.
Spicy—like the smell of cloves.
Ethereal—like the smell of oranges.
Resinous—like the smell of turpentine.
Putrid—like the smell of rotten eggs.
Burnt—like the smell of tar.

Roses are fragrant. Geranium is fragrant, but a little ethereal too. Onion is putrid, but also somewhat fragrant and burnt. Cedar is fragrant, ethereal, spicy and resinous—all four. Grapefruit is ethereal, resinous, putrid and burnt.

That may sound almost as good as the color system, but actually it is not. This scheme is only a rough approximation. There are lots of fragrants: roses, violets and lilies differ. There are many spices: how does clove differ from nutmeg? The system does not make these fine distinctions.

This entire business of recognizing odors is further complicated by the fact that the chemists are constantly creating brand new odors. No one ever sees an entirely new color. Everyone has seen every color sometime. Most of the hues turn up in the rainbow. But no one had ever experienced the odor of illuminating gas until there was illuminating gas to smell. If the use of some substitute should stop its manufacture, children would grow up without ever having that sensation. It is, of course, easy to recognize illuminating gas once you know the odor, but you have got to have experience with that particular object before you can be sure about it.

Another complication arises because the same object does not always smell the same way. Some substances, like the war gas phosgene, have one odor when faint, a different one when strong.

The odors of other substances vary with the impurities that are in them. If a war gas is dissolved in something else, then that something else may be what gives it its odor. In the last war mustard gas of the Germans smelled like mustard, but mustard gas of the Allies smelled like garlic. They had different solvents in them.

The same object sometimes smells differently to different people, and it is said that there is sometimes even a noticeable difference in the smell of an object between the right and left nostrils of the same man.

In other words, if you want to recognize new odors, you have got to learn them, each for itself. It is not safe to depend on a system. It is not safe to depend on what somebody else says is a similarity to the smell of a familiar object. You and he may

145

smell the familiar object differently—or the new one.

To help men recognize the odors of the known war gases, the Chemical Warfare Service, therefore, makes up sample sets for personal identification. You learn the odors in weak harmless concentrations, learn to recognize them instantly. It does not matter if the odor changes in strong concentrations. The time to do your recognizing is when the gas is still weak and harmless.

War Gases

For those war gases that evaporate fast and have smells, there is no chemical indicator so sensitive as a normal nose. A grain of musk can go on scenting a bureau drawer for years with only a barely detectable loss in weight. You can smell 1 seven-hundred-millionth of an ounce of artificial musk. You can smell 2 seven-hundred-million-millionths of an ounce of mercaptan, an evil smelling, especially powerful substance.

All the odorous war gases in the accompanying table, except mustard gas and lewisite, can be detected by smell in concentrations too low to be dangerous. For them the nose is a good detector. Mustard gas can, however, in the course of an hour injure the eye in concentrations too weak to be smelled at all. Lewisite, which has arsenic in it, can be fatal without having been smelled at all.

The table of War Gases attempts to describe the odors of these gases, but it is not a safe guide. The soldier ought to get direct acquaintance with these important odors—in concentrations too low to harm him, of course.

146

Agent	Symbol	Odor	Other Immediate Effects
Vesicants (blistering or burning agent) Mustard Gas.....	HS	Garlic, Horse radish, mustard..	None
Lewisite........	M-1	Geraniums.......	Sneezing, nasal irritation
Sternutators (vomiting gas, irritant smoke) Ethyldichlorarsine.	ED	Pungent; irritating	Sneezing, eye and nose irritation
Adamsite........	DM	Odor from burning smokeless powder, coal smoke.	Canary yellow smoke haze; headache; vomiting
Lung irritant gases Phosgene.	CG	In light concentration, musty hay or cut corn; in heavy concentration, ensilage	Thin white cloud; eye irritation; coughing; tightness in chest
Chlorpicrin	PS	Sweetish, like licorice, flypaper, or anise........	Lacrimation; vomiting
Lacrimator gases (tear gas) Chloracetophenone	CN	Locust, apple blossoms; ripe fruit.	Lacrimation; irritation of skin in hot weather
Tear gas solution..	CNS	Sweetish.......	Lacrimation; irritation of skin
Brombenzylcyanide	CA	Like sour fruit...	Eye irritation usual before odor is noted; lasts some time
Screening smokes Sulfurtrioxide in chlorsulfonic acid..	FS	Acid (strong), burning matches	Prickly sensation on skin; eye irritation; dense white smoke
HC mixture......	HC	Smoky odor, sharp, acrid........	Dense smoke; slight suffocating feeling
White phosphorus.	WP	Like burning matches.......	Glow from burning particles; incendiary effect; smoke
Incendiary Thermit........	TH	None..........	Glow of molten iron

Here are certain rules which, while they apply especially to gas sentries, can be understood with profit by every soldier.

(1) Beware of differences in sensitivity between men. Some men have defective smell, either because of past disease or infection of the nose, or perhaps sometimes by inheritance. A gas sentry should be normally sensitive to odors and know by direct acquaintance the particular odors expected in gases. A soldier ought to get some idea as to whether his sensitivity is normal or not.

(2) A cold diminishes sensitivity; a bad cold may abolish it. No man with a bad cold should be posted as a gas sentry. A soldier with a bad cold should especially beware of gas.

(3) The nose fatigues rapidly to smell. It may become quite insensitive to long continued odors. It is refreshed by breathing pure fresh air. Do not keep constantly sniffing at a suspected odor. Sniff once or twice, and then rest the nose in fresh air. If an odor disappears, be sure it has really disappeared, that you have not merely become fatigued to it. Get someone who has been in odorless air to test for you.

(4) Gasoline fumes dull smell sensitivity. Keep gas sentries away from parking areas, from gasoline tanks.

(5) Tobacco smoke dulls sensitivity. Don't let the gas sentries smoke; when possible, use non-smokers. Don't let other men smoke near the sentries.

(6) When phosgene degenerates, it gives off a substance that dulls smell. Beware of false security after a phosgene attack.

148

(7) Some explosives give off nitric oxide which dulls smell. Again beware.

(8) Since most of the war gases tend to settle down in hollows, ravines and dugouts, don't trust men on high ground to test for the presence of gas on lower ground. In low pockets, test for yourself if you have to enter them.

The test for gas is usually made as follows. The soldier takes a moderate breath while wearing his mask. He stoops and brings his face close to the ground without kneeling. Then he inserts two fingers under the mask's facepiece at one cheek and draws air in under the mask by sniffing, *not by breathing*. If he smells gas, he must clear the mask by holding the outlet valve and forcing air out under the raised facepiece. Then he must breathe pure air through the mask to get recovery from odor fatigue before he tests again.

Camouflage of Odors

There are various ways in which odors can be obliterated or changed. When these effects are introduced intentionally by the enemy, they amount to gas camouflage. In any case they represent principles which the wary soldier should know.

(1) *Fatigue.* Getting fatigued to a gas in low concentrations, or getting accustomed to its presence so that it does not seem important, may prevent the soldier from reacting promptly to a dangerous concentration. The Germans tried this ruse in the last war. They shot over weak harmless concentrations of a gas for several days, until the soldiers were accustomed to having it around and were also some

149

what fatigued to it. Then they sent over a deadly concentration intended to wreak havoc among the troops. The scheme worked with green troops.

(2) *Selective fatigue.* Continued exposure to a mixed odor may cause its quality to change because the nose becomes fatigued to one ingredient sooner than to another. Some perfumes, on continued smelling, reduce to the mere odor of alcohol. Certain changes in odors can be induced by the products of some explosives, by the odors of swamps, pinewoods, orchards, and flowers, by the odors from dumps, field kitchens, hospitals, and garbage.

(3) *Masking.* One odor may cover up another, mask it. The solvents used for mustard gas sometimes mask the characteristic odor of the gas itself. Carbon tetrachloride will mask many different kinds of odors. In fact, almost any strong unimportant odor may, if strong enough, mask an important one.

(4) *Mixing.* A typical odor may be changed by mixing it with another. Nitrobenzine, when used as a solvent for mustard gas, changes the natural odor of the gas to the odor of bitter almonds.

So the moral is: Beware! The nose is a good detector when it is specifically trained to recognize particular odors, but the nose cannot smell the tricks that the enemy has up his sleeve. The nose, in fact, does better in telling you when you must certainly put your gas mask on than it does in telling you when it is quite safe to leave it off.

VII: THE SENSE OF POSITION AND THE SENSE OF DIRECTION

How DOES ANYONE MANAGE to keep his balance when he is standing on a rolling deck or in a lurching tank? How does an airplane pilot flying in dense fog know which way is up? How does a scout find his way surely through a strange woods?

Nobody thinks much about how these things are done when they are done correctly. It is when something goes wrong that it becomes necessary to understand just how the body and the mind work to make them possible.

And the flyer does sometimes fly upside down by mistake. The scout can get lost. Men get dizzy and sick when they get mixed up about up and down and when they spin around. And even when they are not spinning around, they may feel sure that horizon, earth, and sky are flying about them in a mad whirl.

UP VS. DOWN

Drop a cat from five feet above the ground, and she lands on her feet. She has twisted around in the air while falling. She knows which way is up.

Her act is automatic and immediate. She does not take notice of which way is *up*, decide to twist around, twist around, check on her position, and then land. She just lands—correctly.

A paratrooper (Fig. 35) can do the same thing no

151

matter how much he twists and tumbles during his drop.

You do much the same thing every day. You can walk upright over rough ground—even run without pitching over. You keep your balance without ever giving it a thought. If you stumble, you can usually right yourself and recover your balance.

Fig. 35. Which way is up?

You can walk along a plank one foot wide without falling off—if the plank lies on the floor; but perhaps you can't if the plank spans a chasm a hundred feet deep. Or perhaps you can, if you look only at the plank or are practiced. With practice men can walk along tight-ropes. Construction workers walk scaffolding or beams hundreds of feet above ground.

152

Your whole body acts to help you balance yourself. Your skin, muscles, tendons, joints, eyes, and inner ears all work together in the most precise and accurate coordination to enable you to know at any instant where you are and how you are moving.

But most important is your inner ear, the part of it that has nothing to do with your hearing. It tells you when you start to move—ahead or up or down or around in circles. It tells you when you are speeding up, when you are slowing down, and when you have changed position. It tells you which is up and which is down.

Some persons who have something the matter with this non-hearing part of the inner ear have trouble with balance. On a merry-go-round, for example, a man with this ear defect doesn't lean in toward the center to keep his balance the way everybody else does. In fact, he would fly off if not held on. He doesn't get dizzy when he spins around. And he should never risk swimming under water, because then he can never tell up from down and may swim to the bottom when he wants air.

Of course, your eyes help a lot, too, in balance. Nearly everywhere you can see which way is up because there are so many vertical and horizontal things in the world. Walls and trees are vertical. Floors and water are horizontal. But, if you go into a crazy room at an amusement park, where walls and floor are all at an angle, then you will see how confusing that is. Your eyes tell you that up is one way, but your inner ear says something else.

It may be even more confusing to an airplane pilot who is flying partly by instrument, partly by vision.

153

Men wearing bifocal glasses for the first time often have trouble finding the floor with their feet. In starting down stairs, they miss the first step because it looks too near.

Besides the ears and eyes, there is touch. Sensations from the skin, the muscles, the tendons, and the joints, all provide information as to what position the body is in and how it is moving.

An airplane traveler knows the instant his plane takes off because of the increased pressure on the seat of his pants. He knows when it is speeding up because the seat of his pants is shoved back in his chair.

You know when you start dropping in a fast but poorly regulated elevator because you feel your internal organs taking a sudden lurch upward.

And there is also a nice coordination between your eye muscles and your neck muscles. You can keep looking at some tiny object while you turn your head to one side. If your head moves ten degrees to the right, then your eyes move just ten degrees to the left at exactly the same rate, so that they are kept looking at the same thing without blurring it.

All these things cooperate to help you, but it is the mechanism in your inner ear that is of greatest importance.

SPINNING AND BALANCING

In each of your inner ears, is a part shaped like a snail shell and called the cochlea (Fig. 36). That serves for hearing. Besides that there are two chambers and three horseshoe-shaped tubes, filled with a fluid and serving for balance or sense of movement.

154

The tubes which are known as the semi-circular canals are in three different planes, one horizontal, and the other two upright but at right angles to each other, so that the three are in the same relative positions they would be if one were placed flat on the bottom of a box, a second stood up along the end and the third upright along the side.

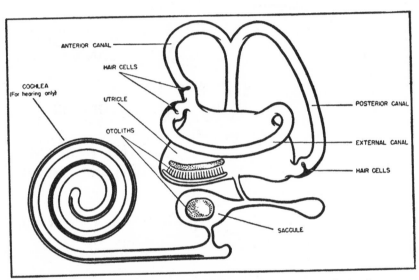

FIG. 36. Semicircular canals and otolith organs of the inner ear.

Because of this arrangement, whichever way the head moves—forward or backward, to the right or left, or up or down—the fluid in at least one tube is disturbed.

Each semi-circular canal has in it a set of hair cells with long hairs that project out into the fluid. The nerve-endings are in these cells.

When your head is spun around, the hair cells have to go along, but the fluid in the canal tends

155

to lag behind. This pushes the hairs to one side, thus exciting the nerve-endings which in turn send their signals to your brain. This is how you know when you are spinning around, even with your eyes shut or in a fog. You know which way you are turning because the feeling is different when the

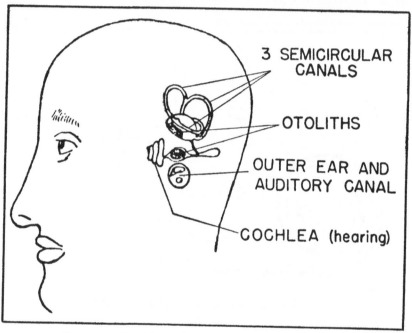

FIG. 37.   Position of the inner ear in the head.

fluid in different canals is disturbed, or when it is disturbed in different directions.

Horizontal rotation affects mostly the horizontal canal, but some canal in each ear would be affected by spinning in any direction. Many kinds of rotation affect all three canals. Of course, you also get clues from pressures on your body and from inside your body.

156

When you start spinning and then keep on going around at a constant speed, the fluid in the canals gets speeded up too. The hair-cells then return to their normal position. This can fool you in a dangerous way. For the feeling that you are spinning stops completely, although actually you keep on going around.

A simple experiment will show you exactly how this works. Let a friend sit in a chair that you can spin around. Blindfold him and spin him. Keep him rotating, as nearly as you can, at a constant speed. After a while, he may be going around quite rapidly and yet feel sure that he is absolutely still—except for the vibration of the chair.

If you talk to him he will feel sure that *you* are sailing rapidly around his chair—very rapidly indeed if someone else spins the chair, and you are far away from him, for then you seem to be shooting around through a big circle at every rotation of his chair.

Now stop him. He will think he is going around in the opposite direction, although the chair is now still. That is because the fluid in the canals tends to coast on when the hair-cells are stopped, thus pushing the hairs over in the opposite direction.

Now suppose he moves his head. The illusion he has of spinning will change. The direction in which he feels he is spinning changes. If you have been spinning him, actually, in a counter-clockwise direction, and he now puts his head over to the left until his ears are horizontal, he will have a startling experience.

He feels as if he were turning backwards, head under heels. It is an alarming experience. He thinks the chair is falling over backwards, and he will throw himself forward out of the chair in an effort to "right" himself—unless he is strapped in. His movement is just as quick as the cat's when she rights herself in falling.

This experiment gives you an idea of how an airplane pilot can sometimes make mistakes in flying his plane due to the tricks played upon him by his inner ears.

The eyes are closely connected with the semicircular canals. When you rotate a man to the right, his eyes move to the left as far as they can, snap back to the right, move to the left again, and so on —as if they were trying to watch some object while he spins. This happens even when the man is blindfolded. When, after being stopped, he gets the illusion of spinning, then his eyes move again, as if the illusory movement were real. If he is not blindfolded, this movement of the eyes makes the visible world seem to rotate. Then it is the room that spins around. If he is flying, the whole world spins around.

The eyes are thus connected with the ears, but the stomach is connected with both. So in extreme dizziness a man is nauseated, gets sick at his stomach. That almost always happens if he opens his eyes when he is spinning in a whirling-chair—unless he is practiced in whirling, as every good aviator should eventually be.

All this seems complicated enough; yet it is necessary to add that the brain also plays a role in getting accustomed to whirling and spinning. Experienced aviators, ballet dancers, and whirling dervishes get, with long practice, so that rotation has less effect
158

upon them than it has on novices. They do not get dizzy or nauseated. Their eyes twitch less on rotation or not at all. The semi-circular canals must still be working in the normal manner, but the eye and the stomach effects have worn off. Some of the standardized brain connections get weakened or broken off through practice. The brain is always adjusting to new situations in this way.

Besides the semi-circular canals the inner ear has, in its two chambers, otoliths, a word which means "ear-stones." (See Fig. 36.) These otolith organs are groups of hair-cells with short hairs. On the hairs rest small stones of calcium carbonate. In the cells are the nerve-endings. The stones tend to lag behind the cells when the head shifts and thus, by moving the hairs, to stimulate the nerve-fibers.

These otolith organs tell you about speeding up and slowing down in a straight line—as you go forward or backward, up or down. Since the semi-circular canals are also affected by straight-line movement, there are five organs in each ear—ten in all —for providing information about movement.

The otoliths, being heavy, are affected by gravity in a way that the hair-cells in the semi-circular canals are not. It is the otolith organs, therefore, that help you most to keep erect and balanced. The eyes, however, help too, and so do the pressures on your feet when you are standing or on the seat of your pants when you are sitting.

An aviator in darkness or fog or at high altitude gets, however, but little help from his eyes in keeping level. There is nothing near at hand to see. Clouds do not have vertical and horizontal lines for guidance. The seat of his pants helps him a little, but it is not enough. So, unless he looks at a level indicator, he is almost entirely dependent on his otolith organs for knowing whether or not he is level.

He may be deceived. For if a pilot flies for some time with one wing too low, his otolith organs become used to it; they stop warning him that he is not vertical. He gets to feel as if he were upright. If now he looks at an indicator and levels his plane up, he feels at once as if he were tilted the other way. These organs in your ears are pretty good, but they can, nevertheless, give wrong information.

In blind flying, the after-effects of movement may be troublesome, if not dangerous. The pilot who has been flying with one wing too low feels crooked when he actually gets the plane level. When he stops turning one way, he may feel that he is turning the other way, although he is actually beginning to fly straight. Sometimes these illusory after-effects are noticed by the pilot, even when the previous movements, which are the reason for them, were too slow or gradual to be noticed when they occurred. No wonder the pilot sometimes gets confused. A real but imperceptible movement can make him perceive later an opposite movement that isn't really there! He doesn't know he has a gremlin working in his ear.

A pilot ought to know about these effects and after-effects of rotation and other movements. Such knowledge helps him to understand some of the surprising things that happen to him.

There is not, however, much value in testing pilot-candidates by spinning them around to see how well their canals and otoliths work. Except for deaf mutes, most men have inner ears that work well enough. Nor is it worth while to test them for dizziness, since a man can be trained out of dizziness.

In handling a plane all the sensory clues are used, all are important—sensations from the semi-circular canals, from the otolith organs, from the eyes, from the muscles, from the seat of the pants. When a pilot becomes a unit with his plane, he is using all these clues as readily and as quickly as everyone does in walking. It is therefore more important to test the pilot-candidate on his ability to learn new elaborate accurate coordinations—to make the right movements for the right reasons—than it is to measure his ability to recognize how much he is spinning and which way is up.

Air-Sickness

Air-sickness, is, of course, to be avoided by aviators It gets less frequent after flyers have become accustomed to the sudden movements of bumpy air and to prolonged spinning and rotation. A sailor gets over becoming seasick in the same manner. Such training, however, takes time, and instructors should try to keep a cadet from becoming air-sick while he is learning to fly, while he is getting accustomed to these new and unusual movements.

If a cadet gets an aversion to flying because of air-sickness, his training is sure to be hindered by it. He may even develop chronic air-sickness and have to give up flying—a disappointment to himself and a loss to the Army.

The instructor must take it easy with the cadet at first. He must not "wring him out." He must not stay up long if the air is very bumpy and the cadet shows signs of getting sick. The instructor can manage mostly to keep the cadet from getting ill, and it is good idea to make the instructor clean up the plane afterwards if he fails. Then he will not often fail.

The causes of air-sickness are many, some physical, some psychological. Here are the principal ones:

(1) The primary cause lies in the effect of slow, prolonged, unusual movements upon the inner ear, especially up-and-down movements. The inner ear can, however, be educated out of this response if its training is not speeded up too much.

(2) The eyes contribute. It is best in a plane to keep them fixed on a distant object—the horizon, a cloud. It is better to keep them closed than to let them watch objects inside the plane—the instrument-board or a book. Exacting use of the eyes fights their natural twitching which is set up when the inner ears are disturbed.

(3) Physical condition enters in. Fatigue is bad. So are constipation and overeating. So especially is an alcoholic hangover. The inner ear wins out when the body is not in good condition.

(4) External factors affect the body. High altitude is bad. Heat is bad. Insufficient ventilation is bad, because it does not reduce body heat, because it does not remove bad odors.

(5) But learning comes in too. You can learn to be air-sick in smooth air, and learn not to be air-sick in bumpy air. Any food that has once produced

162

violent vomiting has a good chance for producing it again. The cadet who has once been sick in a plane gets sick more easily again in a plane. The mere sight of the inside of a plane may come to be enough to start him off. But the cadet who has never been sick after much flying is learning never to be sick.

(6) And then what the psychologist calls suggestion comes in. You can talk a man into being sick in a rowboat on the mildly choppy surface of a lake, and you can talk him out of being sick in the long slow swell of the ocean—provided your talking is about something else than sea-sickness. Many is the man in a plane who has not been sick because a pretty hostess talked to him about something other than air-sickness. And many is the person who has been air-sick because someone else was vomiting. After a few such experiences, the foul odors are learned to be the proper signals for nausea.

The rules for avoiding air-sickness, sea-sickness, jeep-sickness are these:

(1) Never let yourself get sick in the first place. If you do, you lose the power of suggestion and of learning to fight the inner ear and the other physical factors.

(2) Practice the inner ear—on planes, in boats, on swings—but always stop before sickness begins. Go at the job with zest for the fun of it.

(3) Forget about sickness. Do not anticipate it or talk about it. Make suggestion and learning work on the right side. Don't learn to be sick; learn to be not sick.

If you never expect to be sick and can slowly get used to new slow movements you never will be sick.

How Not to Get Lost

People don't have a bump of locality, an occult sense of direction, a sixth sense, an instinctive capacity for knowing where they are, which is north, and how to get home. But they can learn to find their way around, learn to get along without road signs and maps. The only mystery about this skill is that well oriented men are unlikely to know just what clues they do use.

An Army officer, speaking of his own skill in finding the way in spite of detours required by the lay of the land, said that he could always "feel" just where the objective lay and face toward it "as readily as a man with two good ears can face the source of a sound." His feeling for space relations was like that of the man who plays skillful chess blindfolded. The blindfold chess player has a feel for the position of each piece and for the lines and positions that it threatens.

But this officer knew that his skill depended on experience. It did not work in a city with winding streets, like Boston. It did not even work in the woods of New England, but it worked perfectly in the Virginia mountains, where he was at home. Presumably one of his clues there came from the parallel mountain ranges.

Guides in the Maine woods cannot tell you how they know where they are, but they too depend on visual clues—mountains, landmarks, the sun, the wind, and a thousand little items that make up woodscraft.

Blind men also have an ability to find their way

164

that they cannot explain. Their capacity has sometimes been called facial vision, because they think
they can tell with their faces where objects are, how
far distant they are, even something about their
shapes. We know now that they use hearing clues
for perceiving objects at a distance, the echoes of
the sounds which they themselves make, especially
with their sticks or footsteps. Sometimes they snap
their fingers so that the echo can help them gauge
the distance of a wall or some other large object.
They may also get touch sensations from the face
that tell them about very near objects. The point is
that they learn to use ordinary clues without realizing just what it is they are doing.

Ants find their way home by smell. Bees make
a bee-line to the hive at least partly by sight, though
if the hive is turned around they may bump their
noses at the place where the door used to be. Homing
pigeons, released in strange territory, also depend
on what they can see. They follow certain visible
features of the ground, continuing over water until
they find land, and then keep on until eventually
a landmark, visible from a great height, gives them
their bearings precisely.

To get to be a good guide or scout requires practice and interest. The interested man soon learns
many clues. In the woods he uses a compass, but
without a compass he can still note distant landmarks when he gets a chance for a view. On mountains he sees bodies of water, distant towns, distinctive trees. He pays attention always to the direction of the wind, the position of the sun, the slope of
the land, the direction of the streams, the moss on

the trees, changes in the vegetation or in the soil. He builds up in his mind a topographic map (most military maps are topographic, showing ground shapes and wooded areas) of the country in which he is, or, if he has seen a map, he keeps placing himself on it, orienting himself—tentatively, correcting early mistakes by later observation. That is the first rule: Pay attention to all natural landmarks and direction indicators.

The man who is to become a good scout and guide also learns about avoiding common errors. He knows that you seldom go straight on flat terrain in the woods. If you are biased toward one side you circle —and on the average there are a lot more chances of your having a constant bias than of your being set dead ahead. The experienced scout knows that a diagonal path on a slope is apt to get curved downwards. He never assumes that in following a stream he is keeping on in the same direction. Few streams run straight. He expects a tired mile in the late afternoon to be longer than a fresh one in the early morning. He knows all these common mistakes and guards against making them himself.

But most of all—for this is the most important rule—he remembers to keep his orientation *continuous.* As he goes over new ground, he must keep the entire sequence of observed ground in mind, put together at the correct angles. He can do this by always being conscious of where north is, and better by building up a map in his mind's eye, a map with north on it. But if he stops doing this even for a few moments he may become lost, may have turned through ninety degrees without realizing it.

To a man who has developed a scout's mind it is no effort to keep a map in mind. If you think about St. Louis, you know where San Francisco, Chicago and Washington are in relation to St. Louis. You visualize a map, or at least most people do. If you are in St. Louis, you see this map stretching away from yourself, and you could point in the right direction for Chicago, and for north too.

But you have to be interested in space relations to have the map always right. A well oriented soldier is one who likes always to know where he is, and where everthing else is. It is a good habit for all soldiers.

It is surprising what a difference there is between people in keeping aware of directions. You ask one man where north is, and he points instantly. He knows just as surely as an American knows that traffic is going to move along the right side of a street. And if you told him that north was the other direction, he'd be just as upset as the American who arrives in Liverpool to find the traffic on the wrong side of every street. But you ask another man to show you north and he has to stop to figure it out —if he can. He looks for the sun or a star, and then, if he can get no evidence, gives up.

There was a fellow once who arrived in Wilkinsburg, Pa., on the train. The trains going east toward Philadelphia run south through that town, so he thought south was east. But the trolleys going west toward Pittsburgh also go south through the town. So, when he first tried to take a trolley to Pittsburgh, he went the wrong direction. He never did get his mental map of Wilkinsburg straightened out,

167

but a man with better habits for keeping his bearing would immediately have corrected his mind-map and have kept his bearings.

Before you go into strange territory—and every soldier hopes to do that in this war—it is best to study a map, a contour map. From the map you should note how the country lies. See where the hills are. Note what you could see from one place, from another—what hills would mask towns and other hills. Pick out landmarks—towns, hills, streams—especially distinctive high objects. Get further information from someone who has seen the land if you can. Build up your mind-map before you go, and then keep placing yourself on it and seeing the rest of it stretching away from you.

Sometimes you can't see a map beforehand. Or it may only be a worn, dirty map for three minutes as you look over the shoulders of others, all looking at it under a blanket with a flashlight, and trying to see the direction of attack. Then you must rely mainly on what you are told and do the best you can.

The best you can do often includes getting on top of a hill or other high place, taking a look around, and making up your mind-map from the actual map or view of the country itself. Pick out landmarks then, things you will probably be able to see when you are down on lower ground, when you have passed beyond the next hill. Better than keeping north in mind is keeping several landmarks in mind. Have always an opinion as to which direction they lie, and then correct yourself next time you see them.

168

Some men are able to smell and follow their noses to their destination. If you have such a nose, by all means use it, develop it, train it. The salt tang of the sea, for example, can be detected by a sensitive smeller for a considerable distance, and he can be guided by it to reach the water or keep near it. Cattle have a distinctive odor which may serve as a guide to a farm or ranch.

How to Find Your Way When Lost

Sooner or later most soldiers have the experience of getting lost. In heavy woods or jungle it is possible to get lost a few yards off the trail. It gives a man a peculiarly helpless feeling.

You are so accustomed all your life to knowing where you are and who you are and about what time it is, that the feeling of not knowing one of these things comes as a great shock.

For a soldier there is always some urgent military reason for finding the way—to deliver a message, to connect with another unit, or to report information. Hence the need to do something immediately when you get lost is likely, if you are not on guard against it, to make you do something foolish and get yourself lost even more.

The best cure for getting lost is experience in a similar situation. Part of every soldier's training should be practice in getting lost and finding his way back. Much better than a cure, however, is prevention.

A compass is a big help. And knowing how to use it. Learning how to follow a compass course is part of every soldier's basic training. But practice it

169

yourself. And get extra practice in looking at a map beforehand and setting yourself a destination and a route. When you start out, select your general direction by compass.

Then, pick an objective *within sight*. Put your compass in your pocket and walk to that objective, pacing off the distance. Now stop. Make a rough sketch of the distance you have travelled and the direction you took. Picture in your mind where your final destination is with reference to your present position. Then get out your compass and set yourself a new objective. Walk to that and repeat your steps of recording your route and picking a new objective.

Always your new objective must be within sight. Always, you must stop when you get to it to figure where you are, how far you have come, the direction you have come, and the direction you must go. These steps may take you a long time at first. Later you can do them very rapidly. Practice is extremely important.

In the field you may not always have a compass You must be able to do without one. There are other ways of telling north.

If you have a watch, you can use it for a compass. Just point the hour-hand at the sun (or the moon if it happens to be full), or where the sun seems to be behind the clouds. Half way between the hour-hand and 12 is south, approximately—if you are in the northern hemisphere and not too near the equator. In Australia, half way between the hour-hand and 12 is north.

Or watch the shadows, but remember that they

170

shift from west to north in the time between sunrise to noon. If you point the hour-hand of your watch with the shadows, then half way between the hour-hand and 6 is north.

Suppose you have no watch, either. Well, in some parts of the world, prevailing winds at certain seasons are in the same general direction. Whenever you go into new territory find out about local conditions of this sort. If it is a very windy place, and the winds (or the storm winds) are mostly in one direction, you may find traces of the direction in the way all the trees are bent in the same direction —or most of the fallen trees are laid in one direction.

You can tell something by the position of the sun. The sun is never in the north (in the northern hemisphere)—it moves across the sky from east to west through the south. So does the moon at night.

The moss on trees may give you an idea which way is north—it is not too reliable.

If you are in the woods, follow streams if you want to go down hill or if you know where the streams should turn up, but not if you want to go straight. If you can retrace your path to a known place, then do it. If you go ahead, blaze your trail by cutting marks on trees or breaking branches, so that you can retrace later if you wish to—unless you are in enemy country. Don't put the enemy on to your trail. The best rule is, however, to climb a tree or to get out in the open if possible, so that you can see the lay of the land.

At night, if the sky is clear, everything is much easier. The heavens are full of friendly guides. Part of your preparation for duty in a strange territory should be to get well acquainted with a few of the conspicuous patterns of stars in the sky.

Easiest to learn are the great dipper and the North Star—the mariner's friend. Learn the shape of the dipper, if you don't already know it, and make a habit of looking at it and watching its changes of position. Not only can you find the north star with the aid of its pointers, you can also tell the time by the way it swings all the way around the north star every night like the hands of a clock. And that can be helpful too. The dipper isn't visible for some of the night in the lower part of the northern hemisphere, and isn't visible at all below the equator.

But there are other star patterns just as easy to pick out. If you learn about four of these in different parts of the sky, just a glance at the sky at night will always keep you from getting "turned around." You must keep track of them; follow them night after night so that you always know in what part of the sky to look for them.

Here are the ones most helpful—in the northern hemisphere Orion in winter, Cygnus and Scorpio in summer; in the southern hemisphere, the Southern Cross. Orion can also be seen as far south as the Solomon Islands. The rule is: any two stars that point north and south in any constellation will always point north and south, provided the constellation is high in the sky.

MAPS

It is best to have a map in your pocket when you get lost. If you can't have one, then you ought to see one before you go into strange country.

172

The more a soldier knows about maps the better equipped he is for combat duty. His training in how to read them and what to look for on them, if he keeps practicing it, should enable him to find himself if he ever gets lost on any terrain he knows from a map.

Here are a few things to notice, besides the location of villages and conspicuous buildings and roads, landmarks, and points of vantage. How do the streams, roads, and trails generally run? Where are the hills with reference to the streams? Are there big ridges or valleys? In what direction do these run? What is the grade in various parts of the area? After studying the map, could you tell which way you were walking by whether it was generally up or down grade, or by the steepness of the grade?

Also, what kind of growth does the map show for different areas? Where are the swamps, the woods, the jungles, the cultivated areas? These things are especially important in flat, jungle country.

If you have memorized only a few such points about country you get lost in, you can much more readily find your way out.

The paratrooper does not have the advantage of continuous contact with a place he knows. When he comes down he has to make a fresh start. But if he has seen a map and has been able to pick some landmarks in relation to the point where he will land, he should not be so badly off. At least he knows his objective and may try to relate everything to it.

The chief rule to remember is, then, that a good scout and guide, the man with the uncanny sense of direction, has learned to know his way through strange territory because he has always been interested in geography and topography, in the space relations of things on the face of the earth to himself wherever he may be. It takes a constant interest to become expert at this, the kind of interest that works casually all the time in the back of your head. If you can't get up this interest in yourself—it may mean the difference between going to enemy territory instead of finding your own—at least you can practice making mental map-pictures for yourself, pictures with landmarks on them, pictures to use in combat when you do get lost.

But the best way to train yourself thoroughly is to practice getting lost and finding yourself, so that the use of the rules is second nature to you. It is a good idea for every leader of trained soldiers shortly to go into combat, to give his men this practice. He should take them at first in twos or threes, later alone, blindfolded and by a confusing route to strange places, where there is no one to ask questions of, and leave them there to find their way back. Sometimes they should be allowed to study contour maps before such practice, sometimes not. But all men should be taught all the rules in advance, and the first problems should be simple. This builds up confidence. Getting lost is a serious and sometimes life-or-death business in combat areas.

VIII: THE RIGHT SOLDIER IN THE RIGHT JOB

WORK IN THE ARMY is much more than just shouldering a rifle and doing long foot marches. Soldiers work at several hundred different kinds of fighting jobs and at even more kinds of jobs, some directly related to combat and some not, which can be filled with men already trained for them or men who have the necessary aptitude for learning one of the jobs quickly. All leaders have the responsibility for seeing that the right man gets on the right job and, when mistakes are made in this, that the misfits are transferred.

In addition to his basic job of fighting, each soldier has a good chance of filling a job very much like the jobs in civilian life. He may become a truck driver, an automobile mechanic, a welder, a baker, a machine-shop worker. Nearly all the jobs for enlisted men are skilled or semi-skilled. A few are semi-professional, and only a very few are purely professional. Listed alphabetically they run all the way from "Able Seaman" (yes, the Army does have them) to "Yardmaster."

Officers' jobs do not cover such a wide range, for nearly every officer must be a leader or supervisor of men. There are some exceptions, however, and the combat pilot is one of these.

For some Army jobs it is difficult to find enough suitable men. There are shortages of physicists, tool-

175

makers, airplane pilots, crew chiefs, and radio operators—to name only a few.

But fortunately the abilities and skills and aptitudes that America's citizen soldiers have brought with them into the Army are almost as varied as are the Army's needs. These men represent a cross-section of America's working population. They come from farms, stores, and workshops.

Thousands know how to drive a tractor, how to repair an ignition system. Others can weld castings, repair watches, other timing instruments, or road transits, keep accounts, carve carcasses of beef, develop photographs. The Army needs many men who can do these things.

Men from all the 17,000 different civilian jobs at which Americans work, and from all the professions, are available to the Army. Many of them are needed, and some are needed badly. An incorrect classification of one of these much wanted men, putting him where his special ability will be wasted, is an occupational casualty. Such a casualty can be as damaging to the war effort as a battle casualty.

The British found that out in the First World War. At first they neglected to save their specialists. They sent to the front professional men, engineers, and men in skilled trades. Many were killed in the early months of the war. Later the need for them in special posts behind the line became acute.

So a correct classification must be made at the start. It speeds up training and makes maximum use of instructors and training facilities. Whenever a man is picked for a place he can't readily fill, so that he must later be transferred, that keeps a more suitable man out of the place and delays his training. It also interferes with the building up and training of skilled combat or technical teams who must learn to work together.

When errors are made, however, it is important that they be corrected as soon as possible. This is sometimes made difficult by the conflicting interests in the Army. The company commander is anxious to build up an effective fighting unit just as fast as he can. If he has a large number of poor learners, illiterate men with no knowledge of any special work, he is eager to transfer such men to other units even though he may be able to make the best possible use of their limited abilities. If, however, he has a good airplane mechanic at work as an automobile mechanic, he is likely to be so pleased with the excellent quality of the man's work that he is unwilling to give him up to the Air Forces. That's fine for the company, but bad for the Army, unless motor mechanics are needed worse than airplane mechanics.

It is essential that every man be placed where he is of the greatest possible use, regardless of how well he can also fill another type of job.

In picking a man to fill an Army job the classification officer is interested in both what he can do and what he can learn. What he can already do is of first importance. If a man has a license as a radio amateur, that insures him a rating of three grades right off. His particular skill is in immediate demand. If he is an expert duck shooter, but has no other particular ability, he is likely to make a good antiaircraft gunner.

But there are more jobs in the armed services than

there are men already trained to fill them. So it is important to pick the men who are qualified to learn the essential jobs in the shortest possible time.

How Soldiers Differ

Men differ just as much in ability to learn different sorts of duties as they do in size of feet, in height, or in weight. Some are as much as three times as able as others. Most, of course, are just about average.

Some men cannot learn a three-figure telephone number by hearing it once. Some can learn as many as nine figures. The average is around six or seven.

Some men, starting from scratch, can learn in eight weeks to receive and send radio code· at sixteen words per minute. It takes others twenty-two weeks. Some men, used to handling certain type of machinery, can learn to handle certain kinds of weapons much faster than others.

So the problem is to understand and measure *aptitude*. Aptitude is potential skill, the capacity for learning to do something quickly and accurately when given the chance to learn. Both *speed* and *accuracy* are important in learning. A soldier needs to learn rapidly, but also to be accurate at what he has learned. And men differ from one another in both ways.

For one thing, men differ greatly in the speed with which they *learn*. Some aviation cadets can solo after four hours of instruction. Others are not allowed to solo even after fourteen hours. Here the quick learners are urgently needed. Slow learners tie up training planes too long. Besides quick learning might mean a shorter war.

178

Yet the Army cannot do without the slow learners. Manpower is needed, and there are many military jobs which require other qualities than speed of learning, jobs which the slow learners will prefer to have.

Men also differ in speed and accuracy of *reaction*. The average driver requires from one-half to three-quarters of a second to put on the brakes after the stop light goes red; yet some can apply the brakes in three-tenths of a second. Others use up a whole second. These are important differences for riflemen and machine-gunners, as well as for truck drivers Every tenth of a second counts in battle.

Aviation students are given a complex reaction test, one that involves the coordination of eye, hand, and foot. Different men take from 1.3 to 4.8 seconds to perform this reaction correctly. So the time they take becomes one of many measures of their aptitude as pilots. All but fourteen per cent of the men with the longest times get washed out in their pilot training, whereas three-fourths of the men with the shortest times succeed.

Men differ also in the speed and accuracy of *perceiving*. One clerk can check in five minutes a company roster that takes another man twenty minutes. Some men can see a white target in the dark 400 yards away; to others it is invisible at 200 yards Range-finders differ in their abilities to tell the distances of different objects. When the job is seeing, you must choose the best seers.

There is, however, much more to a good soldier than the speed and accuracy with which he learns, acts, and perceives. Every man has *interests,* likes

179

and dislikes. These determine in part what he will do well and how fast he will improve.

A man's interests, for instance, usually determine what he will do with what he learns. Mere exposure to training never made a skilled soldier. It is the interested man who remembers and profits by his

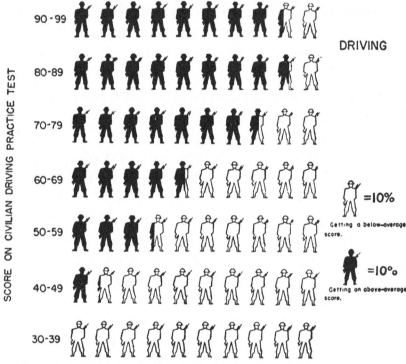

FIG. 38. Predicting Army driving success from score on civilian driving test. Shows the chances in 100 that a man, making a given score on the civilian driving practice test, will obtain average-or-better grade on the Army driving practice test. (Camp Lee, 270 men.)

training and is ready to apply it to new situations. Of 270 men trained as drivers at Camp Lee (Fig. 38) those who at the start knew most about civilian driving did best at the end on the information test for

Army driving. The successful men had a good start and also the interest to carry them along.

The well-educated man, it has been found, generally likes his work in the Army only if he can make good use of his abilities. He also has a deep need to make choices, decisions, for himself. So far as is possible, it pays to give attention to the preferences of such men for particular work. Otherwise they are more likely than other men to become discontented with Army life.

Some Army leaders have thought that the drafted high-school and college men are simply soft, should be made to toe the line, should be taught Army discipline. The more profitable view is that these men should be given chances to advance as far as their abilities permit, and this, as far as possible, in work that arouses their interest. The Army needs their training, needs the interest that they can show if their abilities are used. When men do not like the jobs they have but could like another job that needs doing, then the Army loses. This is the reason why an extensive reclassification of Army personnel is continuously being carried out.

All this doesn't mean that a well educated man won't make a good fighting man, or that places exactly fitted to such a man's specific abilities must be found for him, for the Army to profit most from his services. As this chapter explains later on there are many special military jobs, both in combat and other units, which require a high degree of ability. Many men of high educational qualifications fit into such jobs and find them of deepest interest, and even of especial satisfaction because the jobs seem more directly concerned with the war than other things they might be doing. It is mainly a matter, on the whole, of trying to see that men with good brains get a chance in the Army to use them.

Other personal differences besides interest and likes and dislikes are important, especially for some military tasks. One man may feel completely at ease in the transparent cage in which a bombardier must sit, while another, ordinarily dexterous, is so upset in that exposed position that the pupils of his eyes dilate, his fingers fumble, and he cannot manipulate the bomb-sight properly.

Two equally wise officers may not be equally good leaders. One is at ease with his men, talking with them freely, getting their slant on matters of importance, and giving his orders and directions readily. The other, although he wants his men to like him and respond alertly and willingly to him as a leader, cannot bring himself to feel free and confident with them and open up with them in a way to gain their confidence and liking in turn. The first is, of course, the better leader.

Indeed, leadership is the quality that the Army most needs. All advancement brings with it responsibility, and responsibility for the conduct of others requires leadership.

Army Jobs and Related Jobs

Some of the things men going into the armed services are already skilled in are of immediate and direct usefulness. The trained radio man, the trained airplane mechanic, machine-shop worker, instrument worker, or personnel man finds jobs waiting for him

182

that will put the things he already knows right to work.

But there are not enough of such workers to fill existing jobs in the expanding services.

Other civilian training also fits in, however. Every Army job is complex. Each job, when broken down, is found to require not a single type of special ability but a number of them. And, although men equipped with all the abilities needed for a given job may be scarce, many will have a few of them. The man who has some of them can, of course, be more easily trained for that job than the man who has none of them.

One good source of men to fill these critical jobs is from among those who have been holding related jobs in civilian life. Suppose men are needed to operate a particular military precision instrument such as an artillery range finder. That instrument is unknown outside the armed services. You could not find a new soldier experienced in its use. But other precision instruments are in constant use in industrial plants. So the Army takes a man accustomed to doing fine, accurate work who is familiar with the care and handling of delicate precision mechanisms, and then trains him on the special instrument.

All the relationships of jobs to each other, of civilian jobs to Army jobs, have been carefully worked out in a sort of family tree of jobs. If the Army can't get a man with just the ability it needs, then by consulting tables of related skills it can select the man with the next best combination—the closest relative in that job family.

To speed the selection and classification of soldiers

183

in Army jobs every man registered for the draft checks a list of occupations to indicate all his previous experience and training.

This questionnaire lists jobs by their most familiar names, including 189 jobs which together actually include about 650 different civilian occupations. The man who checks off "airplane mechanic," for example, may have worked at any of eight different jobs—all of them war-important.

Many different jobs belong in the same job family. For instance, a man who checked "toolmaker" is potential raw material for an Army job as a die-maker or as an instrument maker.

The *family trees of jobs* are shown on tables which indicate how closely related different jobs are, and how well different civilian jobs prepare men for a particular Army job.

Take truck driving. A man who in civilian life was an experienced truck driver is not yet a good Army truck driver because he has yet to learn blackout and convoy driving, but he is probably pretty good. He can at least step right into the cab of an Army truck and feel at home. The chauffeur of a passenger car certainly is not a ready-made truck driver, but unless he has too many bad driving habits he is usually better than a man who cannot drive at all. He is merely farther off on the family tree. The jump boy on a delivery truck is still less of a truck driver, nevertheless he may already know about a few of the things required of a truck driver, and he is very likely to be better than a clerk who never owned a car, always rode to work on the street car, and feels strange with a car.

184

The Qualification Card

The Soldier's Qualification Card keeps the record of the soldier's qualifications, his skills, his aptitudes.

All his civilian abilities are entered on it. His education is also noted, any special training he may have had, his performance on certain standard tests, and his progress in Army training. The card is—it must be—kept up to date, for a man is not classified once for all. As he learns, he may be transferred where the new things he has learned to do can be of the greatest usefulness. And as the needs of the Army change, he may have to move from one sort of job to another, wherever manpower is more needed.

At every stage in each soldier's career, from reception center to combat unit, a record is made of what he can do, what he can learn, and what he has done and learned. When he completes any specific training successfully, that goes on his card. If he has a job-tryout, the result is entered. If he is relieved from training as a cook and is trained and qualified as tank destroyer gunner, these things are noted.

Abilities. Aptitudes. Interests. Everything counts in the Army just as it counts elsewhere. These things are the Army's psychological materiel, which is just as varied as the physical materiel. The Army doesn't want just one kind of airplane or one kind of gun To win a war you have to have the proper distribution of weapons and instruments, and other equipment. The aptitudes, abilities, and interests drawn into the Army are its instruments, its human instruments of war. As far as the demands of war permit, they must be in the right places at the right times.

The Soldier and His Job

The right soldier can't be put into the right job unless you know both the soldier and the job, so that you can match them up.

The Army finds out about each soldier by *interviews* and by *tests*. It thus discovers what he has done in the past and how well. When the interview with him is not convincing, or not informative enough, he can be given *trade tests* to see what special abilities he actually does have and how good he is in them. If he lacks any ability for which there is great need, *aptitude tests* will show what he could most easily learn to do well. Every new soldier takes the *General Classification Test* so that general ability and his capacity for learning new things can be found. Expert interviewers can also get at some of the important characteristics of a man's *personality,* his deep-lying preferences and interests. If there is time enough—and it doesn't take so very much time—the Army finds out pretty well what kind of a man has just joined it.

And then, of course, each military job has to be analyzed to see what kinds of abilities, aptitudes, and personalities it requires. This takes study to do it well, and when it is done well you know what shape hole you have and what shape peg you want to find to fit into it.

INTERVIEWS

At the reception center, where newly inducted men are quartered for a few days before they go to a replacement training center, every soldier is interviewed. This was the soldier's introduction to the Army; the Army's first chance to get acquainted with him.

During this interview the soldier is asked to say what he wants to do in the Army, and what his training and experience have been. And what hobbies he has that might be useful, such as radio or photography. And how much schooling he has had.

Interviewers must be trained for this job. Not everyone can conduct successful interviews. An interviewer has to know all about his own prejudices and be on guard against being influenced by them. He must be able to see things from the new soldier's point of view. For if he can do this, then he can gain the recruit's confidence and put him at ease. So he lets the recruit talk, getting him to volunteer the information needed. Later he can ask questions to fill in gaps in the story.

The interviewer seldom has more than fifteen minutes for his interview. In that short time he must find out about age, schooling, jobs held, earnings, special abilities, athletics, hobbies, likes, and any signs of aptitude for leadership. And he observes mannerisms and peculiarities, because they may be very important.

All this information is recorded on the Soldier's Qualification Card.

THE GENERAL CLASSIFICATION TEST

Every man in the Army is also given the General Classification Test. Those who make high scores on this test are among the men who can learn most rapidly and who can succeed in the most complex and responsible jobs. Although this score is not sufficient by itself for making a wise classification of the soldier, it gives nevertheless very important information. According to how he answers the questions on this test the soldier is placed in one of five grades.

If Army men had abilities exactly like the general run of men, they would stack up in these five broad groups about as follows:

Army grade I: very rapid learners: 7%
     II: rapid learners: 24%
     III: average learners: 38%
     IV: slow learners: 24%
     V: very slow learners: 7%

In the Army, as everywhere, many more men are average than are either very good or very poor. But more Army men turn up in grades I and II than in the table just given. This is probably because the Army doesn't accept every man who is called in the draft or who enlists.

In *grades I and II* are found the men who are likely to make good commissioned and noncommissioned officers. Here also are the highly skilled specialists (Fig. 39).

In *grade III* is also found good material for noncoms, for some specialists—especially the less highly skilled specialists—and for basic soldiers.

Grade IV furnishes good basic soldiers and men for routine work in which soldiers from *grades I and II* would be out of place, maladjusted, and wasted.

The soldier in *grade V* also has aptitudes to offer

188

the Army. He often makes a responsible basic soldier. If he is not useful as such, then there are other necessary jobs for which he is usually better suited than other men in the Army.

FIG. 39. Predicting success of officer candidates from their grades in the General Classification Test. Shows the chances in 100 that a man, making a given Army grade on the General Classification Test, will as an officer candidate receive a commission. (14 schools, 5520 men.)

Men differ greatly in the scores they can make on the Classification Test—from below 40 to above 160. But the great bulk of men pile up the average scores, near 100 (Fig. 40).

There are large differences between men coming from different sections of the country and between men with different occupations. On the average the men from the northwestern part of the United States get the highest scores, the men from the southeast the lowest.

189

A close relationship exists between Army grades on the General Classification Test and success in many courses for Army specialists. Students in the electrical communications course at Fort Sill are practically certain to do above average work if they are in grades I or II. But they have almost no chance of being satisfactory if they are in grades IV or V.

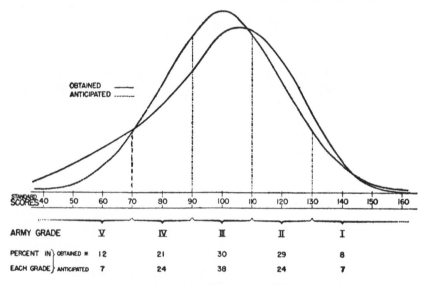

ARMY GRADE		V	IV	III	II	I
PERCENT IN }	OBTAINED ✱	12	21	30	29	8
EACH GRADE }	ANTICIPATED	7	24	38	24	7

✱. 713,000 SELECTEES FOR THE YEAR ENDING FEBRUARY 28, 1942

FIG. 40. Frequency of occurrence of scores on the General Classification Test. Comparison of scores actually obtained on 713,000 selectees with anticipated curve.

Motor mechanics almost always succeed if they are in grade I, are generally above average if they are in grades II or III. They seldom succeed if in grades IV or V.

Radio mechanics at Scott Field had little chance of success if below grade II, but nine chances in ten if they were in grade I. For classification as a radio mechanic, a man should therefore have a higher

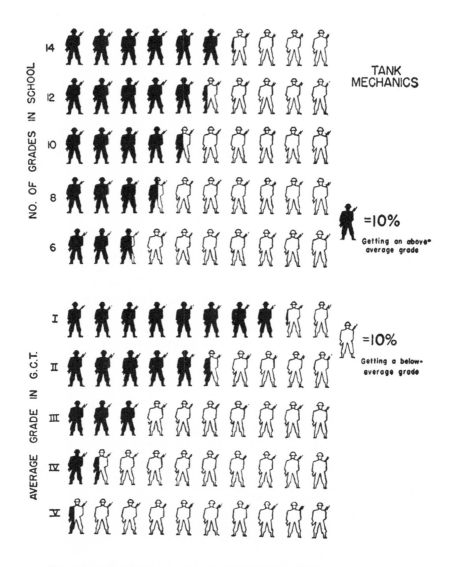

FIG. 41. Predicting success in tank mechanics course from schooling and from grade on the General Classification Test. Shows the chances in 100 that a man, with a given number of grades at school or with a given Army grade on the General Classification Test, will obtain an average-or-better grade in the tank mechanics course. Armored Force School. The General Classification Test is a better predictor than is amount of schooling.

score on this test than for classfication as a motor mechanic.

Figure 41 shows how you can predict the grades of students in a tank mechanics course at the Armored Force School. You can make some prediction from education. With only six years' schooling, his chances for success are less than three in ten. With fourteen years, his chances are six in ten. But the General Classification Test is a much better predictor for this. A man in grade V in that test has less than one chance in ten of success in this course, but a man in grade I has eight chances in ten. So the test result is the right measure to use.

In fact it is never wise to predict from actual schooling if test scores are available. A great many different factors combine to prevent boys from going to school.

Many soldiers who appear to be of inferior quality on the basis of their schooling and of verbal tests turn out to be more competent when given a test that does not involve the use of language. A third of these men are found to be able to learn those various skilled army jobs which do not require much book work.

APTITUDE TESTS

Half the Army's jobs for enlisted men are military jobs which do not exist in civilian life. This means that men with the right aptitudes for learning must be picked for these jobs. And most of these jobs require the ability to learn mechanical things.

Fighting soldiers handle tanks and scout cars, machine guns and rifles. And mostly the men who must fill these jobs are not already trained mechanics. They have been clerks, school teachers, factory workers, farmers, or business men.

When these men have never done anything before which demonstrates that they already have some mechanical ability, they are given a test that shows what aptitude they may have for learning this kind of work. Every man who passes through a reception center takes the *Army Mechanical Aptitude Test.*

Besides this test there are special aptitude tests which help to select men to be trained for particular jobs.

For bombardiers, men are tested in *dexterity—* ability to move their fingers and hands quickly and accurately. Dexterity is needed most in jobs where the same operation is performed over and over again and the hands must move with machine-like smoothness, accuracy, and speed. Most mechanical jobs in the Army do not, however, involve doing the same thing over and over.

For the job of pilot special tests of *hand* and *foot coordination* are given.

For selecting men to learn to be range finders, tests of visual ability to judge distance, heights and depths accurately are important.

The Army has a special aptitude test for *radio operators.* It tests the speed and accuracy with which the individual can distinguish sounds as they are heard over headphones. If a man can't tell one combination of dots and dashes from another when he hears them, he will have a terrible time trying to learn code.

Clerical aptitude can also be discovered by testing,

193

but the Army does not use this test as much as the test for mechanical aptitude. So far, it has been possible to obtain enough men who are already good clerks and to classify them and assign them to jobs on the basis of their proved ability.

Trade Tests

Ordinarily, if a man has learned a trade, the jobs he has held are sufficient proof of his proficiency. It is usually possible to discover, in an interview, whether a man belongs to a union, how long he has been working at his trade, whether he ever got fired and why. It isn't often necessary to give him a test to find out whether he is a printer or an electrician.

Occasionally, however, it may seem to the interviewer that the soldier is claiming to know a job he doesn't actually know. Or the soldier may have worked at a job but can't show evidence of it. For example, he might have learned carpentry or electrical work on his father's farm but has never held a job outside the family.

To clear up any such doubts, the soldier may be asked questions about the job, or he may be given a performance test that gives him a chance to demonstrate how skillful he is at his trade.

The questions are simple, and performance-proved on the job. A plumber might be asked: "What are the *two* most commonly used methods of testing plumbing system?" The possible answers are *water, smoke, peppermint, air*—of which the soldier must name two. This is the kind of thing any experienced plumber would know.

The performance trade test is really a small sample
194

job which the soldier must do to show how good his work is. Only a few such tests have been found convenient for Army use. A man who says he is a typist is given a typing test, which quickly shows how fast and accurate he is at typing. A truck driver can be required to drive a truck over a course with standard road conditions, to turn the truck around, park it, drive it through mud, take it up and down hill.

PERSONALITY

It takes more than brains to make a good soldier; it takes guts. It takes endurance. It takes a willingness to do hard work. It takes a keen interest in doing the job well.

Psychologists wish they could give the Army right now a method of measuring these important personality assets—tests that would be as accurate and reliable as a test for measuring ability to do arithmetic or aptitude for learning radio code.

They can't. Some tests have been tried. Many have been found useless. A few are promising.

One trouble is that a man's personality changes in different situations. For instance, the man who is brave as a lion in the test room at a reception center may not be so brave when he gets into combat. The man who is able to make quick decisions wisely when things are quiet may go to pieces when he is distracted by machine-gun fire, and do something that will result in his own death or the death of others. And difficult situations may have the reverse effect on some men. Men who have never distinguished themselves in training camp may become fired with new spirit when the going gets tough, astounding themselves and the other men with what they can do in extreme emergency.

There are tests of personality, like the one in which the man tells what objects or scenes he can imagine in an ink-blot, but these tests take too much time and require an expert psychologist to give and interpret them. So the Army at present falls back on interviews when it wants to estimate personality.

In such an interview, the examiner tries to find out what the soldier's interests are. He goes beyond mere preferences, finding out whether or not the interests are based on the man's deep-rooted unchangeable likes and dislikes.

For example, about three-fourths of the drafted men would like to go into the Air Corps. Of these, three-fourths want to be pilots. Why?

Most men have heard much about the exploits of ace pilots. They hear considerably less about the adventures of the bombardier, of the Signal Corps man, of the man with the rifle. Flying is popular, even among those who have never flown.

Yet often a man may give the Air Forces as his preference because he is really keen about aviation. He may have been around flying fields since he was a small boy. He may have built model planes. Such a man would be willing, the interviewer discovers, to do any kind of work to get into the Air Forces. He has been studying mathematics and physics in school to fit himself for this job. He wants to be a pilot, but he would gladly be a navigator, bombardier, or gunner—anything, just so he gets a job in the air. His skill in mathematics added to his interest may make him a man the Air Forces need for a navigator.

Another man may give the same preference but knows nothing about aviation or engines or planes, dislikes mechanical work, and hates mathematics. But he has been seeing movies and reading books in which a pilot is the dashing hero. He wants adventure and action. But his hobby is game shooting and he is a good shot. Other things he says all point to the fact that he would be successful and well placed in the infantry, that he would get to be an expert ground soldier.

How to Know the Job

You cannot fit a man into a job unless you know exactly what the job is like. For this reason the War Department has a job analysis of every Army job filled by an enlisted man. The job descriptions are made up by sending an analyst to an Army camp who stays with one trained soldier for a day or two, observing exactly what it is he has to do. If possible he then goes to another camp and repeats his study. After that he records the actual work performed on the job, notes the physical and educational requirements for it, estimates the traits and abilities the worker needs. He puts all the specifications on a form. On such analyses are based the interviews and tests for the selection and assignments of men.

Officers' jobs have also been analyzed. Here, for example, is the description of the job of a lieutenant in charge of a mortar platoon in an infantry heavy weapons company:

197

"Directs discipline, training and tactical employment of the platoon: instructs men in mechanics, marksmanship, techniques and tactical use of the 81mm. mortar; performs essential administrative and supervisory duties for the adequate care and supply of troops. In combat, receives from company commander development orders, special instructions and fire missions regarding employment of mortars; locates firing position areas and determines sectors of fire; takes appropriate measures to assure antiaircraft security, anti-mechanized defense and adequate supply of ammunition; observes rifle troops and coordinates movement and position of mortar squads; directs or executes as directed necessary reconnaissance; advises company commander as to best tactical employment of mortar squads.

"Should know all types of infantry weapons. If in air-borne battalion, must be able to train troops in additional techniques of loading and lashing planes.

"At least six months military experience in line operations essential. Special training in Infantry School, or Reserve Officer Training Corps highly desirable."

Related jobs in the Army, as already described, make up a job family. The most general job heads the family and then, in order, come the other more specific jobs related to it. Thus, there is a job family for *baker—cook, oven fireman, steward.* This order means that a cook is more easily trained as a baker than is a steward.

By using job families, officers can advance men

without wasting the training already acquired. And they can make the best possible use of civilian skills because the job family trees in the Army are traced in the same way. They show at a glance, not only how one Army job is related to another, but how each is related to civilian jobs from which the men have come or those to which they may go after the war.

And that is how the Army gets the right soldier into the right job. It is a complicated process, much more complicated than this brief account shows. Ordnance and the QM do not handle all the Army's supplies. The Army must have aptitudes as well as beef, skills in addition to guns, leaders to use the maps and manuals. You can't use a grenade when you need a howitzer, nor a cook to soup up an airplane.

IX: TRAINING MAKES THE SOLDIER

WHEN MEN ENTER THE ARMY, they are told the importance, in the fighting areas, of taking cover from enemy fire in slit trenches. This point is emphasized in books, lectures, training films, demonstrations and exhibits. By the time the soldier reaches the battle zone, he has learned that he should "take cover in a slit trench" wherever he stops.

That is one kind of learning. In one way it is the most useful kind. With knowledge of how things should be done and why they are important, a soldier is equipped to act in new situations—and there is nothing that produces so many new situations as combat. But this kind of learning, unfortunately, does not always result in action.

A soldier may know perfectly well that he should dig a trench. He may have learned from demonstrations exactly how to go at digging it. Yet, when the enemy planes come overhead, he may, in his excitement, forget what he has learned. In such emergencies, he is much more likely to act from habit than from reasoning and sense.

Habit formation is a further stage of learning. It depends on practice, experience, and repetition. No action ever becomes automatic by learning in words how to perform it but without actually practicing it. But by repetition the operation of a machine or a rifle gets itself reduced to habit so that it becomes almost or entirely mechanical. Like walking. You do not have to think about putting your left foot forward after planting your right foot ahead. That is because you have walked so much. You could not get that way merely from listening to lectures on how to walk.

If, during maneuvers, a soldier practices taking cover instantly whenever he sees or hears the air attack warning or a plane coming close—if he always throws himself flat when he first hears the sudden whistle of a shell or the singing of bullets past his ears—these actions soon become second nature to him. The particular warning sights and sounds become fixed as signals for immediate actions. In a real emergency, the soldier does not have to stop to think what he should do. He just does it.

This sort of learning—of minor importance in high school or college—is basic in the Army. That is why drill is so important, why discipline is so essential.

In war games the soldier gets "conditioned" to all the sights and sounds of battle. In early training it may be possible to simulate realistically the noises of shells, dive bombers, and bursting bombs by recordings reproduced by loud speakers.

In advanced training a soldier may be taught to lie flat on the ground while real bullets strike within a few feet—close enough to cause sand to fall on the back of his neck. He knows he is safe so long as he lies still, but if he should get up and run, he would be killed.

That is good training for combat. A real bullet forms more habits much faster than a lecture about a bullet.

Such thoroughly drilled habits enable the soldier to act when there is no time for thought. They insure that he will act correctly and mechanically even when his mind is confused and thinking is almost impossible.

But knowledge of the science of warfare and practice in solving novel military problems are important too, because they enable the soldier to act wisely in the thousands of unexpected emergencies that arise in battle. Habit is safer than thought for standardized acts, but it won't work for brand new problems.

Drill for combat changes the recruit squad into an efficient fighting machine. Training can convert an unorganized civilian group into an organized unit with deadly power. Military competence, moreover, strips war of its most repulsive and paralyzing horrors. And knowledge takes from the enemy his most potent weapon—surprise.

Drill, combat training practice, and discipline, combined with experience in war, are things that make America's combat troops into "seasoned" troops.

We face as enemies professional soldiers who have spent years—perhaps a lifetime—preparing for their attacks upon us. America's Army is for the most part a civilian army made up of men who gave no thought at all to the business of war until it threatened or actually came.

But since learning-by-unlearning is the most difficult kind of learning, the training of the Army of the United States may actually be speeded up in some technical respects by the very fact that the men com-

202

ing into it are so completely raw and undisciplined.

And we need speed. Democracies always have to hurry at the last minute. The enemy is already facing us, ready trained, and there isn't much time. We must take advantage of every possible short-cut toward the goal of creating seasoned troops, troops armed with adequate training.

The first short-cut is an understanding of a few of the facts about how learning takes place.

The most important requirement of learning is incentive. Men marching to drill reluctantly can no more be taught swiftly and efficiently than a jeep can be taught to run on an empty tank. But fortunately for the Army's instructors, there is a powerful motive furnished by the situation itself. No false incentives need to be thought up and provided.

The enemy has attacked us, we are at war, and no man wants to go out to face that enemy unprepared. No American wants to see American soldiers killed needlessly in unmatched battle. No one wants to see our armies defeated and the Gestapo policing New York City.

What is needed to show the reasons, then, is an insight into how the particular day's task fits into the whole picture of the war effort. To each man, it sometimes seems as if his own immediate job at kitchen police, road building, repairing a motor, or cleaning a gun has little to do with what is happening in those far-away places where there is a battle. For the most part each man can trace for himself the real connection, although he should receive help from his leaders.

As he begins to picture for himself his part in the

whole, he will want to fill in the details of his prospects. Books are available to him that tell him how the enemy fights, what kind of training he will need when he comes up against the enemy, what living and fighting conditions he must toughen himself to undergo. Again his leaders must help him, for this information not only prepares him better but keeps up his morale.

In fact, having a good morale means being headed mentally for success in combat—the eventual success which follows all the minor successes in training which precede it.

The second necessary requirement for rapid learning is an attitude of attention. The frequent army command of "atten*tion!*" recognizes the fact that even the physical attitude plays a part in the way a man absorbs instructions or commands. There must be tension, mental and physical. Slumping in a chair or standing at ease encourages the mind to relax too. And relaxation often means wool-gathering, not learning. Standing at attention or sitting in an alert ready position usually puts the mind at attention also.

Both the desire to do a thing and attention are ordinarily secured by anticipated rewards and punishments. Just as a horse learns to jump to get lumps of sugar or a dog learns to keep out of the messhall by being whipped, so the attitude of any human being is determined by the expected consequences of his action. Promotions and citations are rewards. Extra K.P. and the guardhouse are punishments. Rewards and punishments do not, however, have to be so extreme to be effective.

Success itself is a reward to the soldier. It makes

him proud. His commander may commend him, but it is usually enough if he sees that his C.O. has noticed that he has done a good job. Good morale depends on such rewards—approbation by his officers and approval by his comrades.

In general, reward is much more effective for learning than is punishment. Punishment excites resentment and tends to make the soldier anxious not to comply, if he can get away with carelessness or disobedience. Reward keeps his attention on the business in hand. Punishment tends to shift his attention from the task to his own troubles.

The best kind of reward, because it is most effective in learning, is the glow of satisfaction that a man has when he knows he has done something correctly and well. It has clicked.

The most effective punishment is the surge of disgust that comes when he knows he has missed the target.

For best results, the soldier should know immediately after each shot fired at a target, after each try at performing any skill, just what the score is. Did he do it right or wrong? Did his shot go wide of the mark, did it just barely hit the target, or did he make a bullseye?

Knowing this at the time—not in terms of percentages listed on the unit bulletin board at some later day—links the pleasure of doing a thing well with all the coordinated acts that made the success possible. It enables the man to get the feel of the right way and correct himself when his performance falls short.

But it does not always take practice to form a habit.

205

One experience may be enough when it brings strong emotion. If a soldier has never heard a bomb and then the first bomb explodes near him, his habit may be formed instantaneously. Without thinking he throws himself on the ground for the second bomb, and for every other bomb after that one.

It is also true that learning can be instantaneous when the learner has sudden insight into a relationship. A soldier wonders why his girl is cold to him and then one night he sees another soldier kissing her. It doesn't take repetition and practice for him to know what's up.

Seeing the point of a joke or how a part in a machine works may be just as instantaneous.

Shortcuts in Learning Skills

The simplest sort of learning is the linking of an automatic, inborn way of acting with a new, but similar, way of acting under exactly the same circumstances. Or it means establishing a new signal, or trigger, for setting off the old natural response. This sort of learning is very easy and may take place even without any awareness of learning.

One automatic and natural action is the way the whole body becomes tense and in an attitude of listening at the sound of a sharp, abrupt noise, like a rifle shot.

The corporal makes use of this when he barks out sharply at the new soldier the command "Attention!" At first it is the loud, sudden sound that gets attention. After a short time, the word itself becomes a signal for the same alert listening. It no longer has to be loud or sudden.

Much of army drill consists of building up from this first learning act. A certain order must always be followed by a certain act. This sequence soon becomes as automatic as is the blinking of your eye when something thrown whizzes past your face.

Whole series of automatic actions can be set up in a similar way, so that a single order is followed by a series of actions always performed in the same order and in the same way. It is not necessary for the trained soldier to think of doing each of these acts —they follow each other naturally once the whole train is set in motion—as in coming from order arms to right shoulder.

To learn a mechanical or manual skill, like un-limbering a gun-carriage or sighting a bomb or a rifle, it is necessary to set up a large number of these sets of automatic actions.

For efficient learning of this sort, the same word of command or other signal should be used always to set off the same chain of actions.

When a truck driver becomes used to traffic signals, he gets so that the sight of a red light immediately sets his feet to reaching for the brake. That is because a red light always means *stop*. If the system were suddenly changed so that a siren or bell were used as the stop signal, or if a red light meant not stop but slow, the driver would for a time be confused.

This is why the Army has been right to reduce greatly the emphasis on close-order drill in recent years. In the light of modern knowledge and in view of modern conditions of warfare, this drill conflicts with the methods which must be used in battle.

In the drill of the early basic training, the whole emphasis is on teaching the soldier to respond to spoken commands. Yet when he goes into combat, spoken commands become impossible. The human voice is silent in the din of battle. If commands are given at all, they must be in the form of a nudge, a kick, or an arm and hand signal.

And in drill, the soldier also forms the habit of acting shoulder to shoulder with other men. He comes to rely on being in a group, on doing what the other men do when they do it. Yet in combat, such close order work would be suicidal. Men are then on their own, or in twos or threes. They must keep at a distance from the other men both to do much of their fighting skillfully and to avoid making crowded targets for the enemy's bombs, shells, or bullets.

This means that, in advanced training, men must learn new habits which conflict in some respects with the old. That's not good. The basic rule of all learning is: Do it right from the beginning. Because, if you form wrong habits, you must unlearn them before you can learn what is right. The rule to follow is: Never prepare for combat by learning to act on a signal that cannot be given after combat has started.

How to Speed Training

To speed training means that the man being trained should follow these rules:

(1) *Do things right the first time*. Any initial mistakes in learning a skill mean a false start. Not only do you still have all the learning to do, but you must

also unlearn the wrong way. This is hard. Pay particular attention to the best way of sitting or standing, holding your tools and so on. Once these things are learned correctly, you never have to think of them again.

(2) *Keep constant check* so that you know immediately whether you are right or making a mistake. Don't be content with knowing merely that 60 per cent or 90 per cent of your work is satisfactory. Know, as you do on the range, that each shot is definitely a hit or a miss.

(3) *Make no unnecessary motions.* If you flourish your hands or putter around with your tools, like it or not, these profitless motions will become habit, too. And, incidentally, these ineffectual motions are often more fatiguing than the motions needed in the work.

(4) *Do things in the same order and in the same way.* Stick to this rule so far as possible. It is not always practical, of course, but when it is, it will greatly speed the development of skill and make for smoothness of performance.

(5) *Avoid unnecessary links in the chain of your learning.* In learning radio code, for example, the old method was something like this. First the student learned the letters, which meant that he learned that *V* in radio code was dot-dot-dot-dash. Then he learned to think when he heard the audio-pitch in his earphones singing *dididitdah* that that noise meant dot-dot-dot-dash and that that meant V. He would say these things over to himself as he recognized the signal. Next step in the chain of learning was to learn to write V when he had heard the *di-*

dididtdah and thought that that meant dot-dot-dot-dash and then that that dot-dot-dot-dash meant V. He may have written it first in longhand and later had to learn to type it.

All these intermediate steps are so hard to drop later that they slow up receiving greatly. In streamlined Army training today, men are learning to type V when they hear the signal *dididitdah,* and to pay no attention to the other steps. It soon becomes an automatic response—second nature. It has proved quite possible in mid-Africa during this war to teach natives who still cannot read or write any language at all to receive and type out telegraphic code messages with accuracy.

A similar instance is in adding. The man unskilled in mathematics says to himself, "Three and four are seven, and six would make thirteen. Set down three and carry one." He learned as a child to do it that way and has done all that talking to himself ever since. If he has lots of adding to do, his tongue and throat actually get tired. But the expert accountant leaves out that step. He sees the 3 and 4 and his hand writes the 7, or else in a column of figures he just sees the 7 in his mind's eye and goes right on down the column.

It helps to think of learning as connections established over a system of telephone exchanges. When a signal comes in through the ears, it is transmitted directly to a special message center in the brain devoted to just such auditory signals. If that is to produce a certain action by the fingers, it is possible to make a direct connection from the auditory center to another brain center controlling the finger muscles. And when this connection is made often enough, it is simpler just to leave the wires plugged in, so that there is a standing direct connection or one established automatically as soon as the ear picks up that signal. If, however, before the connection is made to the finger-muscle center another connection is first made through another center controlling the muscles of speech, this delays service and adds to the burden of traffic over the nerve pathways.

(6) *Aim at first for smoothness of performance* rather than speed. Go slowly enough at first so that you don't fumble but get everything right. It pays to work with a certain rhythm—the rhythm best adapted to the particular task. Speed comes with practice.

(7) *Be sure to understand* what you are trying to do—what final objective you are aiming at. Watch skilled performance so that you will know how it should be done.

(8) *Learn series of actions rather than single moves.* If the skill you are learning depends on doing a sequence of acts, so far as possible practice the sequence as a whole. Don't practice each act separately and then try to piece them together. Learning is much more efficient if the whole chain of actions always follows along without break.

(9) *Keep on practicing.* Manual skills ordinarily become automatic only after long practice. So put in all the practice you possible can. Remember it is not always necessary actually to go through all the movements in order to practice them. Once you are familiar with how something is to be done, you

211

can review the motions in your mind, reproducing the feel of them as vividly as you can. When you get back to real practice, you will find that this imaginary practice has helped you in smoothing out the rough places in your performance. Beginners can practice driving a car or tank or plane while lying in bed, but they must sometimes have a real car or tank or plane too.

(10) *Overlearn.* This may seem like another way of stating rule 9. But it is a little more. A great deal of practice is necessary for learning, but a whole lot more is necessary to make it second nature so that you can never forget it and so that you can do a thing smoothly under all sorts of difficulties. The man who says he has learned to load and fire his gun even in his sleep may be speaking almost literal truth. The well-trained soldier can and does go through this action when his mind is confused by the noise and excitement of battle or even perhaps by a head wound or the blast of shells. He can go on with his duties, obey orders, and perform efficiently under circumstances that would make a poorly trained man forget for the time being everything he ever knew.

(11) *Relax.* Tenseness makes for awkwardness and mistakes. Don't be worried if you are tense and clumsy at first. Any beginner learning to do anything works too hard at it. Just watch the way a novice grips a tennis racket or a canoe paddle. But as skill develops, relaxation should come with it. Try to aid relaxation by intentionally taking it easy. When you have learned to relax, you will find that your precision and smoothness of performance pick

212

up. Yet don't overdo and relax so much that your movements have no snap or power.

How to Study Books, Manuals, and Lessons

Men in training in the Army, especially those taking advanced training as officers, have felt the need for a handbook of suggestions on how to study effectively. They are driven by an urgency to acquire knowledge with a speed seldom required of anyone in civilian life.

Ways have been worked out to help cut down the time required to master a subject, to read and understand a book or an assignment, to solve a problem or to memorize a rule or a formula.

The man in the Army should not allow noise or other distractions or interruptions to put him off his work. Working under such difficult circumstances is direct training for actual fighting conditions. In the field the most vital and difficult decisions must be made in the midst of the most violent distractions and under all sorts of physical and mental strains. The officer who had to wait until he could be free of noise or disturbance before he could work out a problem or make a decision would be useless to the Army. If he is used to it, a certain amount of noise and confusion may actually stimulate the Army man to do better thinking.

If it is convenient, a definite time in the day should be assigned for study. The mind can be trained to be ready for work at a certain hour so that this happens in much the same way you begin thinking about food at some other set time. For the same reason it might be desirable to have a certain place set aside for study even if it is just your bunk in a noisy barracks or tent. Then the act of sitting down in that place will immediately from habit put you in the proper frame of mind for mental work. If you are lucky enough to have a desk or corner for your study, don't spoil its value by using it for relaxation or loafing.

But even if they are insistently disturbing it is nearly always possible to ignore distractions and get down to the business at hand.

The mind is an excellent sieve-net. You can read the newspapers and never see the advertisements. You would hear a strange foot-step across the room, yet never notice the loud ticking of the clock on your own table. A telegrapher can sleep through the long continuous sounding of his instrument, yet wake at once when his own call comes in with the right dots and dashes. In the same way it is possible to make yourself deaf and blind to all sorts of sights and sounds except those directly concerned with the problem being studied.

At first it is fatiguing to shut out distractions. You actually make your muscles tense in your effort to attend to business. Later you get so that the things that distract you no longer worry you. Still later they help, and you find that you miss them if they disappear. Like the man who was startled when his clock stopped ticking. Or the radio. At first it prevents you from studying, but if you keep it on continuously, you may get so that you can not study without it.

Having set the stage as well as possible for most effective study, the next important preparation is to develop an absorbing interest in the material to be mastered. It is not necessary to resort to self-delivered mental pep-talks. Enthusiasm grows naturally out of the realization that a study is important in reaching a desirable goal, that it will satisfy your curiosity or that it will give you a chance to exercise some special talent.

Interest is aroused by thinking about the subject, the assignment, or the problem to be mastered—by deliberately searching for all the ways in which knowledge of the particular subject can be applied in winning the promotions desired, in making the work ahead easier, or in eventually defeating the enemy and so ending the war.

For the man who feels himself completely lacking in other motives and aspirations, it is always possible to make things interesting by laying a private bet with some other student on who will find the correct solution to a group of tough problems in the shortest time. Or sometimes a man is stimulated merely by making a bet with himself.

One of the most important ways of creating interest in a subject is to make your study original. Even a bad scheme of study that is your own idea may work better for you than a good scheme that someone else has prescribed for you. Every man respects his own ideas, is interested in what is peculiarly his own. So take notes. Make diagrams. Abstract or paraphrase the text. No matter how, so long as it is the method that you yourself have thought up.

Strange as it may seem, an obscure textbook is sometimes learned more easily than a clear one, for no other reason that that the poor text challenges the student to make it clear. His disgust with the author grows with his pride in himself, as he keeps putting the author right, seeing for himself how the text should have been written.

The chief aid to learning is, however, understanding. When something makes sense—when it fits in with what you already know—then it is easily filed away in the ready-reference system of your memory where it can be recalled later at need.

Learning without understanding is hard. You probably learned the multiplication tables this way.

Learning with understanding may require no effort at all.

So try to understand. Try to see relationships. If chapter 8 depends on chapter 2 and you are uncertain about chapter 2, turn back. See the dependence. Work it out for yourself rather than read it again. If you learn a new scientific fact, see whether you can find instances of it in your own experience. And then, when you think you know what you have studied, say it all over to yourself in your own words. That tests your understanding. Sometimes it gets clear for the first time as you explain it to yourself. And if you can't get it said to your own satisfaction, then the chances are that you really do not understand it. And what you don't understand you won't remember.

Rapid Reading

Since so much of the time of many army officers and enlisted men is devoted to reading of some kind or other, any time that can be saved in mastering the contents of a book, a manual or an assignment is of great value.

Here are a few suggestions:

When you first get a new textbook or manual for study, get a bird's-eye view of the whole book first. Turn at once to the table of contents and see whether the book is divided into main divisions and what these are. You may find, as in one Army Field Manual, that there is a first section devoted to a general discussion of the problems involved, a second on materials, a third on typical practice, and a fourth which is a summary. Then read through the chapter or subject headings in each section.

Next leaf through the book rapidly to see the relative length of the different sections and other facts about the organization of the book—whether it has an index, problems to be worked out by the student, or references for further reading, and how it is illustrated and so on.

Now try to get a better idea of the purpose and scope of the volume. In the particular Field Manual mentioned, this is contained in the first section. In some textbooks it will be found in a foreword. Find out also who wrote the book, if there is a single author, and with what institution or part of the Army he is connected.

Next turn to the summary or conclusions, if the book contains such a section. It is usually at the end of the book. Read this quickly, not with the idea of learning it, but just to inform yourself about what the work contains, what its purpose is.

You are now pretty well acquainted with the job ahead of you—what it is all about, how long it is, how difficult, and how it is related to other things you are studying.

With this background the reading of the first lesson will be relatively easy. Read it through rapidly first to get a general idea of the whole. In this reading don't hesitate over puzzling paragraphs or difficult sections. Get the whole picture first. When you come back to these stumbling blocks later you may find that they are clear when viewed as a part of the whole section.

To speed this first reading, avoid anything that will impede you, such as thinking about the pronunciation of words or the sort of silent pronunciation of words that has unfortunately become an ingrained habit with many men. Reading should be a purely visual recognition of words (or, better still, of ideas). There should be no thinking of how the words would sound or muscular feeling in the throat of how it would feel to speak them. If you catch yourself making lip movements as you read, concentrate for a while on breaking that habit. It is hard to do, but you will be repaid in a greatly increased speed of reading. And don't waste any time on any part of the book that tells you something you already know.

In a second reading, go more slowly. Think now about each paragraph after you have finished it, discovering its meaning and its relation to what has preceded and what will follow it. Work out the problems.

Now another swift reading to re-assemble the complete picture of the assignment and to impress it on your mind. Then close the book and write down an outline or summary in just a few words of all that was contained in that assignment.

You have now learned that assignment! And the chances are that with an occasional review (rather frequent at first, but less often later) you will never forget it.

Unfortunately, the Army student is not always able to complete such a thorough preparation of an assignment. One advantage of this method of study is that, if you are interrupted you are better off to have had a swift view of the whole assignment than you would be if you had spent the whole time on thorough reading of a small part of it.

When, as is sometimes done at an Army school, you are given a large number of lesson sheets and problems to look over in preparation for the next day in the field, it is best to use a similar technique.

Look through the whole mass swiftly. Try to see how they are related—what is to be the general point or emphasis of the next day's work. If that is all you have time to do, that much will at least put you on guard as to what to look for in the next day's problem. Also give a minute to thinking how this new work is related to what you have already learned, how it fits into the whole program of combat training, just what kind of battle situation it is intended to prepare you for, and where you might be using this new combat knowledge after a while.

Ten minutes spent on this kind of preparation is likely to be of more value to you the next morning than twenty minutes would be if spent on working out carefully only a part of the new work.

If previous study habits have developed in you a feeling of guilt at skimming over a page swiftly, you had best get over that. A little practice will enable you to get the gist of a paragraph or a page by hunting out key sentences. The key sentence is usually the first sentence of the paragraph. Read more at that point if you do not understand the connection with what went before or with what comes later. But when it all is clear, let your eye drift on to the next key sentence and find out what the next paragraph or section is about. You can—and should—go back for the details when you have skimmed off the cream of the main facts and general meaning.

In other words, get a view of the general objective first. Fill in the details of individual positions later when you can appreciate their importance in con nection with the whole mission.

In most manuals, you will find key words printed in black type. This aids you in the process of skimming and of organizing the material in your mind. Use their aid if you find them of value to you.

In mastering the contents of a lesson, a textbook, or a manual, it is seldom necessary or advisable to try to memorize any of the words used. Try always just to grasp the facts and to be able then to tell them or write them down in your own words. If you can do this you will be able to remember the meaning without recalling a single word of the original text.

Solving Problems

The method of bird's-eye-view-first applies to the rapid solving of problems, too. Haste too often tempts people to plunge into working out the first part of problem or the easy parts, before the entire problem is clearly in mind. This may result in a

220

false start and needless work. Read the whole problem through first.

Use care in setting the problem down. If you are new at this particular sort of problem, don't try to take shortcuts in this. A little extra time used on formulating the problem in your mind or on paper can save a great deal of time in finding the solution.

The next step is to review rapidly all possible methods of solving the problem until you find one that seems right. Then try that. If it fails to work, try another. That's the way you work with a mechanical puzzle. You should use the same method on a technical problem.

When you are stumped, it may be because you have the wrong approach to the problem. It is easy to get into a rut in thinking. And it is hard to shake yourself loose from one point of view and to see a completely new one. You tend to keep going back and repeating the old kind of attack that has always failed. It's like feeling in the same pocket six times when you have lost your cigarettes and cannot find them.

Especially is it hard to try new methods when you are tired or nervous over your failure to get the right answer. At such times it is best to close your book and work on something else, or to do something outdoors in the fresh air, or even, if you can afford the time, to take a nap. When you come back to your problem, the new approach may come to you in a flash, and from then on the work may go quickly and smoothly.

Such flashes of insight as to what method will really work are not all due to chance. They depend on your experience with other similar problems, on your seeing the particular problem as a whole, on your readiness to abandon methods that have failed, on your coming to the problem fresh from doing something else, or on your lack of fatigue.

MEMORIZING

It pays to memorize certain fundamental rules and formulas that are frequently used. In the long run it takes more time to keep looking them up than to learn them well at the start. Such material should be repeated over and over until it rings in your head like a popular tune. Then, when you want to use the rule, the mere thought of it will automatically start the words going in your mind.

Such memorizing is much more like acquiring new tools you can use than it is like understanding information. It requires many repetitions. And all rules that seem to be arbitrary and seem not to depend on sense have to be learned in this way. But it is much better to get the sense if there is any to get, and to understand the reason for the rule, because then you can reconstruct the rule after you have forgotten all its words.

It is extremely important for an Army leader up as high as company, squadron, battery, and troop commander, to know every man in his command by name, and this accomplishment is quite difficult for some officers. Memory systems have been devised for this purpose. If you personally find them helpful, by all means use them, but for many they are cumbersome and of no particular advantage. They work something like this: The new man in your unit is very tall and thin. He reminds you of a pole. That reminds you of a bean-pole and that makes you think of beans growing in a garden. All that may serve to make you remember that the man's name is Gardiner.

Much simpler and more effective is the direct association of name Gardiner with the sight of the man. Force yourself to speak his name every time you see him. Repeat his name to yourself while you are looking at him. Do this invariably every time you see him for a while and soon the mere sight of the man will make you speak his name without hesitation.

Most effective memory aids are those which occur to you spontaneously and naturally. When you are introduced to a man named King, it may make you chuckle to observe how very diffident and modest the man seems—how very unlike a King. When such associations come to your own mind naturally they help you to remember the name because every time you see the man and notice his manner of deferring to others, you are reminded of the incongruity.

It pays to be on the alert for such natural punning associations with names or dates or other facts you find it difficult to memorize.

PLATEAUS OF LEARNING

In learning to do new things and in all other kinds of learning, progress is likely to be interrupted by a staleness, a mental bogging down which is discouraging to the most stout-hearted, and completely demoralizing to some. Psychologists and educators call this the "learning plateau," a period when learning levels off for a while, but to the student it seems much more like an insurmountable mountain peak.

A medical officer in the Air Corps reports that many men wash out of pilot training courses because they are not forewarned of this experience and become unduly disheartened by it. In aviation training, the plateau is likely to occur when the cadet has already learned to take his plane up and bring it down successfully. Then, just when he feels exultant over this accomplishment and is attacking the new learning of taking the plane somewhere and bringing it back, he runs, as it were, into a zero-ceiling. He can not master the new problems. He makes no progress.

In this case, the reason lies in the fact that, although he has mastered the routine of handling the controls, he has not yet reduced these things to habit. He must still pay careful attention to what he is doing in flying his plane. The actions are not yet automatic, not yet second nature to him. Consequently, when he tries to give thought to the new problems of navigation he is like a young baby who can't hold two toys at the same time. Or the green typist who can't keep on typing while answering a question. Either he fails to master the navigation problems, or he seems to lose some of the flying skill on which he had been congratulating himself.

If this student realizes what is going on and that a slowing-up or plateau is a natural occurrence in his training, he will be patient with himself and spur himself on to more and more practice on the first skills until they really do become so automatic that

224

his attention is free for new problems.

A slowing-up doesn't always occur because a new stage in the learning process is encountered. The student may stop progressing because he has just learned something else that interferes—like starting to study French when he is still not far along in Spanish. Or other matters may take his attention off the learning job—like worry about gambling or love.

In fact, one of the worst plateau producers is falling in love.

Fatigue also slows progress.

Such periods of slowing-up should ordinarily be of very brief duration. Combining new learning with things already learned takes a little time, but if the plateau is of prolonged duration it should be taken as a sign that the student is not getting along as he should, or that the instructor is not supplying him with some aid which he needs at a critical spot in his learning.

In aviation, where so very much depends upon the utilization of previously perfected skills, a cadet may appear both to himself and to his instructor to be stuck on a plateau. In primary flight school, a plateau of long duration is picked up by the supervising pilot who may take the student for a check flight in an attempt to discover the difficulty that is blocking his advance. If necessary the check pilot may assign the student to another instructor.

Some plateaus are more apparent than real. Training courses are ordinarily arranged so that the difficulty of the work becomes greater and greater. Then progress seems to slow down merely because the demands are increasing.

Whatever the cause in any particular instance, the path of learning almost invariably must traverse these trying detours in the route to success. But if the student does not lose heart and keeps plugging away, he will eventually find himself out again on the straight smooth road, spinning along toward his goal.

X: HOW THE ARMY TEACHES

MEN LEARN FAST in the Army. They have to, for a fighting force is needed as soon as it can be built. In war there is no time to waste.

In his twelve weeks at a training center, the new soldier becomes a trained individual fighter or technician. In the first six weeks he gets the basic training that turns him from a civilian into a soldier.

Then, in six weeks more, the Army builds on the foundation of these basic military habits, and gives him the further training through which he learns to handle skillfully at least one weapon or one special piece of military equipment.

After that, when he goes to join a company or a squadron, troop, or battery, he still has more to learn —more about acting as a member of a fighting team or a technical crew. And these things also he has to learn fast.

When an Army is built up almost from scratch, hundreds of thousands of men must learn to be expert at doing things for which their civilian experience has given them little or no preparation.

It speeds up all Army training from the beginning if new men are carefully classified according to what they can do best or will probably be able to learn most readily. And reclassification later on, of men for whom it is necessary, also helps speed training. Interviews and different kinds of tests are used in getting each new Army man into the place where he can learn most rapidly and become of the greatest possible use to the Army.

The demands of war for rapid learning do not permit the use of much extra time to teach a soldier who is slow to learn. If a soldier fails to make progress in the training selected for him, he is shifted without delay to some other type of training at which he will be more likely to make good.

How to Make Rapid Learning Stick

The Army must then have rapid learning. Training must be short, but it must also be thorough and permanent. In addition it must be both rigid and flexible, contradictory as that may sound. Men must know so thoroughly the best way to reach an objective that they will follow the routine in the emotional stress of combat, but they must also be ready instantly to adapt the correct methods they have learned to the special conditions under which they must be applied.

These necessary automatic habits are produced by practice, but the necessary flexibility in using them is got by the soldier's understanding thoroughly the purpose of the habit. When he understands, then he can make changes as the battle situation changes.

The two basic principles of learning anything are *interest* and *participation*. It is not true that repetition alone is the basis of learning something well. A man who repeats an act again and again with his mind only half on what he is doing, may indeed learn it, but he will learn it neither quickly nor well. Fortunately doing a thing and practicing it usually reinforce a man's interest, so that there is really only

228

one important principle—*interest*—at the bottom of learning.

Active *participation* is secured by practice. Lectures are used only when preliminary explanation at some length is needed or when the men cannot be put through the work itself. You are not only told how to fire a rifle. You are helped actually to do the firing, and you work out of doors in the way that you will later work in combat. You do, under instruction, what later on you are going to have to do in combat by yourself.

Interest is secured in a variety of ways.

(1) The personality of the instructor is important. He should be a dynamic and forceful person who appreciates the fact that learning takes time and that some men are slower than others. He must stimulate his men to want to learn.

(2) Instruction must finally become individual. There must be close contact between some instructor and every soldier. When the groups are large they must, therefore, be broken up into smaller groups with assistants, who work under the superivision of the leader, and are assigned to each small group to give the detailed advice and correction.

(3) The relation of the learning to the problems of combat must always be stressed. There are only two reasons for learning anything in the Army. The training must either help to destroy the enemy or help to secure the safety of the soldier and his own unit. When the soldier realizes that this is the aim of all his training, his interest should not fail.

(4) Although non-essentials are omitted in Army teaching, it is very important that the soldier should

229

understand the basic principles of what he is doing. If he is learning how to use a machine, then he should know how the machine works unless it is too complicated for his understanding. Thus he is given demonstrations to see, charts and working models to understand, films which show him what he cannot see in actual practice.

(5) The soldier must also have full knowledge of the purpose of what he learns, of why he needs to know it. Only with such knowledge can his interest be at the highest, and only with such knowledge is he able to adapt what he has learned to the different circumstances that arise in combat.

WHOLESALE DISTRIBUTION OF KNOWLEDGE

All Army commanders and leaders are teachers. All have to instruct their own units. But some, like those who teach at training centers, have the job of teaching many successive classes of men in the same subject. These officers and noncoms are usually chosen because they know the work and are "energetic"—a word often used in the Army to describe a man who has initiative, enthusiasm, interest, desire for action, self-reliance and a personality that makes other men readily follow him and work for him.

Some Army technical instructors are civilians with previous experience in teaching or in the work they impart. But most Army-leader instructors are young men, second or first lieutenants, who never taught before in their lives and who have themselves only learned to give instruction since entering the Army.

Army groups undergoing instruction—platoons, companies, squadrons, crews, classes at Army schools—are often large. School rooms may have to be improvised, and most combat training is necessarily given out of doors. It is mainly out of doors that armies fight. An instructor giving a "lecture," a company commander training his unit, must sometimes try to make his voice carry to the ears of two hundred or more men.

Because of the special problems they face, Army instructors follow specially developed Army teaching methods as they may apply to the work in hand. These differ in some respects from the teaching methods of civilian schools, but are based on the same general basic principles of instruction. There are six steps of instruction:

(1) As soon as he knows he is to give instruction, he prepares for it. He studies what he is to teach, plans his teaching, and sees to it that everything he will need—every aid to instruction—is at the right place.

(2) Then, in beginning the actual instruction, he explains to the group what the instruction will be about and why it is important.

(3) Next, either the instructor or a group of assistants demonstrates part or all of the things being taught.

(4) Practice by the soldiers in the group follows next.

(5) After a reasonable amount of practice—not so much at one thing as to make it very tiresome —the instructor and his assistants examine the whole group to determine how well each man has learned.

(6) The instruction ends with a discussion. The instructor answers questions that puzzle any sol-

diers in the group. And at the end he usually repeats some of the main things to be remembered, gives a glimpse ahead at what will follow next, and says again why the work of that day is important in war.

Some instruction can't be practiced at the time by the soldiers who are being taught. Then, most of

FIG. 42.

the instruction may consist of explanation, and it becomes a lecture.

Any Army instructor may use original ways of capturing the interest of the men and of putting ideas across to them. To supplement his voice he makes free use of charts, photographs, film strips in which each picture is thrown separately on a screen, blackboard drawings, and training films. (See

232

Fig. 42.) In technical work, such as instruction to machine gunners and motor mechanics, he may also use working models of weapons or machinery cut away to show the moving parts.

Or the model may simply be made out of wood or cardboard and colored, being made so that its moving parts can be operated by hand slowly

FIG. 43.

enough for the soldiers easily to see how the weapon or machine works.

Another device often used is a combination of diagram and model (Fig. 43). In signal communication instruction a wiring diagram is prepared, but instead of putting in the symbols for switches and transformers, the real parts are attached at the proper points. The whole thing is thus in actual working order, so that, when a given switch is thrown, the right signalling system is connected or the right lights light up.

Whenever possible in instruction student soldiers are encouraged to take an active part and to ask questions freely, and when called on by the instructor, to offer suggestions, comments, and explanations.

MASSED INDIVIDUAL INSTRUCTION

Strangely enough, individual instruction solves the problem of teaching big classes of men—too big for all to hear the voice of a single instructor clearly. With as many as two hundred men, it is impractical for the instructor to teach them as a group except for short periods and for certain parts of the training. Consequently, in one way or another an instructor has to be provided for every soldier, so that they do their learning in a group, but not as a group.

In one method assistants to the instructor—noncoms or members of the class who have caught on a little more rapidly than the others—walk continually through the group while its members are at work learning something new. They stop and give help wherever it is needed, showing one man how to hold his rifle or his tool, explaining to another who is puzzled, correcting mistakes.

Another way is to separate the class or company into squads. While one squad is receiving group instruction, the others are under the supervision of assistants on practical problems. This is a good method for use in some parts of machine gunnery, in shop work, and in first-aid instruction. The in-

234

structor goes from one squad to another, has the men sit down by their work, and tells them the why and the how of what they have been doing or will learn to do next.

Such small groups, working closely together, can be still further divided up into teams. In a machine shop, for example, two men may work on each machine. These men are carefully matched up. For each new man or each man who is slow at learning, another is chosen who is just a little further advanced or a little better at the particular job. The instructor and his assistants watch to be sure that the better man does only his share of the work. But the less skilled man learns by watching the other, and the more advanced man helps his mate by word and gesture so that he gets the hang of things a little more easily.

A similar method works well in purely military as well as technical training—the "coach and pupil" method. In this a platoon of men is lined up in a double row for instruction in rifle marksmanship as shown in Fig. 44. The front rank men take, for example, one of the positions from which they must learn to fire a rifle. They go through the motions of loading, aiming, squeezing the trigger, and firing, using dummy ammunition or none at all, since it is dangerous for new soldiers to use live ammunition except under careful control on the target range. The other half of the platoon are at this time the coaches—each coaching the man with whom he is teamed.

This works. You may not know how to shoot yet yourself, but that doesn't hinder you from knowing what is wrong in the way another soldier handles his rifle.

The officer instructing the company walks along the line, behind the pairs of men. He instructs the coaches, shows them what faults to look for, how the rifle should be held, how to tell whether a man is

FIG. 44.

jerking the trigger or giving the steady squeeze that hits the Jap or German soldier.

After a few minutes the order is given for all men to change places. Those who were the coaches take their own rifles and become pupils, while those who have been receiving instruction now get the chance to find fault and to give advice.

This, of course, is just one of many steps in learning to fire the rifle, automatic rifle, tommygun or carbine. This method is successful for several of the steps, although other methods may have to be used for the other steps.

ARMY EFFICIENCY IN TRAINING

The simplest kind of learning is to learn by trial and error, but this isn't the best, the most efficient way. It wastes too much time, and so the Army never uses it except in the solving of original problems, where one method after another may need to be tried, at least in imagination. Even then the soldier needs to examine the whole problem first, and limit the number of trials he has to make by discarding those that are not promising.

In fact, a general wartime training rule is to learn nothing that isn't essential but to use everything that helps. Another rule is to look ahead in training. Give every soldier every bit of sensible instruction that can help him to preserve his own life under fire, and to destroy more efficiently his enemy or to serve those whose battle job it is to do so. The more a soldier knows about campaign and battle beforehand, the better he will be as a fighter from his first battle on. Knowledge, not guesswork or luck, is mainly what brings a fighting man safely through combat after doing his full part in winning the battle.

In training, as in combat later, a soldier must learn to make good use of all his senses in different ways. And in the different ways they help him in the midst of battle. An instructor can *tell* his students much but not all. Some things he has to *show* them —with models, charts, working diagrams, field demonstrations, training films. War gases have actually got to be *smelled*—in weak solutions. Weapons, equipment, and tools must be *handled* if their use is to be understood and learned.

In battle, a leader can give orders but only brief ones, sometimes by signal. The soldier receiving such an order must also see the battle situation right around him in deciding how best to carry the order out. His sense of smell is often of assistance too, not only for detecting gas, but smoke of weapons and other signs that indicate something he may need to know. And unless the feel of his individual weapon and its working parts and ammunition have become so natural that he handles them in combat without thought, he is liable to be killed by an enemy soldier who is more thoroughly trained, who is "quicker on the trigger." The same principle applies to handling the controls and levers in a tank or plane or truck, or on a big gun.

The soldier must *do* things to learn them rapidly and well. He must handle the weapons and tools and machines himself or he will never acquire the skill he must have with them for war. He must make the computations himself during his training or he will not make them correctly when the time comes to use them in battle. Hence an active participation by the soldier in the operations in which he receives training is a prime condition of effective learning.

But speed of learning is paramount in the emergency of war. Everything not essential must be cut out.

Army training omits most history, except for such brief references to the battles of this and other wars

238

an instructor may give. It leaves out other interesting but non-essential things which would be taught if there were more time—side-lights of the kind habitually used in the school or college classroom.

In learning how to place the fire of a weapon at different ranges, the soldier needs to learn only how to change the setting of the sights and to use firing tables to allow for such things as up-hill or down-hill firing. He doesn't have to learn the complicated mathematics by which sights were designed and the firing tables figured out.

To learn to keep a plane or tank well lubricated in Russian cold or African heat, a soldier needs to learn only where to squirt the oil, where to inject the grease, what oil and grease to use, and how often to do the job. He doesn't need to know how the oil and grease were manufactured and where.

He does, however, need to learn *why* as well as *how*. For he will remember reasons better than mechanical rules. But *why* and *how* are enough.

In Army training, each subject is prepared in lessons and these are carefully standardized. Officer and noncom instructors follow these lessons strictly. Then, if an instructor gets sick or is ordered to other duty, his classes go right on under a new instructor without any hitch or delay. Thus an Army instructor cannot choose the order and contents of the courses he teaches as a teacher can in a school or college. But he does have full opportunity to use his personality in making his instructions vivid, in building up interest among the soldiers he instructs.

The standard period of instruction in most Army training centers is about thirteen weeks and in some special school courses of training the period is shorter or longer. A school may, however, start a new group of soldiers every week. Thus, if a man becomes ill or has to go home on furlough because of some family emergency, he can come back into the training just where he left off, joining the group that has reached the place at which he left the course. When a slow soldier has to repeat his work, he may only be put back for a week. He doesn't have to take the whole course over again.

On the other hand, if any soldier shows plainly that he already knows well the work he is being taught, his advancement is often speeded up by shifting him to another instruction group. These methods of Army training are efficient. They make it possible to get large numbers of well trained men and units to the war theaters in the least time. Rapid learning means winning the war sooner.

How the Army Speeds Training

The ways in which the Army streamlines its training to make 7,000,000 men fit for combat in a single year can be summed up as follows:

(1) *Will to learn.* A soldier's common sense tells him that he must learn how to fight before he meets the enemy. If he doesn't know this fact when he goes into the Army, he soon finds out because in all training it is constantly pounded in.

(2) *Interest.* The Army selects for instructors the officers, noncoms, and civilian experts who can capture the interest of the men they train. Thus, most new soldiers soon find that they like to learn the things they must learn. Men with only limited in-

telligence, as well as those who catch on quickly, listen eagerly to good Army instruction.

(3) *Discipline.* Soldiers are trained to realize the serious importance of the things they are taught, how much these things will mean in combat later.

(4) *Individual instruction.* In the Army, lectures to big groups of men are few, because this method of training doesn't make sure every day that each man is learning or discover which men are not learning. Army instructors see to it that each man has the chance to learn and does learn if he can. Instruction is modified to fit individual needs.

(5) *Experience of success.* Army instructors try their best to see to it that each man does a thing right the first time—even by holding his hand and putting it through the correct movements if necessary. Mistakes, waste, or wrong learning, failures and damage are thus kept to the minimum.

(6) *Elimination of non-essentials.* In Army training, men are taught only those things immediately necessary to fit them to destroy the enemy and preserve their own lives in combat. Other facts, however interesting, are passed up.

(7) *All-around attack.* Every possible way of reaching the soldier student's mind is utilized. Demonstration and other visual instruction is used where it works best, and lectures and other oral instruction where it is more efficient. All types of instruction are closely coordinated and the instruction is kept close to the job of war in hand.

Instruction is immediately put to use in action on the job. Soldiers learn to do by doing. So far as possible, instruction is kept practical and concrete. Soldiers learn about rifles by handling them, balancing them in their hands, taking them apart and putting them together again, and shooting them. And this instruction isn't complete when the soldier can aim accurately at a target on a rifle range which is remote from any distraction or danger. He must also learn to fire his weapons under combat conditions —from a position flat on the ground in thick brush, from a moving tank or assault boat, after running or creeping with a full pack.

All this activity as the soldier learns the methods of war is constantly accompanied by instruction that enables him to understand clearly just what he is doing and why he is doing it. Every action, whether it is digging a slit trench or assembling the complicated mechanism of an airplane or a machine gun, contributes to the major objective of overcoming the enemy and conserving American lives the better to win through to victory. The soldier must never forget this *why.*

If an instructor puts too much emphasis on training men in the particular details of doing a job, the soldier fails to get a clear understanding of the result aimed at.

A soldier is a better fighting man if he understands the objectives to be reached. Army leaders are, therefore, taught to order results, when writing orders, and not give the detailed methods for getting those results.

Although in training men in the many different Army jobs adequate attention must be paid to the detailed steps to be taken to reach the final objective, the aim itself must also be made entirely clear to the soldier. Otherwise he is apt to become confused if, in battle, the situation changes and he cannot follow the steps in exactly the way he was taught them in training.

The modern soldiers in America's Army are trained so that they combine knowledge of the science of warfare with thoroughly drilled habits of combat in such a way that they are prepared to act quickly and automatically in an emergency, but also to size up the battle situation for themselves and act accordingly, thinking their own ways out of any tight spots. Well established habits, working together, give them all the advantage of a smoothly functioning precision instrument of war. Knowledge and understanding of the aims and methods of warfare give them the judgment, initiative, and quick thinking that enable them to best an enemy—in fighting teams or, when necessary, single-handed.

XI: EFFICIENCY IN THE ARMY

EVERY OUNCE of a soldier's energy should be concentrated on the defeat of the enemy. Whenever he wastes his strength on any sort of activity that does not contribute to that one end, it is, in effect, a casualty.

Nowhere is efficiency more important than in combat. There every man must work at the very peak of his powers. His eyes must see better than the enemy's eyes. His ears must hear better. He must think better. On this victory depends.

Weariness, tired hands or eyes or nervous system —anything that reduces the soldier's efficiency at a critical moment in combat may cost him his life It may cost the Army a position, an advance, a battle.

But a soldier is not always in combat. Much of his time is spent in plain hard work. He may be doing much the same sort of job that thousands of civilians are doing. He must service trucks, repair damaged airplanes, build roads or bridges, load trains and boats, string telephone wires, or cook chow.

Efficiency in all these tasks is important, too. For these jobs are the life and support of the Army. Delay, waste, failure means defeat here as well as in the front line.

In such places as training camps, arsenals, ship yards, and depots, working conditions may be very similar to what they are in any civilian war production plant. There, the lessons learned in peace-time factories for building efficiency and for cutting out waste motions, lost time, and damaged material can be applied. Lighting, ventilation, rest periods, and similar conditions affecting the efficiency of the workers can be controlled, at least to some extent.

In other places where soldiers work, the jobs themselves may be very much like civilian tasks, but the conditions are very different. In advanced bases, in maintenance and repair stations near the front, and in field hospitals, it may be necessary to work long hours without rest and without adequate protection. Combat conditions are likely to dictate how soon and with what tools a repair job must be done. The enemy usually refuses to recognize the end of the working day. Nature often provides the only lighting. Bombs insure the ventilation.

But when a soldier gets into actual combat, what he is called upon to do seems to have no similarity at all to anything he ever did in a civilian job. There is no routine in battle. No standardization. No monotonous repetition. Each moment is a challenging new experience calling for new decisions and fresh insight. It is hard to see where the combat soldier can get any help at all from what he has learned about efficiency in a factory far from the battle zones.

Nevertheless, the experienced soldier realizes that much of what he does is, after all, a smooth performance of well-earned habits. And the extent to which he has learned the most efficient way of loading his rifle, digging a slit trench, mounting a machine gun, or doing any number of other mechanical

245

skilled jobs, determines the extent to which his mind is left free to deal with the split-second judgments upon which life and victory depend.

You may never lay field communications twice in exactly the same way. But you must splice the wires in just about the same way whether you are in training camp or trying desperately to establish communications between a new advanced command post and a higher headquarters.

You may never meet the enemy in exactly the same position under just the same conditions, more than once. But you must hold your rifle, load it, and fire it, and later clean it, in just about the same way every time.

And the speed and efficiency with which you go through all such routine motions will determine whether you get in the first shot—or whether you have already fired your last shot.

That is why a soldier in training must learn from the start to cut out useless and round-about movements that take needless time. Seconds count.

And a soldier's energy counts, too. He can't afford to get worn down before his job is done. He must keep his speed and his accuracy up to top-notch performance. Any blunder in combat may be fatal. There he may not be able to miss and aim again. He may never have another chance.

So it is best to learn the quickest, most effective way from the first because any slow, clumsy wrong methods that a soldier learns must be unlearned before he can master the best method.

To find out what the best way is for any action like loading a rifle or assembling a machine gun, the first thing to do is to analyze the job. That is usually done by the instructor who follows the steps given in the official manual on the gun. These were originally studied out step by step by expert machine gunners who found the best way in the manner described in the next few paragraphs. Any new action or task can be worked out in the same way.

Break the job down into steps—small steps. See what simple actions it is made up of. A job that requires fitting a part into place, for example, may start out with (1) searching for, (2) finding, (3) grasping, and (4) putting the part in its place.

Then study each separate step in the whole operation. See whether there are any waste motions which can be cut out. Can the work be placed so that there is less searching, easier finding, quicker grasping, or moving over less distance. Such improvements will speed the operation. The manner in which the work is laid out is extremely important. If the part must be turned around before it can be put in place, it takes longer and is more tiring than if it can be picked up in the correct position for putting it where it is to go.

See whether all movements are being done so as to produce the least fatigue. Reaching up or bending the back to reach down is harder than reaching just with your arm and without much change of your body's position. If the handle of any tool used is too large, too small, or so heavy that it tires your hand, you will use up energy on that tool which you should save to use where it will count.

If quick, short movements are made, it may be necessary to take motion pictures of them, running

247

the camera rapidly, and then to study the film when it is projected in slow motion. Slow motion pictures not only show up the wrong motions, but also make it possible to measure the time that each movement takes.

Here are certain rules for planning the best method of work in any sort of mechanical job.

(1) Arrange the movements so that, as you finish each one, you are in the best position for beginning the next. Then everything will run along smoothly, and you won't have to interrupt the flow of work to think what to do next, or to make an awkward or tiring movement to begin the next motion.

(2) Make the order of movements one that will encourage easy rhythm, for a succession of smooth swinging motions easily changes into a single automatic act.

(3) Let the movements be smooth and steady, without sudden changes of direction or sudden changes of speed.

(4) Keep the number of movements as few as possible.

(5) Arrange for the use of both hands as much as possible.

(6) When strength must be exerted, arrange, as far as possible, to have the force applied at the time that will take the greatest possible advantage of the momentum of the movement and at a place where the leverage is greatest.

In civilian factory work, such fine breakdowns of jobs and study of movements have been very useful for speeding production and making things less tiring for the worker. In one study it was found that a brick layer used 18 movements in laying each brick. Analysis showed that five rhythmical movements were enough. When that man had learned these new work habits, his speed of laying bricks had increased from 120 to 350 bricks per hour.

That is why it is important for the soldier to learn the best methods of doing any job that he will have to do again and again. When any soldier watches a training film, it will pay him to notice little details like how the demonstration troops hold their weapons or tools and how they use their hands and arms.

The grip on a tool or a weapon is just as important to the soldier as the grip on a ball bat or a tennis racket is to a player. And each movement he makes is as important in defeating the enemy as the player's technique is in defeating his opponent.

It is not, however, wise to insist too rigidly on precise standardization of movements. Men differ from one another as to what the best method is. Each has his own best speed.

And, of course, many of a soldier's jobs are new ones never analyzed by efficiency experts. But he can always make his own analysis. He can perfect his own form, his own technique. And he should.

Special rules apply to carrying loads. And carrying loads is one thing every soldier gets to do. The load should be evenly distributed and so placed that the soldier carrying it can walk erect. For a long march, the load should not weigh more than 40 per cent of the weight of the soldier. For short distances, a soldier should not carry more than half his own weight.

Fatigue

Fatigue is a fifth-column enemy that is always ready to infiltrate and attack. No man can stick at a job for long periods through day and night and continue at top-notch performance, especially if his job involves his using a great deal of strength, keeping alert, and making accurate, split-second judgments.

Just how long men can work and continue to do their best depends upon a great many different things. It depends first upon the man. It depends also on the type of work. It depends upon conditions of work, upon the food eaten, upon rest obtained during the job, upon worry and excitement, and finally upon the necessity for action. A man can run fast and long if death or the devil is behind him. He can fight hard for unbelievable lengths of time if there can be no retreat or if victory is in sight.

Most hazardous is the fatigue which comes from spurts of extreme effort—the greatest of which a man is capable. Such supreme effort seldom if ever occurs in any job on the home front. It does occur in sport. It does occur in battle. Spurred by the necessity to extraordinary violence, a man may actually put out so much effort that he burns up his body fuel at a rate eight or more times the normal rate. This he cannot keep up more than a few minutes at a time. Otherwise the sugar in his blood will fall to a critically low level. His heart will fail. His collapse or even his death will follow.

Heavy work burns up the body's fuel at a rate averaging from three to eight times that of a man at rest. A forced march with a heavy load is this kind of heavy work. So are many of the other jobs in the Army—digging trenches, loading and unloading supplies, running an obstacle course, or swimming with full equipment.

A man can keep such work up for eight hours, but to do so he needs more food. He should have from 1800 to 4800 calories in addition to the diet he would need if he were resting. Especially, he needs extra sugars and starches, and vitamin B and vitamin C. Since he will be sweating freely, he will need extra water and extra salt. He will suffer from heat and lack of proper ventilation more than a man doing less strenuous work.

And it is extremely important for him to have proper breaks in his exertion. There is some evidence that these rest periods should be enforced—not left to the men to take when they please. Men digging trenches in a battle area get more done when they are required to work five minutes hard and rest ten, spelling each other at the job, than if they all work as they please but as hard as they can.

In doing moderate work, your body's fuel is burned at a rate less than three times that of a man at rest. At the end of a day of doing this kind of work a soldier will still feel eager to spend more energy in ball games, dancing, swimming, or wrestling. That doesn't mean, however, that he can go right on working at what he has been doing all day without impaired efficiency.

Many jobs which are light enough on the whole body tax certain small groups of muscles until they are fatigued and the whole nervous system is affected. Close instrument reading, rifle shooting, and drafting fatigue the worker's eye muscles. Other jobs may fatigue his fingers or arm muscles.

Although the rest of your body may not be called upon to do much of any work, nevertheless your whole system becomes tired if these special muscles are over-fatigued. Just standing will tire a man after a long period of it. Or sitting in a cramped position.

It greatly helps efficiency if you can reduce just as much as possible the tiring of small groups of muscles. So, in designing equipment for the fighting man or the quarters in which he is to work, it is of the utmost importance to pay attention to the man who is going to use them. It is just as vital to plan them to avoid fatigue and strain for the soldier as it is to provide for the elimination of friction in a machine itself.

If tall men are to be used on the job, there should be plenty of head room and leg room where they must work. If a man is going to be required to do accurate shooting from a lurching, swinging, or diving vehicle, arrangements must be made to place him so that he can be protected as much as possible from the vibration, jarring, and bumping. For these things are bound to affect his aim. And just the strain of trying to hold himself steady will make him very tired even without any firing.

Another common cause of fatigue is the need of changing the focus of your eyes rapidly from close objects to those at a great distance. And the closer the object at which you must look, the harder it is to change rapidly to looking at a distant target and back.

If you have to look at the open-notch rear sight

on a rifle, only 8 inches from your eye, then to shift to the front blade, about 28 inches away, and then to jump to the target which may be anywhere from 25 yards away to several hundred—if you have to do that, then your eyes are going to get very tired. In fact, you are going to feel tired all over, when you have been doing this for a long time.

This is why the aperture or peep sight is much better. It merely requires an alignment of the front sight on the target. You look through, not at, the peep sight and at the target bringing the front sight and target into proper alignment within the circle of the peep sight without having to look directly at the front sight either.

Best of all for ease is the telescopic sight used by the infantry sniper, and the field and antiaircraft artillery. With it your eyes never have to shift focus at all. It is only necessary to look through it. Both the reticle on which the target is lined up and the target itself are seen by the eyes at the same apparent distance. The periscope used by the Naval officer in Fig. 45 is similar in that the eyes do not have to change focus in using it.

A soldier's hands can get tired, unnecessarily, as well as his eyes. They get tired enough anyway. But the straight stock used on an older type of rifle puts a special strain on the hand and causes fatigue in a a very short time. A pistol grip-stock, on the other hand, can be used a long time without tiring the hand of the rifleman.

In an airplane, the efficiency of both pilot and gunner are helped by providing maximum visibility and minimum noise. The gunner should have a clear view from his window; he should not have to squint around or through a lattice of switches, wires and other gadgets. The pilot should not have to look through discolored or marred plastic. Such obstructions or distortions of vision may seem only minor annoyances in a business office back home, but they may cost lives in a combat airplane.

FIG. 45.

Any men who must sit to operate their weapons, should have the seat adjusted so that they do not have to reach or strain, and so that they do not cramp certain muscles or cut off circulation. Discomfort for the man behind the gun may mean a gradual wearing down of accuracy.

Hard work and intense physical or mental strain have their effects upon your body and your mind. Lactic acid collects in your blood, a product of the destruction of muscle cells by exertion. The sugar reserves stored in your body are reduced, because the sugar is used to burn up the dead cells. You feel tired when you have lots of lactic acid in your blood and are short on your internal supply of sugar. You need then a period of rest in which to build up your muscle cells again and restore the proper chemical balance in your blood. Acute fatigue is relieved by eating sugar. Soldiers on the march are often given chocolate bars or sugar in some other convenient form.

Yet such fatigue does not always make you inefficient, if you have a strong enough need or desire for action. An athlete may break a record in the third heat of the 100-yard dash, after he has been using up sugar and accumulating lactic acid in the first two heats. A soldier may encounter an enemy and subdue him in close combat after he had been on the go in a hard-fought advance all day or all night.

The fatigue changes in your body may occur even when you are not called upon to exert your muscles in any violent way. Mental work and emotional strain are also fatiguing. An airplane pilot

255

gets tired. So does a general, sitting at a desk all night planning strategy.

But the man who gets tired from mental work or the strain of responsibility and worry has an additional problem. He may not consume the sugar in his blood as does the man engaged in violent physical work or combat. His blood, therefore, gets out of balance, and rest and sleep may not readily restore it. It is good for a man who has been under this sort of strain to get some sort of physical exercise—a swift game of tennis, a long walk, or a turn at chopping wood.

A second effect of fatigue is that tired feeling. This is nature's natural protection against over-fatigue. When a man feels tired it becomes increasingly difficult for him to go on with his job. He is more and more eager for rest and sleep, less and less able to spur himself on to go another mile. The best antidote for this feeling of tiredness is high morale and the example of other men. It is the man working alone who has the hardest job in combating his own desire to lie down and sleep.

But the most important effect of fatigue is the effect it has on work. When a man is tired he doesn't, he cannot do his very best. The amount of work he is able to do falls off and the quality of his work suffers too. He does not see as well, does not hear as well, nor is he so alert. His movements may become clumsy and bungling.

Loss in efficiency, strange as it may seem, is not always related to these feelings of fatigue. A man may feel very tired when he has not been working particularly hard, but is merely bored or uninter-

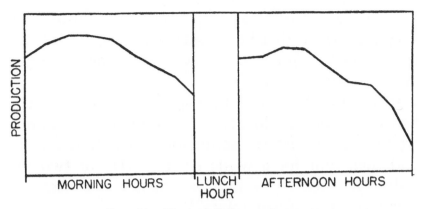

FIG. 46. Typical daily work curve.

ested in his work, or when the ventilation is bad so that he gets "dopey." On the other hand, a man really close to exhaustion may be so excited by his work that he is unable to rest and does not feel tired at all.

Men differ considerably in the rate at which they get tired on the same job. They differ even more in their rates of recovery after work is over. There is almost no general rule as to what will happen, except that recovery is very rapid at first and slows down as the rested state is approached. That fact means, however, that a lot of good can be got out of a short rest, and that many short rests are better than one long one.

The way in which work and rest affect efficiency is shown in the typical production curve of Fig. 46. The rested worker starts off fresh in the morning, but it takes him a couple of hours to get going. Then he is at top efficiency. Thereafter fatigue begins to show and by lunch time he is slowed down. His rest in the lunch period leads, however, to his recovery, and he starts the afternoon almost at peak efficiency.

257

Then fatigue returns and his production diminishes very rapidly, so that he reaches his low point at the end of the afternoon. If he has to work overtime, he does not work efficiently.

It is well to have lots of rest-periods. Students learn best if they do not do all the learning at once, do not try to cram up before examinations but study a little and then quit for a while or for a day or two. In industry, efficiency is highest when rest pauses are arranged at frequent intervals.

If they are not given rest pauses, most workers will manage to take them. A British survey of industrial work showed that workers left to themselves in this regard generally "wasted" (rested) about ten minutes out of every hour. The amount of time needed for rest depends on the job, but it is best to be sure that breaks occur, that men are not made to work continuously. The increased efficiency more than makes up for the time lost, as Fig. 46 shows. In one study which was made in Moscow, production was increased 10 per cent by the introduction of suitable rest pauses.

Complete rest does a lot more for recovery than does mere change of activity. For instance, in one factory the introduction of a 15-minute rest period in the middle of a two-hour period of work was found to increase efficiency 9 per cent when the rest consisted of complete relaxation in a chair, and only 1.5 per cent when it consisted of walking around. Here is a list of the effects of different kinds of rest:

Complete relaxation in a chair..... 9.3 per cent
Rest, the kind unspecified......... 8.3 per cent
Listening to music................ 3.9 per cent

Having tea .... 3.4 per cent
Walking around .... 1.5 per cent

It is best not to work too long altogether, for then efficiency may be cut down so much that the total production is actually decreased. There was a case in a British munitions plant where the reduction of the working week from 58 to 50 hours increased the hourly output by 39 per cent and the total weekly output by 21 per cent. Why didn't the 58-hour men do just as much work in their freshest 50 hours and then a little more in the extra 8 hours? They were too tired. They came back stale in the morning after having worked late the day before.

So it does not pay to overwork workers—or soldiers. Some fatigue is unavoidable and much fatigue must be undergone in the process of toughening a soldier, but chronic fatigue is not to be found along the shortest road to victory. The continuous strain battle usually demands makes it necessary for the commander to relieve worn out troops with fresh -ones. If he doesn't, he will often risk defeat.

Fatigue—both actual inefficiency and the feelings of fatigue—is increased by poor working conditions. Illumination, ventilation, and noise all affect work and that tired feeling.

Plenty of light is necessary for efficient work when visual details must be seen, though too much light may tire the eyes. The efficiency of roller-bearing inspectors was improved 12 per cent by a four-fold increase in the amount of light. The errors saved are worth the light they cost—especially if more light prevents failure of a gun bearing in the midst of combat. But glare and uneven illumination do not help.

259

Dry air in motion and at a moderate temperature is best for work. Hot, damp, still air can decrease work enormously. There is a case on record where hot, moist air caused production to fall off 40 per cent. The soldier cannot always choose his air, but sometimes it can be chosen for him in the shops at the base.

Noise stimulates work and may increase production temporarily, but continuous loud noise generally produces fatigue and causes production to fall off. It creates confusion, partly by interfering with the hearing of speech and partly by distracting the worker. Airplane pilots do not like the noise of the plane. It increases their bodily tension and tires them. And there are some situations in which noise can be reduced, even in mechanized war. In battle you have to do the best you can. Your noise hurts the enemy as much as his hurts you.

Boredom

Boredom is not quite the same thing as fatigue. A man can get bored by monotonous work without having his muscles ache. Boredom means that his attention flags, that his desire to get the work done is low, that his morale for the time being is down. It is not a good thing, and it ought to be avoided whenever possible.

Boredom may actually turn the normal work curve (Fig. 46) upside down. The worker starts fresh and does well. Then he gets bored and his production slows down. Then he sees lunch time coming, or quitting time, and he speeds up again. The bored worker is the clock watcher.

The cure for boredom is variety of work. Many jobs make lighter work. And there are plenty of different things to do in the Army. Variety is possible for many, though not for all.

There are, however, great differences in people in their need for variety of work. Some people like to do the same thing over and over. They find it easier and simpler. It frees them for day dreaming, and they like the company of their own thoughts. Frequent change of work would require their constant attention to the jobs, shutting them off from thinking about themselves.

Often it seems as if the more intelligent men were the ones who want variety, but that is not always true. Some intelligent men are those who like to have time for day-dreaming, for thinking their private thoughts, and such men may prefer repetitive work, which they can do automatically and which is not monotonous for them.

In general, however, day-dreaming is not a sign of a healthy mind, and soldiers should not be encouraged in it. They should have variety of work whether they want it or not. The best morale is found in the busy soldier—the man who has his mind as well as his hands full of his job all day long.

It does not always work out in the Army that variety of work is given to the men who need it, or the repetitive jobs to the men who want to day-dream and can safely do it. There are some men of emotional nature who get assigned to doing the same thing over and over, and who remain desperately bored by its monotony. It is, in fact, almost correct to say that they are bored to pieces by it, for they do almost go to pieces. First they get stale, developing what is called chronic fatigue. Then they become anxious and fearful. They worry, are irritable, can't sleep. And, of course, their efficiency goes right down. They may have the best will in the world to carry on. There is nothing wrong with their patriotism. But they just cannot stand that kind of work. They ought to be given some other way of winning the war, for there are others to whom the same job will not seem monotonous.

Sleep

You can stay up all night and keep awake provided you are active, provided you keep using some muscles, at least the speaking muscles. You can march all night, play poker all night, fight all night, talk all night. You will be likely to get terribly sleepy somewhere along between 0300 and 0600 hours, unless you are doing something exciting or intensely interesting, but you can get through provided you are active.

That does not mean, however, that you can read or study all night, using few muscles other than those of your eyes. If you have to study all night, you may need to read out loud or to stand up to read. It would be easier to keep awake if you could read back and forth out loud with some one else, discussing the reading from time to time. It is very hard to fight sleep if you are quiet and by yourself.

By breakfast time you will be getting less sleepy. You can get through the next day pretty well. You may feel tired, especially if you have been marching or walking about to keep awake. You won't feel

262

fresh. You will feel uncomfortable. But other people will not notice anything wrong with you, unless you sit down and relax with nothing important or interesting to do. Then, very likely, you'll doze off. If you have a job that requires accurate movements or accurate thinking, you will probably make no more mistakes than you usually do.

The second night you won't want to stay up but you may have to. Another march may be necessary or the enemy may attack. And the second night is like the first, but more difficult. It is harder to keep active under your own power; yet you can, if your officers or the enemy furnish the motivation. You don't want to keep your mind on any topic very long. Your thoughts and ideas trail off into irrelevancies. If you can possibly get a chance to relax, you will; and then you will go to sleep. You ought not to be on sentry duty, but you may keep awake by walking. Or you may go off into an inattentive daze while you continue walking. By this time you are probably getting quite irritable. Little things provoke you and you may talk some nonsense. Your anger does not last though, for you'd rather go to sleep.

The day after the second sleepless night is better than the preceding sleepless night, but you'll be irritable, rambling and illogical in speech and thought, inattentive, more than usually sensitive to pain. Your eyes itch. You may begin to see double. You can't sit down and read. Your writing becomes bad and the pencil may drop from your hand. You may even begin to have hallucinations, imagining events that do not really happen, as if you had begun to dream

263

while you are still awake. You can still be spurred to your full mental powers and manual dexterity if the stimulus is strong enough—if your commander demands your attention, if a shell comes over—but the effect of these things doesn't last as long as it would normally. Pretty soon you are back where you were, with the most important thing in the world the need to shut your eyes and go to sleep.

Wounded soldiers coming out of combat after many days and nights of continuous fighting may be so terribly in need of sleep that even the severe pain of wounds does not keep them from going sound asleep as soon as they are allowed to lie down. Anesthetics can be dispensed with.

When soldiers must keep going night after night without sleep, it helps them if they can take food at frequent intervals. To a certain extent and for a limited time, food and hot drinks can take the place of sleep in banishing fatigue. Certainly, when men are deprived of normal sleep, emergency rations, chocolate bars, hot chocolate or other snacks should be freely available. Regular meals should be served often, and all commanders know this and always have it done if possible. At the very least the man who fights or works all night should not go without food from supper to breakfast.

With frequent food, how long can you go without sleep? You can manage a third night without sleep and maybe a fourth, with all the symptoms getting worse, with attention harder and harder to command, with more and more activity necessary to keep you awake. A psychologist once kept himself awake for four whole days spurred on only by the scientific motive for seeing what would happen. With doses of a stimulant (benzedrine) to help him, he actually kept himself awake for eight days and seven nights.

There was a man once who believed that sleep was a bad habit which ought to be and could be overcome. He was given a watchman's clock on which to record every ten minutes the fact that he was awake. He stayed awake almost continuously for nine and a half days, missing only 31 out of 1380 recordings of the ten-minute intervals. Of course, he got some other cat naps during the ten-minute intervals. As time wore on he became dazed. He would keep appointments at the wrong time or in the wrong place or both. He got so that he was not always sure where he was. At the end of the time he was beginning to have hallucinations and delusions of persecution, and had become so cantankerous that the experiment had to be stopped.

Dogs have been kept awake for a week and seem to be normal again after a good sleep. One dog was kept awake for 17 days and then died, but another recovered after 21 sleepless days. They have constantly to be exercised or they will lie down and doze right off.

Rabbits have gone as long as 31 days without sleep. They are put inside a slowly revolving cage which makes them take a few steps forward several times in every minute.

Sleep soon restores the sleepy man or animal. Men who stay awake for two or three days are generally in pretty good shape after a 12-hour sleep, and show no effects at all after two or three normal nights.

The whole trouble in sleeplessness is with atten-

265

tion and thus with the higher levels of the brain which are necessary for attention. The soldier who loses sleep is becoming inefficient because he can no longer keep his mind on his job—on any job except the one job of getting relaxation, closed eyes and sleep. He can be stimulated into attention by activity, by authoritative command, by danger, but the effect of the spur lasts for less and less time as he gets sleepier. When spurred he can do any simple task about as well as usual, unless it is a task that requires attention, alertness, judgment. Then he begins to fail.

Being frustrated by not being allowed to sleep, he becomes irritable, belligerent, perhaps even unmanageable. His morale goes down. He is no longer a good comrade.

But his recovery will be rapid. Give him sleep, which is all he wants, and pretty soon he will be back, his old, competent, friendly, alert self.

That's all right in an emergency, but ordinarily soldiers should have enough sleep. They need to be alert whether for study or combat, whether for driving a truck in America or firing an anti-tank gun in Africa, or Europe. Enough regular sleep from taps to first call should be the rule, except when the enemy decrees otherwise.

There is no rule about the amount of sleep that young adults must have. Some get cranky and irritable when cut down from seven hours a night to five. Others do not. The unit with high morale can do with less sleep, but sleepy men tend to have low morale. These two forces work against each other.

There are also no rigid rules about the details of sleep—no rules that apply to everyone alike. Sleep is deepest and best under conditions in which the

266

man is accustomed to sleep. Men can sleep well in the light. They do not have to have spring mattresses. Nearly any man can sleep soundly on the hard ground. Sailors sleep with curved spines in hammocks and suffer no ill effects. Monotonous sounds tend to lull a man to sleep, but other kinds of noise need not keep him awake.

There is an actual difference between men as to the time of day they work best. Some do their best work in daytime and some work best at night. The day workers wake up early, accomplish a lot before lunch, get sleepy after supper and go to bed early if they can. The night workers get up late (if allowed to), work best after supper, go to bed late and so want to sleep late again (if allowed to). Army life is usually better adapted to the day workers. Unfortunately the night workers are not able to get their daily rhythms shifted around so that they are ready to quit when taps sound—except, of course, when the day's work has been so tough that everybody is dead tired by supper-time, ready to go to bed at once.

Where there is night work to be done at all regularly it is better to pick men to do it who work best at night rather than to give such work to all in turn. For example, a commander's staff of a number of officers and enlisted men will usually have enough good night workers on it to give them the night shifts of work regularly and the good day workers the day shifts. Every staff needs to keep at highest efficiency and alertness for twenty-four hours a day but all must get some rest. Efficiency may be considerably reduced by the mistaken notion that it is best or fairest to rotate the night work among all.

XII: HEAT, COLD, OXYGEN AND
STIMULANTS

GLOBAL WARFARE means the exposure of soldiers to greater extremes of cold, heat, atmospheric pressure, and motion than men are accustomed to endure. And not only must they endure these conditions, they must continue to fight well—to be efficient.

Good morale may help the soldier to push on across the desert in a scorching sun. It may help keep him moving and alert when Arctic cold numbs his feet and dulls his senses. But good morale is not enough.

Men must also have proper clothing. Arctic fighters need fur or wool-lined garments. A flyer may need an electrically heated suit. He must have an oxygen mask. Desert fighters need some protection from sun and insects. Indoor workers need ventilation, not merely to supply them with "fresh air"—oxygen—but mostly to keep their bodies at the right temperature.

And when conditions are very bad, the soldier may need help or consolation from coffee or tobacco or possibly alcohol.

The proper use of stimulants in warfare is still a problem being carefully studied by scientists. Many different factors are involved. Too much alcohol is bad. How about a little? Is the effect of coffee and smoking mostly imaginary, or do they really help or hinder a fighter? Can fatigue be artificially diminished by their use?

Heat and Cold

Efficient work requires an efficient body, and the efficient body must be kept near its best temperature, about 98.6 degrees Fahrenheit. If temperature gets a degree too low, a man gets sluggish, does not work effectively. If the temperature gets too high, then he has the beginnings of a fever, and he becomes inefficient again—because fever means that waste products are being burned up and accumulating in the blood. The fever also makes him sweat, and that's both an advantage and a disadvantage. It's an advantage, because the evaporation of sweat from the skin helps to keep the body-temperature down where it ought to be, but it's a disadvantage because the sweating takes from the blood the water that is needed to dilute the waste products. So it's very important to keep the body at the right temperature, and even a little variation in the direction of heating up causes sweating.

If cold weather tends to get the body too cool, its temperature can be brought up by the oxidation of tissues within the body. That is why exercise warms you. But if the body tends to get too warm, then its temperature is usually lowered again by evaporation of sweat. Evaporation of a liquid from a surface always cools the surface. A porous bag or pot filled with water gets cool in a breeze, even a hot breeze, because the moving air makes the dampness evaporate from its surface.

This is the reason why an outside temperature of 90 degrees feels so much hotter when the humidity is high. The air is so well saturated with water, that it cannot cool the body much by evaporating the sweat.

269

Heat interferes with work more often than cold. Indoors cold can be got rid of by heating systems, whereas the cooling of air by air-conditioning is expensive, new and not generally used. Both indoors and outdoors cold can be combatted by putting on more clothes, but heat cannot always be abolished by taking them off.

And people differ, of course, in what they like. Cold weather peps one man up, makes another shiver. One man can work vigorously in summer

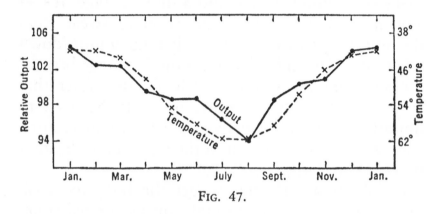

FIG. 47.

heat; another would like to lie around all day waiting for the cool of evening.

Figure 47 shows how output in a British tinplate factory varied with the season of the year and also the average temperature at different seasons. The output was least in August with the average outdoor temperature at 62 degrees, greatest in January with the average outdoor temperature at 41 degrees.

But it isn't outdoor temperature that really matters. It is the temperature of the body, which depends on the temperature of the air next to the body, its humidity and its movement. Men in an unventilated room get uncomfortable after a while. They use up some of the oxygen, but that is their least trouble. They heat up the room and by breathing and sweating make the air humid. The room gets stuffy or even oppressive. If, however, fans are started to keep the same stale air in motion, then the men may get comfortable again, because the moving air causes more evaporation and cools down their skins.

It is the cooling power of air *at the skin* which determines how comfortable men will feel.

The best working temperature is 60 to 65 degrees Fahrenheit with the air not too moist and ventilation assured. The best working climates lie between 25 and 55 degrees of latitude. In the torrid and frigid zones the highest civilizations do not develop. It may well be that Egypt at the height of its civilization had a different climate from what it has now. Especially in the hot climates are men inclined to be listless, uninventive, apathetic, and improvident.

Extreme heat may become intolerable and without ventilation may cause death. As it did in the Black Hole of Calcutta in 1756, when 146 Englishmen were imprisoned one hot June evening in a little room, 18 by 15 feet, with only two tiny barred windows. They were crowded in, standing together with less than two square feet to a man. Heat and humidity rose. There was no cooling ventilation. By morning 123 of the 146 were dead.

Any soldier who has operated a tank in summer in the desert regions knows what heat with insufficient ventilation can do to the efficiency of the human organism.

A certain amount of cold can be combatted by

271

having proper clothing, such as the Russians had in their first winter of war against the Germans, and as the Germans apparently did not. But heavy clothing has also its drawbacks. It makes the man, especially the soldier who is unaccustomed to it, clumsy and diminishes his self-confidence.

Below 10 degrees Fahrenheit clothing begins to be insufficient to protect the body. The hands and feet get cold first, then the body, then the legs. Continuous exposure to minus 20 degrees begins to produce mental distress. At minus 30 degrees there is loss of morale; indifference may begin to supplant distress. At minus 40 degrees continued exposure produces lethargy, which may be followed by stupor and eventually by death.

An aviator in an unsealed cabin begins to be effected by lack of oxygen at about 10,000 feet altitude but may go to 20,000 feet or even higher if he uses an oxygen mask. At high altitudes he runs, however, into the effects of cold, no matter how much clothing he has on. The following table shows approximately how temperature varies with altitude, when it is 60 degrees on the ground:

Altitude (feet):	0	5,000	10,000	15,000	20,000	25,000	30,000
Temp. (°F.):	60	41	23	6	− 12	− 30	− 48

So at high altitudes a sealed cabin is needed for warmth as well as for oxygen, unless the flyer has electrically heated clothing and an oxygen mask.

Exposure to extreme cold may result in frost-bite. The part exposed first feels cold. Then it hurts. Later it becomes insensitive. Finally it turns white or bluish white.

A frost-bitten hand or foot or nose should be

thawed out slowly. The best thing to do is to cover it with clothing and to let the body do the warming, or it may be put underneath clothing in contact with a warm spot of the body. It can safely be wrapped in cloths and soaked in cool water, but it must not be exposed to a hot stove or radiator, nor should the part be rubbed with snow. Rubbing may injure and destroy the frozen tissues, so that gangrene sets in.

If a man has become unconscious from exposure to cold, he should, if possible, be placed in a cool room and covered with blankets. His arms and legs should be moved gently, not violently. And he should have warm drinks when he becomes conscious enough to swallow them.

ALTITUDE AND OXYGEN

At high altitudes, lack of oxygen produces effects very much like those caused by intoxication. Just what happens to the flyer depends on the altitude reached, the rate of ascent, the time spent there, the amount of the flyer's physical exertion, and the physical condition of the flyer at the time.

The effects are much worse at any altitude if the ascent was rapid. They get worse if the flyer stays up a long time, or if he exerts himself vigorously.

Ordinarily you don't notice altitude until you have reached 8,000 or perhaps 12,000 feet. Then you are likely to feel as you might if you had had a couple of cocktails on an empty stomach.

You feel a warm glow of well-being. Nothing is wrong with the world. You are likely to be pretty clumsy in handling any sort of instrument or controls. But you don't know that. In fact, you think

273

you are better than usual. You feel lazy, relaxed. You don't want to be troubled about anything. Your judgment is poorer. Notes written at altitudes above 12,000 feet show poor handwriting, poor phrasing, bad grammar. But you are quite likely to feel certain that your judgment is infallible—it is the others who are wrong.

At 14,000 feet muscular coordination gets worse. The oxygen starved pilot could no more walk a chalk line or shoot accurately than can a man who is drunk. Handwriting is quite bad. Will power fails. You may know what you should do when an emergency arises, but you feel completely unequal to doing it. You may suffer blocks in your thinking —the next idea just refuses to come.

You become emotional. You may laugh boisterously, or weep. You may get pugnacious.

At 18,000 feet your muscular coordination becomes still worse. You may start trembling. Both your hearing and your vision become blurred. Noises seem to come to you from a great distance. And sights are dimmed.

Your field of attention, or of vision, is narrowed. If you are a pilot or navigator trying to watch a number of instruments, you will become unable to pay attention to any except the ones directly in front of you. You will miss seeing anything off to your left or your right.

And you will have to concentrate all your attention on one main task. You may not notice an approaching enemy coming unexpectedly from a direction you haven't been watching. You cannot keep two things in mind at once. Your memory gets bad.

Your judgment is still poorer. Your mood changes more. You lose your ability to know when you do things wrong. You feel fine when you are not fine. You are not aware of danger. You think you can lick the whole world.

Yet all this may happen without your knowledge, especially if the ascent has been rapid. You do not feel your own bodily changes because your senses are dulled. You do not know that you are acting queerly, because your judgment is faulty and because you are in a breezy don't-care mood. It is a highly dangerous situation, and flyers have to be shown their own performance on tests at these altitudes in order to teach them that they *must* put on oxygen masks.

At 20,000 feet the effects of altitude are profound. Hearing becomes very difficult, reaction time is slowed down, muscles twitch or may even become paralyzed. Voluntary control of action becomes very weak indeed. The emotional moods of the flyer are heightened, so that he is really delirious. He loses all sense of time.

Somewhere above 20,000 feet the flyer passes out entirely.

All these effects are due to lack of oxygen, not to the diminished air pressure alone. They occur if a man is deprived of oxygen in a re-breather on the ground. They do not occur if the flyer puts on his oxygen mask at high altitudes. He may not want to put it on, because he does not realize his condition. But he can be taught to do it automatically, from habit, because he must. It must never be left for him to decide whether to put it on or when he needs it.

Alcohol is not really a stimulant; it is an intoxicant.

It certainly has its uses, but every soldier should understand its dangers, too. For alcohol can play havoc with a man's efficiency, especially at some precision jobs.

The first effect of alcohol is relaxation. That is all right when you are on furlough, when you are safe back at your base after a perilous mission, when you are not likely to be called back to duty any time soon. It is fine to be able to let down, to lay aside your responsibilities, and to find comfort—if you do —in a drink of beer or a cocktail. The medical officer may even order you to drink it as medicine.

But all these effects, so pleasant to some men off duty, are a hazard if you are going into combat.

Alcohol dulls your senses. If you were to use it in combat, it would make it harder for you to see faint objects—the enemy patrol creeping toward you in the jungle, and other airplanes approaching at a distance in the dark. It would diminish your ability to perceive shapes accurately—not only fine print, but also the kind of plane or tank that is approaching. It also cuts down on your range of vision, prevents a driver from readily seeing other cars that approach from the side. That is called "channel driving"—the driver just drives straight along in the middle of his field of vision. He has to. He can't see the side of the road or anyone approaching along a side thoroughfare. This is the same thing that lack of oxygen does to the flyer.

Alcohol also dulls hearing. It would thus be bad for any soldier who is listening for sounds of enemy action. It would also be bad for the man who doesn't want to be heard by the enemy, for his own deafness will make the drinking soldier noisy. His voice is raised and his movements are noisy because he cannot hear himself acutely.

In small amounts drinking may increase strength a little, but in large quantities it makes a man weaker. It makes him less steady, reduces his dexterity and skill in complex movements. In general, it slows him up, too.

Drinking also makes it harder to learn new information or movements, and it interferes with memory of recent events.

Alcohol makes a man less alert and it loosens his tongue. If you have secrets to keep and are in company you don't know, beware of drinking too much!

Finally, it makes discrimination and judgment worse. Tests of judgment and of reasoning all show that alcohol does not help, and in sufficient quantity does hinder good thinking. And worst of all, it interferes with self-criticism. The man who is just a little tight doesn't know it when he makes mistakes. He thinks he is doing fine when he is way off the mark. And he is usually completely unaware that he is not in fit condition. He will undertake foolhardy stunts that he is utterly unfit to tackle.

Knowing Your Limit

No one questions the correctness of these statements as applying to the man who has taken "too much," who is really drunk, or who is dead drunk. But how about the soldier who likes to take a beer or two or who wants a shot of whiskey when he has had a hard mission? Is the man who has had just one drink, or two or three, any the worse for it?

Unless a soldier leaves liquor strictly alone, he should certainly know his limit—know what he can take without getting tight or really drunk.

And that is hard to say. It depends on the individual and also on circumstances. A man who weighs 200 pounds can stand about twice as much liquor as a man who weighs only 100 pounds. Like any other drug, the effect is in proportion to your body weight. You get more kick out of a drink taken on an empty stomach than after you have just had a square meal. Fats in the stomach—milk, cream, butter, cheese or olive oil—help to keep you sober.

On the other hand, imagination and what you want, can help the effects along. A man who wants to get a little tight succeeds in getting gay and unsteady sooner than the man who is afraid of what the liquor may do to him. And besides he doesn't have to hold himself in, since everybody knows how alcohol ought to work.

You get drunk sooner in a crowded, poorly ventilated room than you would in the fresh air. You feel the effects sooner if you are sitting down than if you are standing up—and you are less aware of the effects. If you want to stay sober, the best thing to do is to stand and put one foot up on the traditional brass rail or walk briskly outdoors. You get the greatest effect from the smallest drink lying down.

The same amount of alcohol taken in tall drinks well diluted with charged water or ginger ale has less effect than it does taken straight from the bottle or in a cocktail. It has less effect if it is sipped slowly than if it is swallowed in a gulp.

Even the experienced drinker, however, can be fooled about his own tolerance under special conditions. Extreme fatigue has many of the same effects on a man that alcohol does. When a man has been under severe strain so that the sugar in his blood is at a very low level, a single drink may be enough to knock him out cold. For similar reasons, alcohol and high altitudes do not mix well; don't ever drink much if you are going to have to fly.

Whether a small amount of alcohol will interfere with a soldier's efficiency depends a great deal on what he has to do. Pilots in the Air Forces do not touch it unless there is no chance that they will be called upon to fly during the next 24 hours. They know better. Combat flying taxes every sense to the utmost. No man in his right mind wants to take his chances with his senses fuzzed with drink or a hangover—especially not against a sober skillful enemy. After return from a difficult mission, then a drink may be a good thing; it may help him to sleep without going through the whole experience again in his sleep. But if it is necessary, the flight surgeon will prescribe it. Otherwise the combat flyer does not drink.

Any soldier of air or ground with a responsible job ahead of him, a job requiring coordination, keen senses and judgment, had better not drink beforehand, or at most drink but little.

One reason why the Army is liberal in allowing men to drink at their own discretion so long as they do not disgrace themselves or the uniform lies in the relation of alcohol to emotion and morale. It is hard on morale to ask a man to change his ingrained habits. To the man who is used to drinking in moderation, a drink once in a while is a great comfort and pleasure. And the man who is on combat duty earns whatever relief and pleasure he can find so long as it does not interfere with his fighting ability.

And the average soldier can be relied upon not to abuse this privilege.

There is, however, one exceptional kind of person who cannot tolerate even the smallest amount of alcohol without going to excess and getting stupidly drunk. Such men should realize that they cannot take "just one glass of beer." They must leave it alone. It is poison to them just as shell fish or tomatoes may be to other men who are allergic to them.

Some men believe that alcohol makes them brave. They want a shot of liquor before they undertake a difficult mission. But this idea is true only in a very limited sense. Alcohol does make men face hazards more recklessly because it dulls their appreciation of danger—a very hazardous sort of bravery.

And in the case of men very strictly brought up, who have been trained since early childhood to have a deep-seated abhorrence of the job of killing, alcohol may remove such squeamishness.

Tobacco

Heavy smokers who inhale are short-winded, and all smokers inhale some. Probably the lungs get clogged with tarry substances, like a pipe that has been smoked a lot. And a smoker with some of the cells in his lungs clogged up cannot get as much oxygen per breath as the ordinary non-smoker can.

Heavy smokers have less steady hands. Smoking is not good for precision movements. Much of the nicotine in the tobacco gets burned up and does not enter the body, but the products of its decomposition —and of the burning tobacco—pyridine, carbon monoxide and other poisons—make the trouble.

If a man not used to it smokes a cigarette, he finds that his mental work becomes less efficient. But an habitual smoker may work better when he smokes. It is unlikely that the tobacco itself ever helps him. It is more probable that he has learned to work best when smoking so that not smoking bothers him. The man who regularly lights up when he has a serious job to do finds himself actually distracted if he cannot smoke, if he has to make himself keep avoiding the automatic habits of reaching for a cigarette, lighting it, and puffing it. In the same way a man who has learned to study with the radio going is distracted by quiet.

Men in the armed services are generally pretty fond of their smokes. It is not just because of the nicotine in them. It is partly because it is pleasant to have something to puff on and handle in company with the other fellows. It is good to feel a cigarette between your lips, to feel the warm smoke in your mouth, to have the taste of it on your tongue. But if you are on shipboard or other places where smoking is dangerous or forbidden, the urge to smoke can usually be relieved by a chew of gum or a piece of candy. Some men are content if they have an unlighted pipe or a dead cigar to chew on.

For the occasional or light smoker, the pleasure

281

gained probably outweighs the small harm it may do him. But heavy smoking is bad for a man in the armed services or anywhere where peak physical fitness is of prime importance.

There is some evidence that excessive smoking may contribute to the development of stomach ulcers, or may aggravate them once they do exist. And stomach and other peptic ulcers are a principal cause of medical disability in this war. There is also some rather clear evidence that heavy smoking produces temporary defects of vision such as would bar a man from aviation and some other types of military service.

The best rule is not to smoke more than is necessary to avoid that bothered feeling which the smoker has when he longs for a smoke.

Coffee and Tea

Coffee and tea, because of the caffeine they contain, and because they are usually taken hot, are actual stimulants. A large cup of coffee will wake you up, make you more alert, speed you up and improve your muscular coordination. It is a good thing to drink a cup before you go on night duty or when you are very tired and still must go on with your job.

If you drink an excessive amount of coffee, however, you do not add to the good effects—in fact, you may reverse them. You may be slowed down, unsteady, less well coordinated. Especially to the man who is not used to it, large amounts of caffeine will produce jitters.

Habitual coffee drinkers and tea drinkers develop some tolerance for caffeine, however. It takes two cups to do what one used to do. It may take four cups to decrease efficiency noticeably, whereas three cups would be bad for the man who is not used to it.

You won't be kept awake by a little after-dinner cup of coffee. There isn't enough caffeine in it. You are kept awake—*when* you are kept awake—by your belief that the coffee will keep you awake, or by excitement from some other cause. But the caffeine in three full-sized cups of coffee can easily keep a man awake. Two cups may be enough, if he does not drink coffee regularly.

The drug benzedrine sulfate has been widely sold as "pep pills" to keep men awake and make them more alert and their senses more keen. This drug has been used to fight fatigue in troops and it is much more effective than coffee. It should never be used, however, except when prescribed by the medical officer. Like most other drugs, its value and its dangers depend upon the individual and it should never be self-prescribed or used as freely as a beverage like coffee or tea or hot chocolate.

Fig. 48.

XIII: MORALE

MORALE DEPENDS on the incentives to human action, on men's motives, on their emotions and how they react to their emotions. It can be developed in a military unit by the control of those psychological conditions which determine men's desires and conduct, and affect their attitudes toward one another and toward the great undertaking of winning a war.

INCENTIVES

Hunger is a mess call most sure to be heard. Pain is an alert seldom missed.

The most primitive incentives for action, which man shares with other animals, are his bodily needs. Hunger. Thirst. Sex. The need for rest when he is tired. The need for activity when rested. The desire to escape from pain, extreme heat, extreme cold, and other intolerable conditions.

It might be possible to control men or animals by the use of these incentives. You might make a man go hungry until his work was done, and then let him eat as a reward. You might make a man fight by lashing him, then letting up on him as a reward for fighting.

But that isn't the way our Army works. Whenever possible it supplies enough food and rest to its soldiers and makes other provisions for their comfort so that they stay in good spirits and can do their work well.

But in fighting areas it is not always possible to provide these physical comforts. When food or water is short, when the weather is too hot or too cold, when it becomes impossible to bathe and shave, when bombs and shells drive sleep away, and fatigue makes effort a torture, problems of combat morale may arise. And then some other incentive is required beyond their animal needs to keep men going—to make them determined to keep on fighting unto death.

When the primitive needs are no longer enough, it is the social incentives which help a fighting man to do his utmost. There are many social needs, and here are some of them:

(1) Desire for social approval, admiration, recognition, appreciation.

(2) Desire for security, safety, escape from danger and disapproval; fears of all kinds.

(3) Desire for power, mastery, domination, superiority, self-assertion.

(4) Desire for adventure, new experience, freedom; escape from futility, humdrum.

(5) Desire for personal response, companionship, friendship, love.

(6) Desire to help and protect others (especially the weak and helpless, such as children).

(7) Desire for successful achievement, completeness, effectiveness; the desire to do a "good job."

(8) Desire to destroy interference with other desires; aggression, rage.

When a military leader calls a man by name and gives him a simple word of commendation for some task well performed, he is appealing to at least two or three natural incentives. Calling the man by name shows personal interest which almost every soldier likes. The commendation is social approval. If the soldier has been feeling insecure, not quite sure of things, then perhaps his sense of security is established by the event of his leader's approval. He also has assurance that he has accomplished a job well done.

Social approval is a strong motive in human affairs, and in general praise is much more effective than blame. Commendation can get results when bawlings-out fail. Reproof tends to leave resentment. Blame is often, however, effective when used in private and in moderation against a man whose quality of performance is high, for he will work hard to avoid such criticism. A man wants to count, to amount to something, to feel that he is worth while and appreciated. Promotions, citations, and distinctions of all kinds help serve this purpose.

Fear of the disapproval of others or of some other punishment works as an incentive, but it is not good as a steady thing. Troops coerced to action by a snapping martinet become anxious, disgruntled, jittery. There is a loss in morale, in initiative, in judgment, and even in skill.

Men do better in groups whether fighting or working. This is only partly because competition enters. The good performance of one soldier stimulates another to improve. But also, the sense of being engaged in a group activity makes working or fighting easier, even when each soldier is doing a different part of the job so that there is no competition. In most forms of work the worker produces more and is happier if other workers are working alongside.

It is easy to see how the other incentives control Army activities. The desire for superiority works itself out in competition for promotion. The desire for adventure or new experience may lead a man to volunteer for a dangerous mission, or perhaps it merely leads him to ask for a furlough. The desire to help others becomes a loyalty to comrades or help for a wounded friend. This is so strong that it is used in armies to overcome the civilian's natural repugnance to death. A soldier will voluntarily aid in burial of the dead as a final mark of consideration to his friends.

A soldier's desire to do a good job, his sense of workmanship, is helped whenever he can be allowed to understand the nature of the whole undertaking to which he is contributing. A successful leader never assigns tasks blindly when he can reveal their larger purpose. By allowing his men to see the significance of their own smaller jobs, he dignifies the lesser tasks by relating them to the large one. When the workers at the General Electric Company found that certain mysterious plastic somethings they were making had helped General Jimmy Doolittle steer his plane over Tokio, production jumped three hundred per cent practically overnight.

In addition to the social incentives, there are many personal incentives—the kind that might still determine what a man did if he were alone on a desert island. Self-regard is one. A man wants to be a certain kind of person and feels ashamed when he fails. He wants to do what he thinks is right, whether that rightness be the dictates of a Christian conscience

288

or the code of honor of the group or gang. Ambition and aspiration come in here. For the most part it is these personal incentives which tend to make men different from each other and to establish the rule that there are individual exceptions to all the other rules of human motivation.

MORALE

Morale is the capacity to stay on the job—especially a long, hard job—with determination and zest. It is the opposite of apathy.

Morale needs good health—physical and mental. Unless the body is well and vigorous, it is pretty hard to endure hardship and keep up enthusiasm. Fatigue and illness sap mental vigor and moral strength. The body does influence the mind. Yet there is more to morale than that. Men can carry on with strong determination, sometimes even with zest, through injury, disease, and physical privation—through such things as the men on the *Lexington* underwent (Fig. 48). What makes them do it?

For that sort of morale a man needs self-confidence and conviction. He needs to feel sure of himself and emotionally secure. While there are no simple rules for obtaining this sense of security and confidence when the world is blowing up around your ears, some of the conditions that bring it are known.

It helps to have grown up in a home where there was no quarreling or jealousy. It helps to have friends, and to be working or fighting in a group. It is essential for the job to seem important, for it to be related to some of the incentives to human action. A thoughtful man may need to see the job in its

289

larger relations, to fit it into a philosophy of life, to make it a means of satisfying his own code of what is good and desirable. He may need to take a long-range view that extends even beyond his own lifetime and perhaps into another world. All the incentives to human action are potential morale builders.

There is a back-and-forth relation between work and morale. Not only does morale make soldiers work and fight. Working and fighting keep up their morale. Especially in times of emotional stress, as in battle, does a man need to be doing things. As for work alone, men are not naturally lazy. People like to work. Enforced idleness is a cruel punishment.

It has been shown again and again that persons with useful jobs to do in air raids are unlikely to be afraid of bombs. They are busy and their morale is good. They carry on, because they have important useful work to do. Actually they feel secure—even in an air raid, which is a strange place to feel secure! It is the same with a trained soldier in the midst of combat.

But this kind of security is a security of the mind, the feeling of confidence that can become independent of the existence of physical danger.

In some units of an army morale is bad, in some it is good. Everyone knows about these differences when they are extreme, but there ought to be ways of measuring morale and rules for improving it. To some extent there are both.

If an officer wants to assess the morale of his own unit, there are at least two things for him to do.

He can listen. Men will talk when permitted or encouraged to, and they will sometimes speak freely.

290

When they do, they give their leader information that will enable him to answer these questions. Do the troops feel they are being well trained? well led? Do they think their weapons are adequate? Do they want to get at the enemy? Are they proud of their unit? Do they have suggestions for its improvement? Do they think they get fair treatment? fair chances for advancement? Are they worrying about anything back home? or about what will happen when the war is over? From the answers to questions like these an officer can usually estimate accurately the morale of his unit.

He can also study the behavior of his men. Are they ready to volunteer for special duty? Are there frequent violations of discipline? How many are AWOL? How many in the guardhouse? What is the rate of venereal disease? How do they receive bad rumors? Are there many fights, and are the fights based on religious or racial differences?

All these things are symptoms. If he notes them systematically, an officer or noncom may even be able to correct his own earlier beliefs about the morale of his unit.

Morale building is a primary task of leadership Any leader trying to improve the morale of his unit will find these rules helpful:

(1) Make each man feel he is needed by his unit, that his job in it is important.

(2) Never let a man forget that he is a soldier and that a soldier of the Army of the United States is an important and respected person.

(3) Make it very clear that the unit has its own important function in winning the war.

(4) Encourage the expression of pride in the achievements of the unit.

(5) Give commendation and encouragement when it can sincerely and appropriately be given, for fair appreciation usually works better than condemnation.

(6) Never belittle or humiliate a man in front of others except when a military emergency, as in battle, may require quick correction. When rebuke is necessary, do it in private, and make it clear that it is the act that is punished, not the man.

(7) Keep idleness at a minimum, but make recreation possible.

(8) Train each man in every useful task and action that actual combat will require, and teach him that these habits will reduce his fear when combat comes, as well as make him a trained and able fighter.

(9) Let men work together in groups whenever possible, because the social relation increases effectiveness.

(10) Let the soldier on isolated duty feel that he is an indispensable man, not a forgotten one.

ZEST

Zest is the fabric from which morale is made.

Zest. Vigor of spirit. Love of life coupled with a willingness, an eagerness to risk life itself in a good undertaking. A spirit of high adventure that turns a difficult mission into a rare chance to show the stuff of which men are made.

This is the weapon that makes a military unit unbeatable. Without it the best trained army would be a lifeless automaton incapable of deeds of splendor

—unable to put forth the "last full measure of devotion" that brings victory.

Zest depends first upon physical fitness. It demands a sharp appetite that will make a soldier eat plentifully and digest his food. It requires physical exercise that brings plenty of oxygen into the lungs and plenty of red blood circulating to brain and back and hands and legs. If a man is to meet the sunrise with any sort of spirit for the new day, he must have sleep at night, sound and undisturbed by anxious dreams within him or by vermin in his bed.

Fatigue can quickly reduce a fighting spirit. Medical officers in this war have begun to talk about a new disease—flying fatigue. But fatigue, and its deadly effects, is by no means confined to leaders of flying men. The symptoms of mental fatigue, whether in the air or on the ground, are a staleness, a lack of interest in the job to be done, lack of enthusiasm, a heaviness of limbs, eyelids, even of the will that make it well-nigh impossible to drag through the day's duties, and with it shortness of temper, irritability, and the blues.

All leaders have to be constantly on guard against this insidious spiritual fifth columnist among their men and among themselves. Regardless of how invaluable the man, when fatigue has made this attack on his fitness, he must have relief. He must be required to sleep, to take respite from responsibility, to get away from the strain he has been under. Otherwise the price is a psychological casualty. And the more important the man, the greater the price to the Army.

Hidden hunger—that body starvation for essential

food elements, particularly the vitamins, from which a man may suffer though his stomach is full—is another killer of zest. Much has been discovered since the last war about vitamins. Of particular concern to the Army is the "morale vitamin" known as B-1 or thiamin. This is the vitamin contained in good red meat and in whole grain cereal—oatmeal and wholemeal bread. Without it men become gradually listless, dispirited, unconcerned with whether they win or lose, fight, or lie down and give up.

Excessive physical discomfort can also eventually deaden all zest for life and for battle. Men can fight with their socks stiff with dirt or frozen to their feet, with hands so swollen and cracked they can barely pull a trigger; they have fought when baths are unknown and shaves almost as scarce, when marching must be done through seas of mud and clothing never dries, or when the eyes are cut and the lungs choked with never settling clouds of dust and sand. Men have fought, and are fighting, under such conditions.

But it takes an unquenchable spirit to keep its zest when things are like this. Whole armies have shown this spirit, but such conditions prolonged deaden zest in the end, and therefore must be relieved whenever possible.

And just as physical ills can bring the spirit low, so also mental ills can affect a man physically, make him lose weight, go off his feed, become easily fatigued, and suffer sleepless nights.

Although most of the mentally and emotionally unfit men are weeded out before they get into the Army or in their early days at training camp, severe

294

advanced training conditions and combat itself can put new strains upon any man. When he has his first encounter with the immediate threat of death, when he must kill and see men killed, when he must steel himself to hear the unheeded cries of the mortally wounded and endure the stench of battle, a man may become sick in his very vitals. He may lose his interest in food, and yet this will be no sign of squeamishness. The toughest of leathernecks may feel intensely the inward revolting and horror the battlefield can provoke.

The defenses against these physical and mental foes of the spirit are a faith in good leaders, a loyalty to them and to comrades, and a shoulder-to-shoulder feeling of solidarity with the other men of the outfit. "I can go anwhere and stand anything my Captain and the rest of my outfit can."

And a man can pull himself out of the lowest depths of fright by a sudden powerful realization that he is adequately equipped with weapons and training. Here is a description of such a poignant moment during the World War as related by Colonel (then Lieutenant) Elliot D. Cooke in *Americans vs Germans: The First AEF in Action:*

"The air was alive with deadly splinters. They tore at the trees, furrowed the ground, and all too often found a target in human flesh. Men called for first aid, frantically, pitifully, pleadingly. Then another sound arose and grew until it dominated all the others. It was the crackle of machine-gun bullets and meant but one thing—the Boche were coming over to pay us a visit. . . .

"I knew I had to get up out of that hole and I

didn't want to do it. Nothing about me wanted to. Every inch of my anatomy shrank from being exposed to so many different kinds of death. My arm muscles acted like wet dish rags and my feet were numb, but somehow I did pull out of the hole and wriggle down to the forward line of men.

" 'For Pete's sake, Lieutenant, get in here before you get your can blown off,' one of the kids yelled, and generously made room for me in his foxhole.

"Together we peered out into the haze of smoke hanging over the still smouldering wheatfields. Shadows formed, weaved, and vanished. Machine-gun bullets pelted at us with the crescending hiss of steam pouring from a hose. Yet the expected wave of charging, grey-clad figures did not appear. Somewhere out there they lurked behind that screen of smoke while we waited tensely for them to come and fight.

"The boy beside me suddenly lifted his Chauchat rifle, aimed, and let go a full clip.

" 'Say,' he grinned, 'that feels good.'

" 'Give me a try.'

"The chug, chug, chug, of the heavy weapon against my shoulder was indeed soothing to the nerves. We both felt and expressed the hope that each of our bullets had got a German, right in the belly."

FEAR—ALLY OR TRAITOR

The first battle, the first experience of having an enemy machine gun aimed at you, the first time an airplane swoops low to lay its deadly eggs in your particular patch of ground.

296

That is an experience anticipated by the young soldier with mingled dread and eagerness. He is eager by that time to get at the enemy. He has learned a great deal about the science of war and wants to use this knowledge to wipe out the enemy and gain victory.

But he always wonders—every man does—just how he will behave when that time comes. He doesn't feel like a hero. If he is honest—completely honest—with himself, he knows he will be scared —terrified.

The experienced soldier who has been through all this the first time and many other times has found out for certain that every man going into battle is scared. His hands tremble, his throat is dry, he must swallow constantly because his "heart is in his mouth." He does idiotic things like looking at his watch every few seconds or examining his rifle a hundred times to be sure it is loaded. The soldier green to battle may think he is the only one so disturbed, but it is true of the veteran as well. And it is true of the enemy. Germans and Japs get just as scared as Americans and British.

The bad moments do not come during actual combat, however, but in the time of tense waiting just before. As soon as the frightened man is able to go into action—to do something effective against the enemy, especially if it involves violent physical action —his fright is apt to be dispelled or forgotten because he is too busy fighting to remember it.

Airplane pilots who had distinguished themselves in action against the Japanese said, when asked whether they were scared during those moments of acute peril, "Why, I don't know. There was too much to do. We didn't have time to think."

"Most of us were scared at first," wrote a member of a torpedoed ship, "sure we were. But when the torpedo hit us we forgot all about it. There wasn't much time and then there was too much work to do."

Encounters with the enemy are most terrifying when they are unfamiliar. As the soldier becomes used to gunfire, to explosions, to the sight and odor of death, he gradually acquires the power to meet these things more stoically. He does not actually lose his fear, but he learns to ignore it sufficiently to keep his attention mainly on the business of combat. And if he has in his trained hands a good weapon which he knows will put the enemy out of action, this gives him a feeling of confidence—a sense of power—that in large measure outweighs his fear. He knows it will soon be the other fellow's turn to be scared.

Fear, when it is experienced, is intensely uncomfortable and seems often to be incapacitating. If the period of fright is prolonged, a man may feel that his nerves are "all shot" by it. For fear is disintegrating, demoralizing. It shatters morale. The soldier may be rooted to the spot, paralyzed or immobilized by fear.

Nevertheless such awful moments before an attack, when each second seems an hour, may actually be useful to any soldier. They may really add to his efficiency.

For fear is the body's preparation for action. The heart pounds faster, pumping blood more rapidly to the arms and legs and brain, where its oxygen

298

is needed. The lungs do their part by quickened breathing. Blood pressure goes up. Adrenalin, which is nature's own "shot in the arm," is poured liberally into the blood stream. Sugar is released into the blood to act as fuel for the human fighting machine.

Subtle changes in body chemistry, automatically effected by powerful emotion, serve to protect the soldier in action in ways he would never think of, if he had to plan them himself. His blood clots more readily. He loses temporarily the sense of fatigue even though he may have been dog tired.

It is sometimes difficult for a tense, frightened soldier to get started into combat—to begin the action that will relieve his fear. That part is taken care of by Army training and discipline. Months of training have taught the soldier to respond from habit to definite battle orders, even though in battle commands often cannot be given as in training. It has become second nature to him to carry out his own job as a member of the fighting team.

The parachute trooper, jumping from the plane, has learned to follow the man ahead. At first his "jumps" were from a mock-up only a few feet off the ground, but then he learned timing. He learned to take his cue from the man ahead. When he received his slap behind, it was his turn and out he went.

The fact that any action is so drilled in that it is mechanical helps when you are scared. No matter how distracted your mind may be by unfamiliar and terrifying sights and smells and sounds, you act, from sheer force of habit. In fact, it is habits which take care of a man if he is too frightened to think clearly, like the habit of diving for cover when bombs come down.

Then, presently, you are in action. You are fighting! You are at last using force against the foe! No more are you a cowering, abject soul. Fear is forgotten—provided you are well trained.

How to Fight Fear

(1) *Action dispels fear—do something.* In the time of suspense when men are all ready for action but are waiting the signal to start, fear is at its height. If the period of waiting is to be prolonged —perhaps a delay until the weather changes—the time should be occupied with preparation for action Fight fear with work—when expecting combat, when waiting on a raft for rescue, when waiting for enemy bombers to return.

(2) *Physical contact with friends helps.* Men should, if possible, stay within sight in time of peril, but not bunched up enough to become a bomb target. Just the presence of another man, not far off, when no word is spoken, minimizes fear.

(3) *Roll calls help.* Men in peril should be reminded that they are not alone, that they are an integral part of a close-knit organization, that each is important to it. The artillery's "call out your numbers loud and strong" reassures each man that in the smoke of battle the others are still in their places, doing their parts. It also lets him know that the others, too, are keeping track of him. They will miss him if he is lost, will look for him. They are "all for one and one for all."

(4) *Knowledge is power over fear.* Surprise is the most important element in battle. Thus men should be kept constantly informed of the dangers they may meet, of the weapons that may be used against them, of the tactics which the enemy uses. Every moment of leisure should be used by the men to find out what they can about what battle will be like, what the enemy is like. The known is never so fearful as the unknown.

(5) *Control of action helps.* To be afraid does not mean that a man must act afraid. Fear is contagious when it is expressed in action. If a man goes to pieces and becomes panicky, he must be removed from the sight of the other men if that is at all possible. It is each man's responsibility to control the signs of his own fear if he can, so as to spare the others. And if he can manage to act as though he were calm, he may actually become more calm. At any rate the opposite is true: giving in to fear tends to increase it.

(6) *Even statistics help.* It is reassuring to know that of all the men in the army comparatively few are killed. The chances that any one man will be among those mortally wounded in any one battle are relatively small. Unless a man is such an egoist that he believes that the enemy will single him out for special attention, he can be relieved by the thought that he has a good chance of coming through. And the longer he remains unscathed, the surer he becomes about those chances.

Fear just before combat is not, however, the most trying fear that men in the armed forces must sometimes face. That is, after all, a thing of the moment, and men are helped to face it by the excitement of action.

There is another kind of fear that must be endured for days and weeks—perhaps months or years—if men are besieged, cut off from help, deprived of adequate defense. Then the ever-present peril from the enemy may be aggravated by the greater perils of disease, famine, exposure. And there may be little chance for action.

Men in the present war have endured primitive sorts of hardships that would seem to be beyond human endurance—in Bataan, on Corregidor, alone on a rubber life raft for five weeks in blistering sun and drenching storm without food, without shelter, without water, without any aid but their own unquenchable spirits, their fortitude and their faith.

This means terror mixed with despair. The misery cannot be relieved; it can only be endured. Then they must maintain sanity, courage, and life itself by their ingenuity in originating occupations for hands and minds that will relieve the tension and seem to reduce the hazards.

Men battling alone against the sea welcome a chance to learn something of navigation, to contrive means for keeping track of the directions and distances they are being carried by current and wind. They think of songs to sing and of games to play. The captain of one-torpedoed boat reported:

"Our lifeboat was shelled for two hours. It had 24 holes in it. The crew plugged 7 but that still left 17. So the men in the boat held a meeting to discuss the problem of buying sheet metal to plug up the other holes. The meeting lasted two days and was conducted under strict parliamentary laws, according to Robert's Rules. The discussion was finally tabled on 3 counts: (1) The ship's treasurer was in another lifeboat and they couldn't reach him; (2) All their money went down with the ship anyway; (3) There weren't any stores there in the ocean. However, the debate made 48 hours pass quickly."

Thus a resourceful leader can exercise considerable ingenuity in keeping his men occupied. If physical activity is impossible, keeping minds occupied with talk on some subject unrelated to the immediate threat of danger relieves tension.

In such trying times and in tense moments, a laugh can be a lifesaver. An Army officer relating experiences of the World War tells of a time when badly frightened, untrained soldiers of that war had taken refuge in a roadside ditch against an unforeseen horror—the fire of American guns turned on them by mistake.

"Panic sent the blood pounding into my head and emptied my stomach of courage. It was bad enough to be shot at by the Boche, but there was no sense in being killed by friendly troops. My men looked wild and fingered their triggers, ready to return the fire of our other battalion. Something had to be done and done quick. And Captain Wass did it. Unintentionally, but still he did it.

" 'Jackson!' he yelled.

" 'Yes, Captain.'

" 'Where are you?'

" 'Right here. Across the road.'

" 'Stand up; so I can see you.'

" 'Captain,' Jackson shouted above the crackling

roar of machine-gun bullets, 'if you want to see me, *you* stand up.'

"American humor can lick anything. Smothered chuckles ran down the line. Orders were given and listened to. Men wriggled backwards out of the zone of fire. The first to reach the trees dashed down the line of the 3d Battalion, shutting off the guns."

Nor may we forget the power of religious belief as an antidote to fear. When men get into a tight spot they pray. They pray hard and from the heart, and they feel the better for it. Prayer works.

Fear is nature's way of meeting in an all-out way an all-out emergency. It is useful in mobilizing all the body's resources. Obviously, prolonged fear is horribly fatiguing. Long periods of anxiety are damaging in the extreme. But fear within limits increases strength and endurance.

And fear is an ally in other respects. It is of value to the army as well as to the individual soldier, for it serves the same purpose as the red signal light on a railroad—to give warning of danger and to promote caution.

The purpose of warfare is to destroy the enemy, and to gain this end with a minimum sacrifice of our own forces. The soldier who needlessly puts his own life in jeopardy is committing an act of treachery. The officer or noncom who imperils the safety of his men through his own foolhardiness or his failure to appreciate a danger is also betraying his country.

There are a few men in every army who know no fear—just a few. But these men are not normal. They would be recognized by a psychiatrist as not quite right mentally. They have a callousness of mind that makes them incapable of emotion.

Such men are recognized as a danger to the Army. Wise leaders watch them zealously and are con-stantly on the alert to prevent them from exposing other men to peril. But in spite of—or because of—their complete lack of caution and common sense, these crazy dare-devils, by taking the enemy com-pletely by surprise, sometimes accomplish amazing things and cover themselves with glory before going to a premature death.

Their mad acts are not, however, feats of cour-age. They may collect a few medals, but they are not heroes.

True courage is the ability to act as you believe you should in the face of recognized danger—to act in spite of fear—to risk your life in order to keep the soldier's faith.

A man may succeed as a soldier without broad vision. He may be an efficient dependable fighter with no interest in the larger objectives of the war. If he feels loyalty to his unit, that is enough. Train-ing and experience teach him to be interested in the means of fighting without being concerned with the reasons for fighting. Such a man cannot be said, however, to be without ideals. His loyalty, his sense of responsibility are more than mere obedience and a sense of duty.

Thus the soldier who deliberately chooses to be blown up in order to wipe out an enemy tank or machine-gun nest that would otherwise cost the lives of his friends, has ideals—has indeed, all it takes to make a soldier. The commander of a ship,

305

who coolly sends away the last lifeboat and goes down with his vessel rather than abandon it while some of his men are helplessly imprisoned in one of its compartments, is afraid, but governed by something more powerful than fear.

You may call this force idealism, conscience, religion, philosophy, tradition, code, or even habit, or you may be modern and call it ideology. Psychologists sometimes call it the triumph of the social over the selfish instincts. They recognize this force as the most potent weapon an army can possess.

Men fighting for their homes and armed with this spirit can stand their ground and win against tremendous opposing forces.

Courage and fear are not opposites; they may fill the same breast at the same time. But armed with courage, no soldier need worry about his own fright. The coward, who must run when he is scared, is the one to dread terror.

None but the brave can afford to fear.

Why Men Fight

Lower animals fight from a variety of causes. Some fight because, as beasts of prey, they live by killing and devouring. Animals may fight their own kind in a tussle over a mate. They fight to defend their young, their homes, or their own lives. Some are aggressive and go about seeking what they may devour; others fight as a last resort when they are cornered.

Men, being two-legged animals, may fight for any or all of these reasons. But, because they have minds capable of being moved by abstract ideas such as honor, glory, freedom, sympathy, justice, and patriotism, men fight also for what they believe to be the right.

Greater than the fear of injury and death, Napoleon said, is the fear of shame.

When one nation fights another, the motives stirring each individual soldier and driving him to battle will naturally differ. The strength of the force within each man depends largely on the strength of his loyalty to his country and to his own army and to his leaders.

When a man begins to think of himself not as John Smith, the man, or even as John Smith the salesman, or plumber, the teacher, church member, or Rotarian; when he becomes John Smith, American and soldier, then the advances and defeats of his Army become his own individual successes and failures.

He is then eager to give himself to the utmost to serve the needs of the Army and the nation, quite regardless of his own personal advancement.

In a draft army, it must be recognized that not every man feels himself so completely a part of it. Although Americans, as a nation, voted for the draft and wanted it, some individuals have left their jobs, their schools, or their homes with reluctance and found the change to military life difficult and not entirely to their taste.

Before the drafted man throws himself wholeheartedly into his work as a soldier—before the civilian makes up his mind to enlist in the Army, he is stirred and influenced by one or perhaps by many of the following forces:

(1) He may be carried away by mass suggestion. An infectious martial spirit spreads throughout the community roused by Government officials, speakers, or writers. Flags are waving, bands are playing, drums beating, and crowds cheering. There has not been much of this in the present war, but in other wars men have been excited to a point of frenzy by such methods. They enlisted in a condition almost like drunkenness and some woke up to find themselves under arms and with a headache.

(2) He may become involved in a wave of war hysteria. Like the fervor of martial spirit, war hate is infectious. Men rush to arms at news of the enemy's evil designs or brutalities, of a treacherous assault or intended invasion. Stirred to a high pitch of hate, a man wants to get at the enemy as soon as possible. This is what took many a man to the recruiting officer on the day after Pearl Harbor. But still this influence is not so powerful in this war as it would be if the enemy were actually on the shores of continental United States, or if New York or Washington had been bombed.

(3) He may be urged by a strong spirit of adventure, a thirst for the excitement of perilous enterprises, a hunger for primitive experience. Despite "debunking" of war as a glorious experience, the exciting drama of life as an aviator, or as a Commando, has a glamour that draws the adventurous man irresistibly.

(4) The ambitious, self-centered man, especially perhaps if he has been unable to achieve success in civilian life, may see war as an opportunity to gain personal glory and power. He is seeking a chance to

308

command men or to be an individual hero—a Sergeant York, an ace.

(5) He may be driven by his own combativeness. Some men delight in fighting for its own sake. Some may even be killers at heart. Because murder is outlawed in civilian life, and because in many circles even taking a poke at a man or cursing him freely is frowned upon, some combative men may find their first thrill of release in an attack on the enemy.

(6) He may be unconsciously trying to relieve a grouch by violence that is considered legitimate. The man who has spent a lifetime enduring an unending series of disappointments, failures, and obstacles, and who has dammed up in himself ever-mounting grievances and resentments may be able to turn all that ill will against the enemy.

(7) He may have joined the Army as he would apply for a job. If he has been unemployed or his job is uncertain, if he doesn't like his business or is afraid of failure, the steady pay and sureness of food in the Army may draw him to it.

(8) He may have been driven into Army life by a regard for public opinion. He may feel keenly the way his friends, especially the girls, regard a military uniform and a fighting man. He may hate the thought of being considered a slacker.

(9) It may be the desire to maintain his own self-esteem that moves him. He may have to end his secret shame at the thought that others are doing his fighting for him, especially if the "other" is a brother, father, or close friend. He may want to prove to himself that he has the necessary courage to make a fighting man—that he is not a coward.

(10) His action may be based on a feeling of one-ness with the nation and on faith in the nation's leaders. He may be intellectually convinced that our war is just and justified, that wrongs must be righted and abuses corrected, that the nation's integrity and territory must be defended.

(11) He may be acting out his faith in democracy. Even though he may have no personal desire for war or for taking part in it, he may still feel himself bound by the decision of the majority of their elected leaders. He may enlist because he regards it as his moral or patriotic duty. It is a matter of conscience with him.

(12) He may be compelled by the spirit of sacrifice. He may be moved by an enobling emotion that some men feel—the willingness to give his all for his ideals, for an enduring institution, for a righteous purpose—the willingness to die for his country.

All these are reasons why men join the Army, why they accept training, in many cases why they keep on willingly when they go overseas to a fighting front. Yet by then motives usually change, or some of them do. Here are the chief reasons why a man fights at the front.

(13) In a unit with good morale, he fights out of loyalty to his comrades and his unit. There is a job to be done and cooperation is necessary for success. He is proud of his part in the common undertaking, he wants his group to succeed in its battles, in all it attempts. He never wants to let the others down.

(14) Or he may fight because he is led. Men at the front face danger and are often uncertain what

to do about it. This is especially true in a unit with uncertain morale. In the turmoil of battle men often become confused. They may not know where the enemy is, where the objective is. They may be lost. At such times men accept any seemingly competent leadership that presents itself. They will follow a stranger to attack a machine-gun nest if their officers are gone, if the stranger but speak and act with assurance.

(15) Finally a man may fight because there is literally nothing else to do. He and his comrades are in the war, at the front, in battle. No one stops to figure out why he should escape from a burning house. So with fighting. *Why* was a question perhaps, long ago, back in America, in the training days. Now the fighting has come and the only question there is left is *how* to fight best. When choice no longer exists, motives are no longer conscious. They hardly matter.

A mixture of several of these motives may impel a given man at the same time, or in succession. Some of them go much deeper into the roots of a man's life than others do. Some may impel a man to join the Army and yet not make him devote himself fully to the hard training, the toughening experiences, the high pitch of performance Army life requires. In general, however, it is the deeper motives that can best carry a man through the hardships and emotional tests of war.

For this reason it is important for officers and enlisted men alike to understand the war aims of the nation and become convinced that these aims are in harmony with their own ideals, their beliefs about what is best for the nation and for the world. A dim outline of a better world to be achieved by supreme effort has the power to call forth the last resources of the fighting man. And so have some of the other deep motives.

But the lesser things count importantly too—loyalty to the unit, group pride, ambition for the group, acceptance of leadership. And then training—the sort of training that puts the question "Why should I fight" back in the remote past, and substitutes for it "How can I fight best?" The fighters, the seasoned battle troops, have forgotten motives. They are concerned with means.

How Men Meet Defeat

Washing out of flight training is no blow to a man who never really wanted to fly anyway. But it may be the symbol of eternal failure to a man who has had his heart set on flying ever since he can remember.

Disappointments, failures, obstacles—small and large—stand in the way of every man's advancement in the Army. How serious they are, what they do to the individual, and how they affect the morale of the whole outfit depends upon many factors, some of them obscure and little understood by the ordinary fighting man. An obstacle may stir in one man a grim determination to overcome it and excite him to vigorous action. Another man facing what looks to the outsider like the same sort of frustration may become apathetic and a poor fighter, may "go over the hill," or may go on sick call.

The way a man stands up to a blow depends

partly, of course, on how heavy the blow is. It is much harder to take the news that your sweetheart is sitting under the apple tree with somebody else than it is to learn that the whole company is to be confined to barracks for one evening.

But a continuous round of small disappointments and annoyances can add up to a surprising total out of all proportion to the importance of any one of them. After having food you don't like for dinner, getting reprimanded for a clumsy salute, getting grease on your clean uniform, and feeling the smart of a sun-burned face, a little razzing goes a long way. Yet the other fellows, unaware of what has gone before, may be astonished at the explosion that results.

The onlooker is puzzled to see what happens sometimes after such a simple mishap as having a wrench slip off the nut a man is trying to tighten. He throws the wrench violently to the ground and starts trembling all over or swearing. He has perhaps been told by his sergeant that he is too clumsy to make a good mechanic—that he will have to give up his ambition to be a technician unless he does better.

When a man is faced with a very difficult problem or a series of them, with any sort of obstacle or frustration, when things become too difficult there are just three sorts of things that he can do. He can work at it harder, attacking the problem from new angles and with increasing vigor. He can get mad and attempt to destroy the obstacle or himself or something else. He can give up in despair and sit in apathy or run away.

The first way is the way of learning. It is the

way the laboratory cat behaves in a puzzle box. She jumps around, scratches, meows, pulls at ropes and repeats these actions and many others until finally she hits on the solution, and steps on the release that opens the door out of the box.

The human animal faced with the problem of making a dead automobile engine run again doesn't have to push and pull or turn everything inside it (although he actually may before he is through). He can imagine or think out what would happen if he did each possible thing without actually going through the motions. This is planning.

When what seems like a good plan is hit upon, it is tried. If this fails, it is a signal for more thinking.

When a good working plan is finally evolved and the engine finally turns over, success is achieved and the man has learned.

All this activity is healthy unless the individual becomes so engrossed with a single problem—so obsessed by it—that he fails to eat or sleep or pay attention to other necessary problems.

But suppose the problem he has set himself is an impossible one—a goal he can never reach. Then as plan after plan fails, his distress and excitement mount, especially when there is an urgency about getting out of the jam. Then the man may keep on working but his activity begins to have less point to it. He may try rash or foolish things. Or he may do the same thing over and over endlessly, despite knowing already it will not work.

The shipwrecked man who has tried vainly to signal for help and finally reverts to calling his mother's name over and over until he is exhausted

314

is an example of how thinking breaks down under the strain of continuous failure. So is the way a man will search again and again in the same drawer for important papers that have disappeared.

Getting mad over disappointments or failures is generally not profitable. It is particularly hard on the "innocent bystander" because of the way men have of shifting their grouch from the original obstacle to other persons or things.

The man who fails to get the promotion he has been working and longing for doesn't take a poke at the officer who refused to recommend him, much as he would like to have it out with him. Instead he is likely to kick his buddy in the pants if he so much as raises his eyebrows.

Leaders, too, may "take it out" on unoffending men, who then wonder "What's eatin' him?"

Because of the essentially pyramidal nature of the Army organization, it is particularly unfortunate when an officer who is by nature cruel, sarcastic, incompetent, happens to get into a place high up in the pyramid. Such a man can cause more friction and do more to hamper morale than many men lower in the pyramid could do all told.

When such a man by his incompetence sets up lack of confidence among his immediate junior officers, or when he keeps them on edge by stern punishments for minor infractions of discipline or by arbitrary and unreasonable decisions, the power of his position and respect for his rank prevent their direct retaliation.

In consequence, sooner or later, some of them "take it out" on men below them and this process goes on until it finally reaches some of the buck privates at the base of the pyramid.

Such a piling up of grouches and aggressiveness is not only valueless in a fighting army; it is likely to be dangerous and costly. By draining into countless petty personal quarrels and frictions between individuals the fighting energy that should be spent to destroy the enemy, a whole unit may be placed in jeopardy.

There is another common way of "displacing" the resentment aroused by rebuke or punishment from superiors, to whom it is impossible to show anything but meekness. That is in imaginings. Outwardly compliant and calm, a man may be inwardly seething with the things he would like to say and do to "get even." He may even half convince himself and tell the other fellows what he "came right out and said" to the leader.

Such imaginings can drag out into long daydreams in which the resentful man is placed in a position of authority and retaliates. Under certain circumstances such day-dreams may become all-engrossing; efficiency then drops and a casualty may result.

Aggression may also be turned inward onto the self. Many a man goes about "kicking himself," usually figuratively, but sometimes in real self-punishment such as banging the head or punching or kicking a hard object until the flesh is bruised. Of course, the extreme of self-punishment for disastrous failure or frustration is suicide, but mostly suicide is just giving up.

"If at first you don't succeed, try, try again." This

adage may be useful to maintain courage, but the process is actually governed by natural law.

The number of times a man will attempt to accomplish a certain job or to reach a certain objective is governed in one direction by the importance of that particular success and in the other direction by the effort and pain involved in trying.

When the successful achievement means less to the individual than freedom from the strain of trying to attain it, any man will abandon the struggle. "Giving up" is nature's way of protecting the organism against too much pain.

Time is a factor which also enters into this natural law. Distant goals have less appeal than those within sight. For this reason it takes tremendous fortitude for men to spur themselves on to do their best to overcome great obstacles in a war of long duration. As soon as a victory, even a minor one, seems close, however, they summon all their resources for redoubled efforts.

Giving up may mean defeat, but it does not always mean surrender. In most situations what is given up is some particular way of reaching the goal, rather than a complete abandonment of the objective. This sort of defeat results in thinking, in fresh striving, and in eventual progress. A man who has been unable to get a commission in the Army may enlist, earn his stripes, and later reach an Officer Candidate School.

Another kind of giving up results in compromise. The original objective is abandoned, but another more easily achieved is substituted. The man who washes out of his course in pilot training may decide that after all he'll make a better bombardier or mechanic, or whatever special work he is selected for.

Ability to accept defeat in such ways is no fault of character. In fact, a man who can "take it," and still do his best without bitterness, is as highly regarded in the Army as in civilian life.

But there are other ways of meeting defeat or disappointment that are destructive and may result in a "psychological casualty." The familiar "sour grapes" reaction is what happens in a man who has set his heart so firmly on a particular achievement that he can't give it up and face the fact. So he belittles or "runs down" the very job he wants so much to have. He says pilots are all "crazy" or "fools" and the whole flying game is a "gyp."

When the disappointment is much too severe for a man's strength to stand up under it, he may literally run away—go "over the hill"—even in the face of punishments handed out for desertion in wartime.

More likely to occur is a sort of symbolic running away through feigned illness or physical defect. A man, faced with failure to pass an examination for a promotion he has longed for, may suddenly announce that he is color-blind, night blind, or has some other previously undiscovered defect that would prevent his success.

Or he may actually become ill and be honestly unaware of the connection between the sudden sickness and the frustration. Most of us have caught ourselves in this sort of self-deceit in the face of failure. In an important examination which turned out to be much more stiff than was anticipated, a

318

violent headache, a nauseated stomach or burning eyes often develop to make a good alibi.

Such mentally caused illnesses are real enough even though they have no organic basis. And it is in the most conscientious persons—those who try most earnestly to succeed—that they occur.

The hysterias—hysterical blindness or deafness or paralysis—and war neuroses, miscalled shell shock in the World War, have this sort of origin. When a soldier reaches the point where he can no longer stand up under the horrors he must face, when he can walk no farther, and can fight no more, and yet his spirit will not allow him to turn back, then he may suddenly go blind, lose the use of his arms or legs, or he may forget his name and everything connected with his identity and wander off.

Such physical ills, psychological in origin, have their parallel in psychological ills which are physical in origin. This is the kind of thing that sometimes hits an aviator after a crash and makes him unfit to fly again.

An aviator, after a crack-up in which his pilot and two mechanics were killed, soon recovered from painful but superficial physical injuries, but afterward he could no longer fly. He could not even imagine himself going through the motions of flying a plane. Furthermore, he developed an intense fear of planes and everything concerned with aviation. In other ways he seemed all right.

Not always, however, are the effects confined to just one field.

A sailor complained much of numbness, pain and cold, but more especially of sweating from the waistline down. He was irritable and unstable emotionally. He became aggressive suddenly and without sufficient cause. He was blind at times for five to fifteen minutes. He had attacks of dizziness. His sleep was disturbed by dreams of drowning. This seems like a lot of complaints, but it is not unusual for one man under such circumstances to suffer from a number of different symptoms.

Although this sailor insisted he had suffered no serious shock, his symptoms first appeared after his ship was torpedoed.

When he was induced to tell about the experience, he became excited and swore. His anger seemed to be connected with the rescue. He said that officers in life-boats had received preference by those in the small rescue boat. This man and his mates were forced to cling to a life raft for another twelve hours.

He admitted that when he allowed himself to close his eyes and think of his present sensations, he still imagined himself clinging to that raft, half submerged. Several of his comrades had lost consciousness and drowned. Probably this sailor owes his life to the concentration of his attention on the painful sensations of cold in his half-submerged body. Small wonder that the pain and cold continued to persist as hallucinations after their service in keeping him from unconsciousness and death was done.

His blindness, interestingly enough, occurs whenever he encounters scenes of violence such as an auto wreck or a fight. It keeps him from witnessing another horrible situation which might cause him more pain than he could stand.

Each man, no matter how strong mentally and

physically, has his limits beyond which the strongest will cannot drive him. The wise man learns his own tolerances and cautiously retreats, if possible, to a more defended position when the hazards and obstacles he is in danger of are too great. This retreat may be mental only instead of physical, or both. And he may, by gradually becoming accustomed to dangers, increase the ability of his mind and body to stand the emotional strains of war. But for the foolish and the heroic who ignore all physical limitations, nature may have to provide these peculiar forms of escape from pain or emotion too intense to be endured.

Rage—A Two-Edged Weapon

A group of tanks stands in a field, silent, motionless, and dead. Suddenly switches are thrown, motors start and they become alive. Noise bursts from their exhausts and they roar to attack.

A gun is inert and dead until high explosive powder is set off in its chambers. A bomb without nitroglycerine is a dud.

All weapons are mere useless pieces of metal until the release of energy brings them to life.

Man, too, as a weapon of war must have energy released to galvanize him into an acting, fighting soldier. And the high explosive that sets off man's fighting power is emotion.

There are certain things that a man can do in an automatic way without the fire of emotional energy. But these things would win no wars. Without fear and without rage he could not even defend himself if the enemy were aiming at him and about to fire.

Slap a man's face and he will become enraged. Drop a bomb beside him and he may be terrified. But, although the two feelings may seem to the man very different, inwardly the changes that take place in his body are similar.

His heart beats faster, his blood pressure rises, his blood is shifted from internal organs to the muscles, his digestion stops, sugar in his blood increases, his hands tremble, his voice quivers, the body wastes in the bladder or bowels may be expelled—he becomes alert and ready for instant action.

Whether all this extreme preparation for action by the body is a good thing for the soldier or whether it will actually endanger his life, depends upon the circumstances.

In primitive hand-to-hand combat when the last ounce of energy of which the body is capable must be summoned instantly for one tremendous spurt of running to get away from peril, or for one outburst of physical strength to down the foe, rage or fear will pour into the blood the adrenalin necessary to rouse that vital energy.

If immediate vigorous physical action is impossible, however, and if life depends instead upon the coolheaded use of skill, self-control and discipline, then violent emotion can put the soldier in mortal peril.

It is as possible to be literally blinded by rage as it is to be paralyzed by fear. A prizefighter knows that he can win against a stronger and more skilled opponent if he can rouse his opponent to violent anger in which he strikes wildly and fails to "use his science."

322

The main purpose behind all the long routine of military training and the pre-conditioning of troops to simulated battle conditions, is to drill into soldiers fighting habits so deeply ingrained—so intimately "second nature"—that they will persist in the face of the most overwhelming provocations to rage or panic. Long practice in shooting coolly at a target without undue excitement, without blood lust, makes it possible for the soldier to shoot calmly at his target when his very life and the safety of his pals are at stake. His hand must not tremble then, his keen eye and steady nerve must not waver.

Fortunately, men in a civilized society have been trained since early childhood to control and discipline their natural impulses. For the normal adult it is entirely possible for intelligence to remain in command of his behavior, and for even recently acquired habits to be retained in opposition to the instinctive impulses to run or to drop his rifle and flail out with his fists.

There are many degrees of anger, however. And although the violently enraged individual may be at the mercy of the enemy, a milder form of resentment of injustice and calm determination to avenge cruelty can serve to fill men with a fighting spirit that knows no defeat.

The difference between this cool anger and rage is like the difference between tempered steel and molten iron, like the difference between a raging torrent that destroys blindly and the harnessed power of a Niagara that can be directed intelligently to wipe out the enemy.

Such deep and controlled anger is not to be roused

323

artificially by any harangue before a group of men. It is the automatic result of an unpardonable offense. It rises like an unquenchable fire when a man's house is attacked, when his wife or his children are abused, when his own native land is invaded. This is the spirit which has kept the heat of battle raging on the frozen soil of winter-bound Russia and on the plains and in the valleys of China. It is what accounted for the heroic defense of Greece against overwhelming odds, and the never-ceasing campaign in the mountains of Jugo-Slavia.

Such anger can be used not only for actual killing of the enemy, but also to provide the energy needed for work behind the lines.

A soldier who is determined to defeat the enemy will do anything that he feels contributes to wiping out the foe, whether it is changing the tires on a truck or unloading shells from a packing case or policing barracks in his training camp. He will fight at his job. He will do that job well, and will use his own initiative to volunteer for extra duty or to think up ways of doing his job more quickly or more efficiently.

An effective leader, whether he is a corporal or a general, will know how to recognize and utilize this active force in his men. He will see to it that it is directed and given useful outlet. He will be on the alert to prevent its diversion or dissipation in personal quarrels.

Anger is infectious and can spread from one person to another through personal contact. Just to see the flushed face and the tense expression of a wrathy person may be enough to stir anger in others. The

324

sound of anger in a raised voice or the sight of angry behavior is even more catching. Anger spreads most readily when the beholder is sympathetic—when he is able to put himself in the angry man's shoes, when the injured person is "one of us."

For this reason the roused anger of a people is much greater and more moving than the sum of the individual angers within the group. They reenforce one another.

Anger shared, controlled and directed to the single purpose of destroying the enemy, is a powerful force for survival and for victory. ·

FIGHTING OUR COMRADES AND ALLIES

Hatred of the enemy makes sense.

The Army is organized throughout for one single purpose—fighting. Soldiers must be fighting men with a fighting spirit.

But some acts of aggression by soldiers are useless to the war effort and actually dangerous to the Army.

When competition between companies or regiments turns into bitter rivalry, when soldiers in town for Saturday night pick quarrels with each other or with the townspeople, when race prejudices are permitted to develop within a camp, or when officers stoop to professional jealousy, the harmful results can be as bad as those dealt out by the enemy.

Such conditions make rifts in the solidarity essential to fighting morale; they cause a deterioration of discipline, produce a state of anxiety and insecurity among the troops; and, worst of all, they actually drain off in ineffective petty squabbles the fighting energy, every ounce of which is needed, to bring victory.

The thoughtful leader, knowing that no group or nation can long survive if it is torn by internal strife or dissension with its allies, is seriously disturbed by any tendency toward personal or factional friction within his command. He well knows that victory can come only if the whole group puts all its efforts into a unified cooperative battle against the common enemy.

Single incidents are difficult to trace to their cause, but wherever there is an outbreak of private fights and disorderly conduct either in camp or off the post, the trouble can usually be traced to a focus of infection. There is sure to be some agent from which the discord is spreading, just as typhoid can be spread from a carrier in the mess kitchen.

There may be a trouble maker among the men. Such a person may be the sort of mental or moral misfit known to medical officers as a psychopathic personality—a man who should never be allowed in the Army in the first place because he is never any good as a fighter and can demoralize an otherwise effective fighting unit.

Or the men may have some legitimate grievance. The food may be unpalatable. Mails may be late. Opportunities for relaxation too infrequent. In an organization so strictly disciplined as the Army, men may not always present their gripes to the leaders who could correct such conditions. Instead they may become grouchy, irritable and short tempered with each other.

Most serious of all the causes for an epidemic of

dissension is the bad leader. When, as sometimes happens in any organization like an army, men have placed over them a man they do not trust, one who loves to show his authority and "throw his rank around," or an unreasonable martinet, the whole outfit will be filled with resentment. Since it is impossible to show this antagonism to the officer who is at fault, the troops go around with chips on their shoulders daring each other to knock them off.

The only way to wipe out such an infection of dissension is to track down and remove the cause. If men believe they have a grievance, even if the complaint is unjustified, they should be permitted to tell their troubles to someone in authority. If an officer gives them a patient hearing, investigates conditions with a fair and open mind and explains his findings to the men, they will usually be satisfied even in cases where it is impossible to do much to correct the objectionable state of affairs. Just telling their troubles to a willing listener serves to get the air cleared. And in cases where the men make constructive suggestions for correcting conditions, they will take in the organization a pride that they never had before.

These are the reasons why for many years in our Army any officer or soldier has been free to tell a grievance to the inspector general sent periodically to each place where there are troops.

Just as a child can be taught that saying "please" will get more favors from his parents than will kicking and screaming, so an adult can be taught that a courteous request meets with more favor and success than does sulking or griping.

327

This is the best way to reduce wasteful aggressiveness—by rewarding cooperativeness and courtesy and constructive suggestions.

Incidentally (but importantly) this method of dealing with disaffection cheats the fifth columnist and saboteur who may lurk in camp. It is much safer for the Army that men should pour their gripes into the ears of an officer than that they should spill them in a beer joint in town or in any other place where outsiders can listen.

Another method of handling dissension and overt aggression is by punishment. This is the chosen method of dictatorships and autocratic organizations generally. The method is commonly used even in America, and most children have to learn that, when they feel aggressive, punishment is not far away. As a result, Americans are, on the whole, relatively unaggressive as far as physical actions are concerned.

Quarrels and word battles are another matter, however. These are not so severely punished in American children. Consequently adult Americans are behaving normally when they give vent to their annoyance at the many frustrations of strict discipline by grouching, bickering, yelling insults, swearing and bawling one another out.

This sort of thing is not generally considered anything to worry about. It is just the American way of letting off steam. It may actually get resentments "off the chest," so that the group can build up a strong feeling of united action impossible when some continue to nurse grievances.

From the standpoint of the superior officer, it is much more desirable to control dissension by rewarding cooperative behavior than by punishing unruly acts. It takes more forethought, but when a man is induced to talk over his complaints in a cooperative and constructive manner, the cause of the difficulty is often removed.

On the other hand, when he is punished, he may be prevented from giving expression to his anger, and the anger—far from being dispelled—is increased.

Suppose a man who is expecting a Sunday of freedom is put on KP duty instead. This is one cause for annoyance. But if he is accustomed to grouch about such disappointments, and this time his "bellyaching" meets with a gruff rebuke, he is given a new cause for feeling sour. He may shut up and go about his duties in an orderly way, but the double frustration may make him seethe inwardly.

If there should be a chain of such restraints and restrictions, the later consequences of the bottling up of his feelings may be serious. Especially if he takes a drink too many he may beat somebody up.

Sometimes the soldier's troubles cannot be attributed to any one person. They are due to the conditions of war or of Army life. An ambitious and energetic man may find himself so wound up in red tape that he cannot do a good job. An organization may be all set to go forward to an objective, but is hindered by failure of supplies, by shortages, by weather. No one is to blame.

But it is well nigh intolerable to be angry without having someone to be angry at. A man who is thus held back and interfered with is eager to find some person or group of people who can be blamed for the miserable state of affairs.

This natural need for someone to blame and punish when things go wrong—responsible for much race and religious prejudice—is also the cause for most quarrels that grow up between allies and between one branch of the service and another.

Since it is such a natural need, it has been seized upon by our enemies and capitalized to the utmost. Hitler could count it his most important campaign if he could succeed in turning the American's natural resentment at being required to change his way of life and at being deprived of members of his family and things dear to him into resentment against the labor organizations, the farmers, the manufacturers, or some other national group.

Axis propagandists are constantly striving to make the soldiers of the United Nations forget their fight against the foe in disputes—British against American, Indian against British, Army against Navy, Whites against the Blacks or Browns, Christian against Jew.

An occasional individual in any large group appears to contradict all the rules about how aggression was built up. He will turn nasty when he is treated with kindness, and becomes very docile under punishment or frustration. He is excessively polite and cooperative as long as he is kept in a subordinate position, but when he is put in command of other men, he becomes tyrannical and overbearing.

A superior officer who has these characteristics will not treat with sternness a subordinate who rebels against his show of authority. Instead he meets such insubordination by becoming very pleasant or even propitiatory.

Such peculiar behavior is often the result of too severe punishment of self-assertion or aggressiveness in childhood. This man is carrying around his own grouches and resentments bottled up inside him. He is deeply anxious to punish and hurt other people. But as long as he is faced with the threat of punishment himself, he retains his childhood fear of showing his feelings. As soon as other people treat him decently, and appear no longer like a threat to him, then his meanness lashes out.

People who have this curious reversal of the normal reaction to other people's kindness or aggressiveness often like to boast that they are "tough" or hard, and that they "respect a man who will stand up to them." This boast is an explanation that fools many people—even including the explainer himself. Actually the "respect" they claim to feel is nothing but an unconscious fear—a secret fear that the rebellious subordinate will punish them.

Such men make poor leaders. They are unable to maintain discipline. They make their subordinates angry and uncooperative. They work best when alone.

The good leader is not afraid of criticism from his subordinates. He will encourage it as a constructive and cooperative way of eliminating causes for resentment and dissension. And he will use it himself in dealing with his subordinates. But the criticism should be constructive and directed at the true cause of the difficulty—not at some imagined evil or some harmless and defenseless person or group. It should not be a means of "passing the buck."

Here are some rules for critics to keep in mind:

331

(1) Stick to things that *can* be corrected: don't criticize dead issues or unalterable situations.

(2) Be *specific:* keep to concrete issues. Say *what.*

(3) *Limit* the issue: don't blame "the brasshats" or "the men" in general. Say *who.*

(4) Suggest *practical* solutions to problems: don't arouse emotion without suggesting what to do about it. Say *how.*

(5) Stick to *facts:* don't swallow rumors, especially Axis-inspired rumors.

(6) Criticize leaders or men for their *acts* and policies, not for their personalities.

(7) Put blame where it belongs. Don't find scapegoats.

XIV: FOOD AND SEX AS MILITARY PROBLEMS

In the Army the needs of the vigorously exercised body—sleep, food and sex—become matters of primary urgency and concern.

The rule that a well-balanced diet is essential to the sustained efficiency of the soldier has never before been so generally acknowledged and applied. Except under hard conditions of combat or prolonged siege, and during periods of training for hardship, a soldier in the Army of the United States can count on being provided at all times with an abundance of nourishing food. If he eats what is set before him, he will get all the proteins, carbohydrates, fats, vitamins, minerals, and water he needs to keep him in good fighting shape.

And men, like children and animals, are so constituted that if all the different elements of diet are available to them, their own appetites will urge them to eat what they need if (and this is an important if) they have not acquired peculiar likes or dislikes, addictions or aversions, as a result of past experiences.

But a man can suffer from hidden hunger in the midst of plenty if he eats only meat and dessert and leaves untouched the spinach, the eggs, the carrots, or whatever he may have taken a finicky dislike to.

And psychologists know that men can also eat all their bodies require of good food and still come away from the table hungry. This is often observed among men in any army, especially among those recently come into the service.

They feel hungry and think the hunger is for food, but actually it is for other satisfactions which throughout their lives have been intimately associated with eating. They may not realize it, but often the truth is they have become homesick. They are longing for those upon whose presence and affection they have long depended. They want their wives or mothers.

Because they are not completely aware of what it is they need, they may smoke or drink to excess or may eat quantities of candy or ice cream. Or, paradoxical as it seems, they may do just the opposite and develop a sudden aversion to food.

The confusion in men's minds as to just what they want is due partly to the fact that the two great desires of the flesh—hunger for food and hunger for sex—become joined or mixed in curious ways and modified and extended through experience, so that hunger for one is frequently expressed as hunger for the other.

Every young man has, from the time of his birth, satisfied his hunger for food by sucking, biting, and chewing. That is why these activities are so pleasant even though they do not actually serve to relieve hunger. That is why men find such pleasure and release from tension in sucking on a pipe or a cigarette, or in chewing gum or nuts or candy, or in drinking either soft or hard liquor.

But the satisfaction of hunger has also been closely associated ever since the earliest months of his life with the loving care and affection of another person —first his mother, later, perhaps his wife.

It is for this reason, quite as much as because of actual nutritional needs, that an army marches on its stomach. Well-fed, the soldier feels valued as an individual, his morale is high. Ill-fed, he tends to feel lonely and rejected and discriminated against, unless he understands clearly about such feelings or has been trained to undergo hunger.

Recognition of these facts will enable the soldier to use the post exchange with discretion. When he feels in the dumps or under strain, or tense, whether in camp or in the field, a smoke, a chew of gum, or a bite of candy gives him a temporary consolation. But if he does too much of this in the unconscious hope of satisfying deeper needs for nourishment or love, he will merely upset his stomach and deprive himself of getting a good square meal at his mess.

The second great desire of the flesh is sex. The purely biological basis for this need is in the more or less periodic swelling of the sex glands which drives the individual to seek relief. But in the course of a man's life, this need is modified, changed and disguised.

In training films, instruction booklets, and man-to-man talks by medical officers, the soldier gets what information he needs about the physiological side of sex life. He learns about the dangers of venereal disease and what is necessary to avoid them or to cure them promptly. He learns about the way prostitutes can contribute to the defeat of an army.

Some men are disgusted by this instruction and some are scared. It is important that they have the instruction, but seeing the films can have either good or bad results. The instruction may help to keep them free of venereal disease, yet it may also make trouble for them psychologically by increasing their personal problems. It is not easy for a man to get his sexual life into wise and proper adjustment.

But the purely physical side of the Army's sex problem is only part of the story. The average soldiers' sex needs are only partly physical.

The sex drive is one of the most plastic of all human desires, capable of an almost infinite number of combinations with other needs. Craving for affection, attention, and love may disturb the life of a fighting man as much as the purely physical urge of sex. This happens for the same reason that the needs associated with hunger are in many ways as important to a man's well-being and military fitness as his purely biological need for food.

The strength of the sex drive varies in different men and at different times in the same man. At one extreme it is apparently absent; at the other it is an abnormally intense compulsion. All normal men feel it keenly at times.

In some men the sexual instinct is expressed as a direct and not-to-be-denied demand. When excited strongly, especially under the influence of alcohol, almost any woman, the easier the better, will serve to reduce the pent-up tension. It is chiefly these men who acquire and spread venereal disease, the control of which has become a medical problem of the first magnitude throughout the world. In other men the sexual drive is as a rule more strictly governed, more selective in its choice of satisfying object. In still others it is largely inhibited for one reason or another; sometimes being sufficiently stimulated and appeased by moderate halfway practices, such as dancing and necking.

The soldier whose standards are such that he can indulge in promiscuous sexual activity without disgust or feeling of guilt may have a good fighting spirit and be an efficient soldier. Provided the urgency of his need does not drive him to go AWOL, or become so careless he catches a venereal disease, he may have high individual morale.

Such a sexually promiscuous man may, however, seriously disturb the morale of other men compelled to associate with him. His behavior and loose talk may rouse the sexual needs of men of more complicated character who cannot resort to such direct satisfaction without a resulting mental conflict and remorse.

The typical man in the Army cannot find true satisfaction with prostitutes or in other promiscuous relationships. Most men choose a sexual partner, not solely for the relief of purely sexual tensions, but for the satisfaction of much more complex needs.

Many men will have already chosen such a person before they come into the service— a sweetheart, fiancée, or a wife. Separation from home, for soldiers of this kind, means much more than merely sexual deprivation. It means the loss of innumerable and unnameable delights of feminine companionship and love.

If the cherished one at home sends constant reassurances of undeviating faithfulness, expressions of pride in what her man is doing for his country, and gifts and letters in abundance, the soldier will find it much less difficult to keep his spirits high and resolutions firm.

If, however, a soldier is denied these substitute satisfactions, then the feeling of aloneness, especially if he half-consciously wants to make his own girl suffer for her neglect of him, may drive him to seek sexual satisfaction with other women. Yet he will not be able to do this without conflict with conscience and feelings of guilt which lower his efficiency and morale as a soldier.

For men who are dependent upon the company of women, but who are trying to be faithful to the girl back home, dances, parties, dinners, and entertainment in private homes may keep them from feeling starved for feminine companionship and so help them to get along without resort to direct satisfaction of their sexual needs. This holds true, regardless of the length of separation from sweetheart or wife or the degree of deprivation of the sexual need.

Soldiers with normal sex drive who have had no contact with women for long periods of time, regardless of whether the deprivation is due to isolation from women, or to a self-imposed denial of sex impulses, may have sexual fantasies. This should not cause worry. Such fantasies are as natural as are the hungry man's preoccupation with thoughts of food during the day and dreams of feasts at night.

The sexual fantasies which occur as night dreams may be accompanied by emissions. There is nothing abnormal about this under conditions of privation. It is a harmless and natural outlet for sexual tensions which at the time cannot be relieved in any other way. They are a substitute form of satisfaction even though they are not sought, and a man need not be worried about what he does in his dreams.

Though a more active and willed expression of sex, it is still a substitute when a man relieves his sexual tension by himself. To do this is not abnormal or physically harmful if it is only resorted to as a temporary outlet, and if the man does not feel guilty or worried about it. But if a man exaggerates the physical or mental consequences of this act, or feels that it has deep moral consequences, he may thus gain his sexual relief only at the cost of great mental suffering. If, in spite of such fears of the consequences, he still can't control this impulse, a state of anxiety may result. The worry and sense of guilt and shame may be enough to exhaust a man and interfere with his work. It may actually incapacitate him for army life. Yet this failure would not be due to the physical effect of the soldier's act itself, but to his worry about it—worry based either on misinformation as to the effect or on a strong moral sense of guilt.

When, however, this habit is resorted to not as a substitute, but as the man's preferred form of sexual gratification, it is definitely abnormal. It is a sign of the kind of ingrown personality which makes a man capable of sex interest only in himself. Such men avoid women even when their company is available. They are abnormally girl-shy. They can't mix with others. They may be actually mentally ill.

Because of his eccentricity, a man of this kind in the Army may easily become the butt of jokes and gibes from others, and may suffer a degree of unhappiness that may in turn lead him to other "crazy" behavior and perhaps even to suicide. For that reason it may be necessary to discharge such persons from the service.

Although medical officers at the induction centers try to keep them out of the Army, a sexually abnormal man who finds satisfaction only with other men may get in. Some of these men have no feelings of inferiority or shame, no mental conflict, over their homosexuality, and readily apply their interest and energy to the tasks of army life. If they are content with quietly seeking the satisfaction of their sexual needs with others of their own kind, their perversion may continue to go unnoticed and they may even become excellent soldiers.

But if, as not infrequently happens, such a man forces his attentions upon normal men, there develops a situation of such gravity for the whole group that the court-martial and discharge of the man from the Army is necessary. Attempts to reform such men are almost always futile.

The man whose homosexuality develops for the first time in a situation where he cannot have normal sexual satisfaction may be only mildly disturbed by what he has done, but it is more likely that he will suffer from mental conflict. He will feel inferior to other men, ashamed and worried for fear he will become a confirmed homosexual and become unable to enjoy normal sexual intercourse when he gets back home. Or he will feel afraid of being found out and punished by dishonorable discharge and a long sentence; or he will suffer strong feelings of guilt. Or he may have all these feelings at once.

340

So long as he is thus seriously worried and dissatisfied with himself, the chances are that he may be all right again when he returns to normal conditions of life. But he should put up a strong fight with himself to control his homosexual impulses and find some other outlet for his sex drive as soon as he can.

Strictly speaking, there are no real substitutes for sexual satisfaction. And there is no way to kill the sex need. The best many men can hope for is to succeed in avoiding the things that will stir up or increase their desires to uncontrollable extremes. They should keep their minds off feelings of deprivation as much as possible by hard work and strict attention to the job of winning the war, and should find what helpful outlets they can for the release of their emotions.

A soldier can take what comfort he may in the knowledge that other men are confronted with just about the same problems as he is, and that, while they may never find an escape from them, most men manage to endure them and do not allow them to impair their efficiency seriously.

It helps to work hard.

It helps to avoid the company of those who are preoccupied with sex.

It helps to get as much fun as possible. Companionship with the other men and the varied social activities of camp life keep a soldier from lonely brooding and day-dreaming. So does the intensive physical activity of campaign and battle. For those who enjoy them, athletic sports—boxing matches or ball games—are diverting and healthful.

Band concerts, mass singing, and dancing are ways of "letting off steam" by stirring and expressing emotions other than those of sex.

Religion is the greatest help to many men. The Catholic man may find comfort and new strength through telling his worries and confessing his acts or his feelings of guilt to his priest. Many devout men find relief for their loneliness and tension in prayer and the songs and services of the chapel.

Some men think their troubles out seriously and decide that they are pretty small compared to the great troubles of the world that have caused this war. And they figure that personal deprivation is simply a part of the service their country and civilization need of them.

But since the only real permanent relief for the pangs of sex longing can be obtained through speeding the victory and return to home, the soldier will find that putting his whole heart into the business of training for war and destroying the enemy will give him the greatest peace of mind. Whatever he does in this spirit to speed victory will also serve to strengthen the emotional ties with those at home who are also working for the same end through sacrifice and war production.

Such ties help. And it helps if the loved ones at home—his girl, his mother—keep sending him evidences of their affection in letters, pictures, and gifts. These are aids but not true substitutes. For love there is no substitute. For the pangs of separation there is no perfect cure, except winning the war and getting home to the loved ones again.

XV: THE SOLDIER'S PERSONAL ADJUSTMENT

IN A DEMOCRATIC, civilian army, millions of men are suddenly, abruptly thrown into a new way of life. It is in many ways a tough life.

Men, used to going their own ways, choosing their own jobs, associates, neckties, times for going to bed, now have to follow military orders about all these things.

Men accustomed to a comfortable litter of belongings around them, find the bare neatness of policed barracks hard to get used to. Those used to steam heat, warm shower baths, and breakfast eggs cooked just three and a half minutes at home, may be pretty uncomfortable when they have to put up with a bed on the ground and cold water for shaves.

There is, moreover, no privacy in the Army. If a man oversleeps and his corporal dumps him out of his bunk, the whole company knows about it. If he looks at his girl's photograph a lot, they know that too. The business of living in a gold-fish bowl and having to take razzing from his fellow soldiers is about the hardest thing for a sensitive recruit to get used to.

Not every man, of course, meets hardships for the first time when he goes into the Army. Some have known hunger and cold and hard work. Some never saw a flush toilet or a shower bath before they got to camp; some never had a good square meal, well

343

cooked. For them, the Army is providing luxuries.

But farmer, lawyer, banker, section hand, college man or man of little schooling—they all must adjust themselves to an entirely new way of living. All must learn new habits.

Young men may find it easier to make the adjustment than older men, because they are ordinarily a little more flexible, with habits a little less fixed. But most men can fit themselves into the new life and work without too much friction. Those who do it most easily are the ones who accept the new life at once, throw off civilian habits with civilian clothes, and put themselves wholeheartedly into becoming soldiers.

One of the hardest adjustments comes with the loss of contact with friends and family. The soldier who misses friends at home is slow about making new friends at camp. He may hear from home, but letters are not full comfort to a homesick soldier. He probably wouldn't admit it, but worst of all for him is the fact that there are no women in the Army. He misses his girl friend, his wife, or his mother. And he secretly longs for someone in skirts to bake him a cake, mend his socks, put away his belongings, or comfort him when he is tired and aching from the hard work of training.

The Army is as liberal with furloughs as war permits for such homesick men, when they first go into service. But the real remedy is not in hurried trips home or long-distance telephone calls. It is in the building up of new interests and ties in and around camp. If the war and the safety of the world didn't demand their services, most American soldiers would rather be home than where they are. But they are all in the same situation, are all doing the same big job together. And this bond of sympathy often leads to friendships much closer than those made in civilian life.

Men in the first AEF sometimes came to think and speak of their units as "all one family." That is morale. It is the same in this war. To the growth of such morale each man can contribute something. An officer can contribute more. The best kind of leadership supplies the sense of solidarity—one for all and all for one—that goes with enthusiastic cooperative working and fighting.

INDIVIDUALISM AND COOPERATION

One of the fears that many men have to overcome or adjust to, when they first go into the Army, is the feeling that they may lose their identity—their freedom of individual expression.

From reveille to taps, there is little if any opportunity for the new recruit to do anything he is not told to do. Whether he wants to or not, he must get up at the sound of the bugle, put on the prescribed uniform, march when he is commanded, stand at attention when he is ordered to do so—even with a mosquito biting him. No longer does he eat when he is hungry or go to sleep when he is tired. All conduct seems to be according to order. Is this really a fight for freedom and democracy?

Of course it is. But conformity and discipline are necessary for the efficient operation of an army. They cannot be relaxed for the benefit of the new recruit who chafes at constraint. Habits will have to

345

become so firmly set that they will not fail when the violent emotions of battle drive everything else from the mind. They form a "backlog" of conduct, a set of essential, life-preserving actions that can be depended upon no matter what the emergency.

The soldier's best ally in adjusting to this imposed restraint is humor. Perhaps he will never quite grow to like it, but, when he realizes that routine is necessary for his own welfare as well as that of the Army, he can put up with it and even grin when he is assigned to the more unpleasant jobs that have to be done.

After all, what kind of Army would we have if every man did what he pleased—if soldiers were permitted to throw their clothing in a heap, to spit on the floor, to burn lights at all hours, or to sleep until noon?

Most men soon work out their own ways of getting along under discipline without fretting too much or blowing up and landing in the guard house. Some take it out in endless griping. They gripe about the coffee, the K.P., the bus service, the sergeant and innumerable other small things that do not really matter in the war. They let off steam.

And most new soldiers take full advantage of weekend or evening passes and of furloughs to get a change from a regulated existence and let loose a bit. They get relief then, so that when they go back to duty they can accept the discipline with a good grace—even with enthusiasm.

For the best way to find individuality again in the Army and to stand out on your own in among thousands in the same uniform is to do a bang-up good job of soldiering. In this new Army of the United States, a real attempt is being made to find individual skills and aptitudes in order to place the men who show any sign of special abilities where they will be of the greatest use to the Army. Officers are constantly on the lookout for the man who is a little out of the ordinary, who has a special knack at some certain job. And the man, who takes pains to do a little more than he is required to do, and who does it a little better than what will just get by, will soon be wearing stripes.

The greatest relief from irksomeness of constraint is, however, to like it. And why not? It is not so bad if you look at it the right way. Especially for the man who has had a great deal of responsibility in civilian life, it is a relief to have much of his thinking done for him. In the Army he need not worry about where tomorrow's dinner is coming from, whether he will have any money left to buy a winter overcoat, or how he is to find time to do all the work piling up on his desk.

A SOLDIER'S WORRIES

As a unit gets nearer to combat new worries develop. Actual battle is likely to increase them.

There is, first, the fear of death. It is best met by accepting the possibility of death as a natural part of the job, and by being careful not to lose a sense of proportion about it. No soldier is so important that he is justified in thinking the enemy is aiming every bullet, bomb, and shell at him. Besides, there are a great many men in the Army, and only a small proportion get hit in battle. And the greater part

347

of those who get hit will live and get well-earned relief from the strain of combat. After that there may be a purple heart decoration and some glory.

And soldiers who have been through the worst of warfare are inclined to say that only a fool wants to live forever. They usually add the warning: "But, if you must die, make your death count for something. Don't throw your life away by taking needless chances."

There is also the civilian's natural horror of the unaccustomed sight and smell of death and bloodshed. A major in the first AEF, who was one of the greatly loved officers of that great adventure, helped his men to overcome this repugnance by teaching them that consideration for their friends must go on after death. He taught them to see to it that the body of a friend gets thoughtful care and a decent burial. This is also taught in our present Army.

This inspired officer had built up excellent morale in his battalion. The men in it were welded together into a close-knit group of friends and comrades. They would crawl out into the hazards of no-man's-land to bring in the body of a comrade who had fallen even if they had to gather it up in a basket. This sort of affection made death seem a less complete cutting off. And each man came to think of his own death with less horror because he knew that the tie of comradeship would carry on even then.

Sensitive men may also worry or feel guilty over killing enemy soldiers—other men in action. Unless they understand this worry and face it squarely, they may head into trouble, because killing is the main job of a combat soldier.

348

From the earliest childhood, American boys are taught that it is wrong—the greatest wrong—to kill. This principle is learned so early that it becomes a part of them. As boys grow up they forget most of what happened in infancy and early childhood; few people, in fact, can remember much of what happened in their first three years. Yet they retain within themselves the attitudes formed during their earliest years. They don't remember ever learning them—it seems as if they have always felt that way. If a man did not learn that it was wrong to kill until he was grown, he would learn it then with his mind, and it would be easy to lay aside that rule when war or emergency make it necessary for him to kill.

But the don'ts learned in earliest childhood become the voice of conscience in the adult. They seem to be absorbed rather than learned. And, even though his mind tells a grown up man that the execution of criminals is justified, his emotions may rebel. Then, if duty forces him to kill, he may go ahead and do it, but afterwards he will feel a vague uneasiness, an anxiety—his conscience won't rest.

Some men, strictly brought up, may even get sick at the stomach at the sight of the limp, pathetic body of a rabbit that has been shot.

The cure for the anxiety that results from this kind of conflict between conscience and reason is to understand it. Once a man realizes that the feeling is natural in men brought up, as the average American is, to respect human life, this particular worry won't haunt him so much. He may have a few bad dreams, but that won't interfere with doing the job ahead, disagreeable though it may be.

The Healthy Mind

To be at his best, a soldier must keep his mind fit as well as his body. He must be mentally alert and accurately aware of his surroundings. He must shoulder responsibility willingly, and accept the dictates of superior officers without resentment. He must be able to get along with other men without undue friction and with mutual pleasure.

The marks of a man with healthy mind or personality are:

(1) He uses his abilities with enthusiasm and satisfaction, although not always with happiness.

(2) He wants to do something worth while, to pull his load and not be carried by others.

(3) He gets along with other persons, including his superiors and those with whom he has a difference of opinion.

(4) When he is disappointed, or meets with deprivation or strain, he faces the situation with constructive ideas and a fighting spirit, not with fear, rage, hopelessness or suspicion. So then he does not suffer from indigestion, headache or pain, which, though not at all voluntary, may be produced by mental troubles.

(5) He perseveres in the effort to solve a problem or complete a task in spite of difficulty and disappointment.

(6) He likes to give as well as to take.

Why Some Men Break in the Army

Men selected for induction into the Army are picked because they are strong and in good health, mentally as well as physically. Yet in spite of careful

350

selection and expert care, men in the Army do fall ill. They may catch something like measles or influenza, but they may also develop non-infectious kinds of sickness such as heart disease or mental disease.

Some break down mentally, because they are just not fitted for Army life. They never should have been inducted in the first place. Physicians at induction centers watch carefully for the signs of beginning mental illness, but nevertheless some do slip by.

Detection of mental illness is not quite so clear-cut as the detection of some disease like tuberculosis. You can't take an X-ray plate that will show up the weak spots in a man's mind.

The physician who is trying to judge whether a man is mentally fit must decide how that man would act when put with other men—how he would behave in training camp—in battle. Experience with many other men who have failed to stand up under strain teaches the physician many of the subtle symptoms of coming breakdown. He can spot these. But the specialist on mental and nervous illness is accustomed, in private practice to devote many hours to examination of a man before he is ready to declare him fit or not. In an Army induction center he has only a few minutes. And he must examine a great many men on the same day. As one physician put it, "When you have examined 70 men on the same day, you may miss some of the tell-tale signs in the 71st man. A physician gets tired, too."

But physicians making the Army induction examination try their best to reject not only men who are

351

already in the early stages of an illness, but also those who, although they can get along all right in civilian life, would break down under the tough life of a soldier. Naturally, they miss a few, nevertheless about eight per cent of all men examined are rejected on this ground.

Even in ordinary civilian life, a great many men break down and become mentally ill. These illnesses may not show up until a man is in his twenties or thirties or later. Before that, it is not obvious to most people, not even his family or intimate friends, that he is not quite well and normal.

It has been estimated that one person out of every dozen in the United States can expect to go to a mental hospital for at least brief treatment at some time before he dies. Of course some of these men get into the Army. Army physicians know that they must expect some mental illness among the troops, just as they must expect some heart disease and tuberculosis. But because its men are carefully selected, there is less of mental illness in the Army than there is among civilians.

In addition to those men who seem foredoomed to develop a mental illness, there are other men who break in the Army under battle conditions. These are real battle casualties, just as much as if they had lost a leg.

A man in battle may receive a blow on the head that will cause injury to the brain. That is serious, particularly if he is a leader responsible for the direction and safety of his men. Since the brain itself has no sense organs, a man does not feel pain when his brain is injured, and he may think he has not been badly hurt. But even what seems like a slight wound in the head must be looked after carefully. Usually the wounded man should be relieved from duty. If even a small part of his brain is hurt, or if his head has received a hard blow which does not even crack the skull, nevertheless he is likely to be confused or to act in a peculiar way in battle.

A direct blow on the head is not the only way a man's brain can be injured. The blast of a shell nearby can cause harm to the brain. Modern helmets, however, protect a soldier's ears and his brain very well.

Besides these direct injuries to the brain, men in battle can suffer shocks to the mind. Every man has his limit, mentally as well as physically. There are strains which no man, however tough-minded, can endure. Modern battle has pushed closer and closer to these final limits of man's endurance.

Gruelling hardships, great fatigue, prolonged loss of sleep, blistering heat, intense cold, high altitudes, great pressures below the sea—these are all conditions that put a dangerous strain on mind as well as body.

When a man must go through these things and then in addition suffer the strain of seeing his friends killed, of being in constant peril of his own life, of dealing out death with his own hands, there may come a time when the strongest man's mind will sicken.

Such a sufferer from war shock is not a weakling, he is not a coward. He is a battle casualty. If given psychiatric first aid promptly, he will probably recover to take his place again in a battle unit. If neglected, however, he may become permanently ill, or

353

may even seek relief from his mental wounds in death.

MENTAL DANGER SIGNALS

Mental first aid is just as important as physical first aid for preventing casualties and losses to the service.

If a man can be relieved of duty for a time, given a rest when he needs it urgently, he can usually be counted upon to come back to the combat presently with fresh zest and vigor. If, however, he is allowed to go on past his mental breaking point without let-up—if he is permitted to wait until he collapses or until the urgency of his needs makes him go on sick call voluntarily—the chances are much smaller for his rapid recovery.

Emotional or mental fatigue follows the same kind of law as muscular fatigue. When a man pulls a weight of about twelve pounds with one finger and gets a rest of ten seconds after every pull, the finger muscle shows no fatigue. But if he keeps on pulling until his finger is completely fatigued, it will take him two hours to recover. And if he should go on trying to pull the weight even after complete fatigue, the recovery period is prolonged even further.

It is the responsibility of the company officer to spot the men who need help and to see that they get help from the medical officer before it is too late for speedy recovery. Here are some of the danger signals run up by the mind that has had too much punishment.

The first thing to look for is anything that makes a man stand out in an awkward or queer way from

354

the others in his unit—anything that makes him look odd to the other men, marks him as "not belonging." Does he stay by himself too much? Does he go for long periods without speaking? Is he known to other men as having queer ideas? Does he find conditions intolerable that other men get along under all right? Is he a problem in the outfit —refusing certain foods, wetting the bed, following strange or peculiar practices? Does the sergeant regard him as peculiar?

Another thing to look for is any sudden change in the soldier's own personality. If he is a man who has been in the outfit for a while, it is easy to note a complete reversal of habits or attitudes. When the ordinarily cheerful man becomes moody and depressed. When the quiet, orderly soldier becomes boisterous and noisy and a disciplinary problem. When the neat, well-groomed man becomes dirty and disheveled—lets his shoes go unshined, his uniform unbuttoned, hair uncombed. When the dependable man goes AWOL, starts drinking hard. These things are signs of mental trouble. They should be looked into. The guard house may not be any help at all—sometimes it even makes things worse.

When a man has been through a particularly trying experience, in combat without relief for a long period, under steady bombing or gunfire without protection, cut off from other troops, or lost at sea, more acute signs of war nerves may show up. All the men should know that these signs are the natural result of fear and war strain. They do not mean that a man has gone "insane." But they do mean that he needs care, rest, medical attention and mental first aid. These signs are:

Inability to sleep. Terrible nightmares in which the battle is repeated over and over. Inability to eat. Buzzing or humming in his ears. Shakiness, general weakness, weakness in certain parts of the body, as the knees or the wrists. Dizziness. Peculiar feelings in the heart—fluttering, pounding, skipping a beat. Difficult breathing. Restlessness combined with a feeling of being penned in—an overwhelming desire to push people and walls out of the way.

Rest is the principal cure for these indications of "war nerves"—rest and the care of a medical man who understands such cases, and an understanding on the part of the soldier of what is wrong with him. These feelings are natural enough in anyone who has gone through the difficult conditions of combat, but they are very frightening to a man who did not expect them—even more distressing than the shells or bombs or torpedoes themselves.

Officers who understand these matters can do a great deal to relieve the men's fears of war nerves and to prevent them by their own calm recognition of the fact of nerves and of their cause.

How the Mind Protects Itself

The body has defense mechanisms. So has the mind.

Touch a hot piece of metal and instantly you have withdrawn your hand before you know what you are doing. If something flies toward your face, you shut your eyes without stopping to decide to close them. These are natural means for self-protection.

356

When the mind is attacked by unpleasant ideas, dangerous fears, it, too, has its way of withdrawing or of turning away and shutting out what cannot be endured.

When you see a man of ordinary good common sense become strangely blind to facts—refuse to believe that his lost brother has really been killed, or refuse to see that he himself is to blame for a disastrous failure—that man's mind is automatically protecting itself from a truth so bitter that he can't take it. It might be dangerous, even were it possible, to convince such a man of the actual facts. He might, if compelled to face them, commit suicide. That has happened more than once.

An obstinate refusal to accept the truth on the part of a man of ordinary good judgment is a danger signal, just as a fever of 103 degrees is a signal of serious physical danger.

Don't try to argue with such a man. He should be given rest or a furlough from the duty and strain. It is apparent that his mind is hard hit. When he is fit again, he will be able to see clearly once more. He will rid himself of his delusions just as the fever patient does when his temperature goes back to normal.

But it is only when the mind's natural protective mechanisms are used to an excessive or unreasonable extent that they point to a sick or exhausted mind. Every normal man uses them daily to some extent.

This is the way they work:

1. *Passing the buck*. You see this every day. When a man fails or is humiliated, he can shrug it off or freely admit his own fault only if the failure is trivial

and did not mean much to him, or if he has a strong character. If the failure is a great personal tragedy, all but the man of an extraordinary strength of character will try to put the blame on someone or something else. The man who thus fails will seize upon any plausible excuse. He blames the weather, the man who gave him wrong advice, or the man who got in his way. Sometimes he may even imagine a plot against himself, and persuade himself that "everybody is down on him." Humiliation and defeat are hard to bear. Instinctively, every man wants to try at once to get out from under when blame hangs over him.

Habits of good sportsmanship usually prevent him from doing so, but still in his own mind or among friends he will say, "But it wasn't my fault."

2. *The false front.* When a man is worried by the fear—perhaps only half consciously but deep in his heart—that he has a serious fault or weakness, what does he do? He puts up a great show of being just the opposite sort of person. If the man is stupid or ineffective, yet feels the need to be strong and sure, he will overdo in his efforts to impress people—he will be loud, boisterous, and cocky. A naturally effeminate man may try to demonstrate his virility by telling smutty stories or by recounting daring adventures or sexual exploits. These adventures and exploits, in fact, may never have occurred except as tame events which are exaggerated in his imagination. The timid person may do foolhardy stunts seeking to prove his bravery. The man who is really courageous, strong and manly seldom feels any need to demonstrate it. He just takes himself for granted.

358

3. *Taking it out on the dog.* The man who suffers an injury and is not strong enough to hit back may literally take it out on the dog, or may go around looking for trouble with someone he can talk back to or punch in the nose. This keeps happening, with some men in the Army, because disappointments and punishments are necessarily handed out by superior officers against whom there is no way to get even. Or it may happen in a unit under continuous enemy bombing or shelling. The strain of having to sit and take it may cause a high degree of irritation and friction among the men—unless they can keep busy. Then they take it out by energetic work.

4. *Borrowed virtue.* A more constructive or helpful sort of mental self-protection mechanism is the action of a man who feels weak or inadequate by himself and who gains a feeling of strength and superiority by attaching himself to a stronger man or to a strong group. It was this that sent so many men to the recruiting stations on the morning after Pearl Harbor. As a man, alone, you feel powerless in the face of threatening dangers. As a United States soldier, you know that you can go anywhere in the world, avenge wrongs and protect your treasured way of life.

5. *Sick call.* When your mind is called upon to face something you dread terribly, your body may come promptly to your rescue. The aviation student who really dreads to go up for his first solo, feeling sure he is going to crack up his plane, may develop a convenient but real headache on that day. But when the situation involves something more serious

than a student's cold feet over going "on his own," the ailment that develops is likely to be more serious, too. Some Jews in German concentration camps have gone blind when faced with the necessity of looking at a fellow-prisoner's torture or other things just too horrible to watch. Men may become paralyzed for similar reasons. It is easy to accuse such a person of faking, but what has happened to his mind is not the result of any conscious attempt to get out of dreaded duties or experiences. It is Nature's way of protecting man's mind against those things that it is just not strong enough to bear.

6. *Transferred feelings.* The mental habits of childhood are usually carried on in more or less disguised form all during life. This is sometimes good and sometimes bad for the adult, depending upon what sort of childhood he had. If a boy is abused by his father so that he learns to hate him, the man he becomes will go on hating not only the father, but anyone who looks like him or is a reminder of him. Since the father is so often the one who gives orders and is the head in the child's home, anyone in a position of authority—an officer, say—may become the object of unreasoning hatred from such a victim of parental abuse. It is this characteristic of the human mind that accounts for many of the disciplinary problems in the Army as well as for much crime in civilian life.

THE WAR WITHIN THE MAN

It might be much easier to defeat the enemy if men could only win in some way the conflicts that very often go on within themselves.

A man so often wants to do two opposite things at the same time. And he wants desperately to do both. He wants to dominate other men and yet be liked by them. He wants to give vent to his anger, but he doesn't want to get into hot water. He wants to gain promotion, yet he doesn't want to do hard work. Above all, he wants to be a brave and true soldier—to keep the soldier's faith—and yet he wants to live.

How to be brave and safe—that is the greatest psychological problem for the soldier. Most of the war neuroses (mental illness) result from the failure of men to find any sort of satisfactory way out of that dilemma.

Many of those who do find the answer find it in the mental security of cooperative bravery in the fighting Army unit. Or they find another substitute —they learn to want permanence for the things they love instead of trying desperately to hang onto life itself.

Every man is equipped with two kinds of deep-seated desires or instincts. Often these two conflict. One set has to do with his relations with other men —he wants to be one of the gang, appreciated and admired by the others, and he even likes to sacrifice himself for the good of the group to which he belongs, whether it is family, church, Army or nation. But he has also another set of desires that cannot ever be entirely denied, desires connected with himself—his life, his comfort, his personal freedom.

When war starts, when the nation is threatened or parts of it endangered, the desire to be patriotic, to be with the other fellows fighting back becomes a major driving force. The social instincts are very strong. They are reenforced when at every turn we see men in uniform and the flag waving, hear bands, speeches, propaganda, the Star Spangled Banner and the stirring service songs.

To join up gives men a sense of important service and security—for the time being.

But no amount of patriotic fervor can wholly kill or drown out the calls of the more personal instincts. Only a few rush to enlist with no misgivings. For most men there is some concern or distress in making the decision to leave home, family and job in order to join the service of the country.

In the course of the tough, hard work of military training and all the personal sacrifices involved, the social instincts nearly always have to take some punishment. The newness or glamor of military life fades. The personal instincts are reinforced. Then a man may begin to ask himself what he is getting out of it anyway.

But a move to the war theater and an advance to close contact with the enemy usually brings a crisis in the battle within the soldier as well as in the battle against the enemy. When a man finds himself close indeed to death, then his instinct of self-preservation, one of the most powerful urges every normal man has, makes every fiber of his being protest against facing the danger.

Yet his comrades, his officers, his country are all counting on him to do his bit. A pretty big bit—risking his own life. Yet they are counting on him.

If the personal instincts win the struggle, the man, when contact with the enemy forces is made, will run away or will surrender. If the social instincts prevail, then he is the stuff of which all good soldiers, all heroes are made. Most men who have traveled the hard path of Army life up to the front lines put up a good fight once they get there.

For a few, however, this struggle ends in a stalemate—a compromise. That is what a war neurosis is—a compromise in this internal conflict. If a man goes on being torn by his conflicting desires—if he cannot bring himself to go forward, yet is too conscientious to give up—he will suffer from the type of neurosis characterized by anxiety. He finds he can no longer concentrate. He becomes confused. The expression on his face, his pulse rate, his rapid breathing betray the fierce battle going on within him. He himself may not be fully aware of the cause of the terrible sense of fear and horror that seems to hang over him. Yet he is, in a way, solving his problem. He is making himself too inefficient to continue in the fight, yet giving himself so much suffering that his conscience cannot accuse him of taking the easy way out. Yet, even so, he does not know that he is doing all this. His nervous system does it for him.

Another result of unsolved mental conflict is the loss of memory. A soldier in such a predicament may be found wandering aimlessly around. He can't remember what regiment or company he belongs to. He may not even be able to tell his own name. He may be blind or deaf or partly paralyzed.

The man who suffers in any of these ways is not to be blamed. He is not a coward. If he were, he would have no conflict. He would see to it that

363

he was not at the front but in a soft, safe job somewhere at a good distance. If necessary, he would desert. But he does not desert and still he does not fight. He compromises with a difficult unpleasant alternative—one which he does not choose, but which his nervous system chooses for him.

It is, therefore, the failure of the nervous system to withstand such a terrible strain as modern warfare imposes,_that causes these breakdowns—these unfortunate compromises between self-preservation and a genuine desire to sacrifice the self in the cause of right.

The neurotic—it is hard to emphasize this point too strongly—does not understand what is happening to him. He cannot control it. The leader who lectures him, bawls him out, or punishes him for neglect of duty is likely only to increase his trouble.

On the other hand, coddling such men is a mistake, too. What they need is understanding help, the reassurance that comes from a firm, but friendly attitude on the part of those who deal with them. They need the encouragement of assurance that such things happen to the best of men, but that men may get over such difficulties with aid. They need to be told that they will be helped by a good night's sleep, perhaps drug-induced by the medical officer—by a good meal—by rest. And that then they will be expected to return to the fight and do their duty with the others.

In the Spanish Civil War the doctors in the Republican Army got many of their neurotic patients back to the lines in short order. The men whose legs were paralyzed could often crawl. So the doctors arranged for crawling races with prizes, and some of the men got so excited that they got part-way up and half ran to the goal. The men who were blind were given night duty, in which they did not have to see. The doctors were sympathetic but they did not let the men escape all responsibility. It was a good treatment. Lots—not all—of the men got well.

Men differ greatly in their abilities to stand up under this internal, personal conflict. Most men can come successfully through terrorizing experiences, revolting scenes, and exposure to death. War is older than history, and all nations and tribes have resorted to it. While statistics show that the war neuroses present a serious problem to medical officers in the Army, modern methods of psychiatric first-aid treatment continue to salvage the mental casualties produced by these intolerable conflicts.

The average soldier has conflicts, but he settles them himself with no one else the wiser. So he finds himself free to fight with his whole strength. On him—the average, free soldier—victory depends.

Fortunately, the first contact with the enemy is the hardest. In seasoned troops internal conflict diminishes. They have faced the worst and know it is not intolerable. Even soldiers who have to retreat are not defeated, if they have learned to conquer their own fears. They will advance another time, having once won the fight with the inner man, and having faced the reality of battle, finding in it less terror and more opportunity for success than the green recruit could ever have believed possible.

XVI: LEADERSHIP

You Can't Boss a Brick

You can't even boss a dog unless the dog has been trained to obey and has formed habits of responding to commands. And before you can boss him you must know what commands he will respond to. The famous Seeing-Eye dogs can do wonderful things to aid the blind, but both dog and master must first go through a period of training.

Authority is not power. No amount of legal authority over the grizzly bears of British Columbia would enable you to get yourself obeyed by them out in the woods.

Men can be commanded only after they have acquired habits of obeying, and after their leader has learned to give them the commands that make these habits work. All successful leadership thus depends on the habits of those who are to be led.

The officer standing before his men is limited in the direct exercise of his authority by what the troops are able to get through their eyes and ears. And what the men do, in response to what they see and hear the officer do and say, is just exactly what their previous training and their previous experience with him insure that they will do.

When authority is not obeyed, the fault may lie in the manner or speech of the leader or else it may be that the men are in need of basic training.

It is often said that a good leader knows how to

handle his men. Actually, however, it is not possible for any leader to *handle* men. It is himself that he handles. Then the men react to his deportment. And the way in which they react depends, in turn, upon their habits of thought and action.

Discipline

In an army much of this training on which leader-ship depends is established by discipline. Discipline is training in the right habits of attention and obedience. Without such habits we might have a crowd or a mob, but not an army.

It is quite possible to lead a mob, yet such leader-ship is uncertain, depending largely on the accidents of personal appearance and on fortunate timing. In an army, however, there have to be many leaders of many ranks, and they have to be interchangeable. If a leader is killed, another must be ready to take his place and lead his men. And the men who lose a leader must be ready to follow without question the commands of a stranger.

Training in discipline is training in giving attention and obedience to authority, regardless of individual personality. That is why armies are uniformed, why the insignia of rank are standardized. Also, it is why commands and the manner of giving them are fixed. Discipline makes it second nature for the soldier to give attention to the insignia of rank, and obedience to commands.

Learning Obedience

The first requisite of command is attention. What a soldier does not see or hear, he cannot obey.

Attention means stopping all activity that interferes with looking and listening.

If this attention did not become second nature through long practice, an Army leader would, in an emergency, have to compete for attention—by shouting, or gesticulating. That would not do—he might not succeed.

So discipline is calculated to insure this preliminary attention by placing certain restrictions on behavior whenever an officer is present or enters the scene. If loud arguments or profanity or occupation with the soldier's own affairs were permitted to occur in the presence of an officer, then the soldier would learn to disregard the officer, and the officer would lose his ability to command attention and thus his ability to command at all.

If, on the other hand, the presence or arrival of an officer is always the signal to the soldier to come to attention, or, in combat, to pay attention, then no confusion of battle or distraction of pain or noise or close danger can cause a soldier to ignore his officer or his command.

What men do invariably and repeatedly is finally drilled into them—becomes for them second nature. They learn to perform acts or maneuvers in response to command or order because the command or order has always been accompanied by the act and the act by the command.

Mere lecturing never trains men in action. At best it makes them learn mere word sequences, except when the listeners already know enough about the required action to perform it in imagination. Learning something new, in other words, requires participation. You don't learn to swim by taking a correspondence course.

Unfortunately, bad habits, as well as good, can be learned. If, on a spoken command, men do not respond, then they are learning not to respond. Whenever they are ordered to do something they cannot do, they are learning to disobey. Military manuals embody this fact in a rule: *Never give a command that you do not expect to be obeyed.*

Thus a young leader, when he finds himself so situated that his command might be disregarded, must refrain from giving it. He must try first to change the situation, to capture attention, or he must merely wait until he is reasonably certain that, when he gives his order, it will indeed be obeyed.

So attention is the first requisite of command, and practice is the second. The leader must see to it that his men get the right kind of practice. He must never give conflicting orders. He must give only directions that can be executed and then he must see to it that they are executed. Otherwise he loses his own power of command, and discipline is broken down among his men.

The Leader

Through training in discipline the Army prepares its men to carry out its ultimate missions under command and according to plan. Leadership would be uncertain without this discipline.

But a good leader does not depend solely on the authority that discipline gives him as an officer or noncom, for good leadership goes far beyond discipline. A good, experienced leader inspires respect,

369

confidence, and loyalty in his subordinates, all of which enable him to get from his men performance far above what a new leader could command.

In this the leader can rely on the generous co-operation of his men, for men have a natural longing to respect and have affection for their leaders. They want to be proud of their officers and noncommissioned officers, just as they want to be proud of their unit and their branch of the service.

So soldiers look to an officer for that sort of bearing and behavior that leads to his being known as a "grand old man." They don't necessarily want him to be a model of all the virtues; they can forgive him for bursts of temper, for occasional arbitrary commands, for a rare show of weakness—even for tears over the loss of a friend. What they do demand in him is unfailing loyalty to duty and to his men —and the same sort of respect and confidence that the leader expects to receive.

When the new Army was first being formed, many of the officers had had little experience in command. They had learned the words—were capable of giving directions and instructions—but they had learned neither the action nor manner that go with command. A young officer would utter an order, but his manner would betray his lack of confidence. This uncertainty was in effect a signal for not carrying the order out promptly and effectively as military orders must be carried out. All our lives we have depended on the manner and behavior of others, as well as on their speech, to know what was in their minds. Army discipline cannot change human nature.

370

What a soldier does in response to a leader's command depends not only on the words spoken by the leader but also upon the way in which they are said —it depends upon everything the soldier sees and hears.

The leader's facial expression, his movements, his posture and the firmness or quaver in his voice all have their effects. And these effects may completely nullify the effect of the spoken command.

A leader is actually giving conflicting orders if his uncertain manner hints that he does not expect obedience or that he thinks he may not be obeyed.

Although it is possible for the new leader who has lacked experience to imitate the manner and tone of wiser leaders around him, only practice in command develops the appropriate manner and tone.

A good officer or noncom ought to have many imitators of his effective style, yet not of his irrelevant mannerisms. It is hard to keep the two distinct. Every man, unfortunately, forms and keeps many useless habits in gesturing, grimacing, and manipulating. It is not these that should be imitated, but his habits of direct address, clear speech, military manner, confident air, enthusiastic interest, friendliness mixed with reserve both in command and greeting.

Lack of a confident manner inevitably interferes with command. So also may a manner that betrays indecision, for men respond to the signs of indecision by withholding or delaying action. The rule is that a leader should make up his mind and arrive at the decision *before* he gives orders. When he confronts his men, he must be ready to commit himself to this course or that. Men will accept assurance for competence, and they do want competence in a leader.

A judge in a high court recently heard one of the trial lawyers say: "If the Court is in doubt . . ." The Judge rapped the bench and said: "This Court may be occasionally in error, but it is never in doubt." It is the business of a judge to decide cases. No matter how evenly the issue is balanced and no matter how much trouble and time is required for him to reach a decision, the decision, once given, must appear final.

The leader of soldiers finds himself in the same position. On him depends the direction of men's actions. That direction must never be ambiguous. Always it must be clearly indicated.

What Soldiers Think of Leaders

For the first time in the history of armies, the Army of the United States has undertaken to find out what its enlisted personnel think about a large number of things important to the Army.

Some thousands of soldiers have been interviewed at length, and one of the subjects about which they were questioned is Army leadership. What the soldiers said makes it very clear that the quality of leadership in an army is the most important single determiner of morale and performance. The relationship between men and officers, commissioned and noncommissioned, determines the fighting spirit of an army quite as much as the ability of the soldiers to take training does.

In fact it turns out that these human relations are much more important to morale than beefsteak, warm socks, ball games, and vaudeville shows, or what the men believe about war. Among the 150 or so items covered in the interview, 77 proved to be definitely associated with morale, and of the 20 most closely related to morale, 16 have to do with man-officer relations.

What the men think of their leaders is, then, of the utmost importance to the Army and to the successful prosecution of the war.

Roughly, in the order of their association with good leadership in the minds of the enlisted men, are the following points:

(1) Ability. Competence comes first. The good officer must know his stuff, for on this depends the men's confidence in his leadership.

(2) Next to ability is interest in the welfare of the soldier. The officer who can be trusted to help the soldier in time of need, or who would be accessible for personal advice, is a good officer.

(3) "Promptness in making decisions" is next.

(4) "Good teacher or instructor" follows. The leader who has the patience and the ability to make things clear to the men under him is valued for that reason.

(5) "Judgment," "common sense" and the ability to get things done follow next in order.

(6) The good leader does not "boss you around when there is no good reason for it." Soldiers dislike an officer who throws his rank around, who tests his own authority continually. They sense that he is not sure of himself.

(7) "The man who tells you when you have done a good job" rates well as a leader. Failure in commendation is a common complaint among men in the

ranks. The best incentive to good work is the prospect that it will be noticed and remembered by the leader.

(8) Physical strength and good build come next.

(9) "Good education," "sense of humor" and "guts or courage" follow in that order.

(10) Impartiality is next. Leaders who do not "save the dirty jobs for the fellows they don't like" are valued. The good leader is fair to all his command.

(11) Next in importance is industry. Leaders who "do as little work as they can get away with" are not respected by the enlisted men.

(12) When an officer "gives orders in such a way that you know clearly what to do," that too is a mark of merit as a leader. Soldiers also like an officer with a "clear, strong voice."

The remaining qualities which the soldiers mentioned came toward the bottom of the list. They are undoubtedly related to good leadership, but they are less important. Not "hot tempered," do not "drive you too hard," "keep promises," "the kind of fellows you could have a good time with," "not too proud of their rank" are all characteristics which some men want in their leaders, but there is no general agreement about them. Many leaders are considered good in spite of failure on these points.

The chief things a man wants from a leader are thus, competence and interest in his welfare.

The orders of a man who does not know his stuff cannot be depended on. They are subject to change and countermand. An incompetent leader teaches caution and hesitation in following his lead. He

374

becomes a signal for lack of action on the part of the soldier.

Indecision in a leader has the same effect on a soldier as ignorance has. No soldier can follow a leader who is uncertain which way to turn. The essential quality of any leader is to take the lead and show the direction—quickly, clearly, emphatically, and with enthusiasm. Without these qualities a man is not even a good leader for his hunting dog.

THE RÔLE OF THE SOLDIER

Part of what makes a man a good soldier is his own adoption of the soldier's rôle. He comes to think and speak of himself as a soldier. He is progressing in military training when he stops thinking of himself as a plumber or a salesman who is now in the Army, and begins to regard himself as an infantryman or an artilleryman or a tank man.

What a man thinks of himself affects his behavior. The rail straightener—the skilled worker who runs the machine that straightens railroad rails —is one man when he thinks of himself with pride as a rail straightener. He becomes another when he begins, as he may, to regard himself as a mere "wage-slave." The rail straightener takes pride in his work, does a good job, is happy. The "wage-slave" lets crooked rails get by because he doesn't care. In the same way, the soldier, who thinks proudly of himself as a soldier, is doing a service to both himself and the Army.

Certain forms of punishment, public disgrace, ridicule, all disturb the rôle of the soldier and may lessen or destroy his usefulness to the Army and his amenability to leadership. The noncommissioned or commissioned officer who rides one of his men in such a manner as to make him doubt his own value as a soldier is shattering the man's best motive for good performance. The senior leader who reprimands a junior in the presence of his men reduces that junior's value to the Army.

Good leadership, on the other hand, causes men to build up, each for himself, a particular rôle—a specialty. It means a great deal to a man to take pride in being a soldier, and in being a sharpshooter, an aviation mechanic, a truck driver, a cook, or a radio operator. Competent leaders criticize a poor piece of work, condemn a mistake, but take care never to make a soldier feel he is a failure in his job. When a man has accepted his leader's statement that he is "no soldier," then indeed he falls back to perfunctory work and the mere effort to keep out of trouble.

When a soldier begins to regard himself as being a part of his unit and when his job has become part of his rôle, then team work is enormously improved. The soldier who thinks of himself as only a private, temporarily on this or that assignment, is a different man from the soldier who thinks of himself as a necessary member of his outfit. Good leadership always takes advantage of this essential of team work and common effort.

The leader's easiest and most important contribution to the personal recognition that the soldier needs is the use of the soldier's name in addressing him. When an officer is unable to call his men by name there can be no chance that a man's good performance will be noticed and remembered. It is one of the first duties of a company officer to make clear to his men that he knows each of them.

A leader need not always speak of specific good performances. It is often enough for him to make it clear that he saw the good performance. Continuous public commendation of one man may put that man at a disadvantage with the others and have a bad effect on them. Public praise should be reserved for important and occasional performances.

COMPLAINTS

Soldiers are notorious gripers, and the griping may be useful not merely because it lets off steam but because it gives valuable information to the leader ready to profit by it. Only the smug or the incompetent leader dismisses complaints because they are common.

A collection of soldier comments on noncommissioned and commissioned leaders offers some food for reflection. Here is a selected batch of confidentially treated opinions expressed by a number of soldiers early in the War:

"This army can't be driven; it must be led."

"Break up the old Army noncom clique and put advancement on a merit basis."

"Officers bluff too much."

"Let noncoms be chosen for what they know, not who they know."

"Our first lieutenant is dominated by the first sergeant."

"No reward for good work; old soldiers learn never to volunteer for anything."

"They treat us like children."

"When an officer tells his men he doesn't like the army any more than we do, he's not the one I look to."

". . . instead of changing his mind every few minutes. . ."

". . . should take a little interest in what we eat . . ."

". . . give us some idea of what's going on in maneuvers."

". . . hurry and wait!"

"We come from just as good or better families . . . say a good word now and then . . . call a man by his name . . . show a man they know their stuff."

"After all we're the ones who are going to fight and we want to be respected in uniform."

". . . don't tell what it's about."

". . . shames us in front of other batteries."

Such complaints cannot always be taken at their face value. The complaint that a soldier makes of his food, his officer, his quarters is often not concerned with the basic trouble that makes him complain. When he is depressed or annoyed, some complaint comes to the surface. The real trouble may be news from home, or a quarrel with a squadmate, or a slight from a leader that makes his future look insecure. Complaints may only be symptoms and may very often completely hide the real trouble.

Nevertheless, any collection of complaints will reveal the chief faults of leaders, because in the Army the most important part of every soldier's environment is his leaders. What officers and noncoms say, what they do, the manner of their speech and acts, what they think—all these things are closely observed. It determines the attitudes of men toward duty, toward the Army and toward the war.

No completely satisfactory system for selecting all leaders will ever be developed, for one man responds to one type of leader and another man to another type. The college leader might do quite badly if put in charge of the gas house gang. There are, moreover, different ways of leading the same group of men.

If the Army were to introduce a uniform system for the selection of leaders, this system would have to be based on those few qualities of soldiers which are—because all the U. S. soldiers are Americans— widespread in the Army. There is no one person who embodies all the qualities for leading everybody.

Nevertheless leaders must be chosen somehow— the commissioned and noncommissioned officers and the officer candidates. How is the job to be done?

No good tests exist for the measurement of leadership ability, except the General Classification Test. It has been found that a high score on this test indicates that the man will be likely to succeed as an officer candidate in the Quartermaster and Adjutant General's Schools. A score below 110 indicates, moreover, that the man lacks the general ability to make good officer material in any school. There may be exceptions, but this is a safe rule.

In most of the arms and services, however, many other qualities besides this general mental ability are necessary for good leadership. These capacities cannot as yet be measured by any test; the only way

379

of finding out about them is by observation and interview. Selection has to be made by the personal judgment of a superior officer or by a selection board.

There are, however, ways of safeguarding the fairness and of improving the accuracy of such personal judgments.

In the first place, good judgments require *competent* judges. Rank is no guarantee of ability to judge leadership in others. Nor are good leaders necessarily competent to assess good leadership in others. The test of a competent judge is his successful predictions in the past.

The second requirement is that there should be a number of judges, not one. This is a case where a jury is needed. A jury of five is likely to average out the personal biases and hunches of each of its members and to come near the truth—provided the five are competent. Wisdom is, of course, something more than the average of five incompetent opinions.

The third requirement is that the decisions of the judges should be based upon the *actual performances* of the candidate in practice and not upon what he does or says in an interview or his bearing on that occasion. If the judges have to rely upon interviews without direct observation of performance, then they should try to bring out in the interview concrete information about the candidate's past achievements.

The interview itself is not a fair or accurate test of a soldier. The man who would make a good leader may be a modest man who fails in an interview to exhibit those qualities that would make his men believe in him, trust him, admire him. And the man who could never secure the loyalty of subordinates, may nevertheless by assurance and poise, by voice and manner, mislead inexperienced judges as to his capacity.

It is easy for us to say what will *not* work in predicting leadership.

The tests have been tried and failed thus far.

Making out a list of leadership qualities, rating the candidate on them, weighing and averaging them is an impressive procedure. But the trouble is that it does not work. At any rate not now. There are too many different ways of being a good leader, of securing loyalty. No one can yet name the traits upon which success depends—except that a good leader is a good leader and can develop further with time and opportunity. In other words, the only proof of leadership is leadership, and the best thing to do is to give it a chance to emerge and then to have competent men judge whether it has appeared.

For similar reasons no single successful set of questions has ever been devised to assess leadership in an interview. The competent judge adapts his questioning to the individual candidate knowing when to discard one answer and when to give another much weight.

This much, however, is known. Although young men can make excellent leaders, leadership develops with experience. Higher standards should, therefore, be set for older men. The man of thirty, who is only just as good as the man of twenty-two, is not going to improve as rapidly as his younger competitor. It has taken the older man longer to get where he is and it will take him longer to make the next advance.

There is one source of information about leadership which the Army has too often overlooked. It is possible to get the judgments of subordinates about a superior. They know whether the superior is a good leader or not, and for the most part subordinates do not grudge honest appreciation to a superior. If the leader has the loyalty of his men, they will want to express it. The use of estimates by subordinates is generally supposed not to be conducive to good discipline, but that objection lacks force when the manner of getting the estimates is the proper one.

It is known, moreover, that the men of a platoon can size each other up effectively, can pick the men who deserve advancement more consistently than the leaders can. The men know competence when they see it.

Thus it appears that the officer who fails to find out quietly the opinions of his subordinates when he is selecting a man for promotion is overlooking a valid source of information, one that is in the long run far more accurate than his own judgment. For this reason a good leader always has an advantage in picking potential leaders, because the good leader has the loyalty and confidence of his men. He can get their judgments of one another without jeopardizing discipline.

LEADERSHIP CAN BE LEARNED

There are no born leaders. All leadership is based on learning how to deal with men. Nearly all leaders improve after they have had experience in command. Some improve faster than others, and some continue to improve while others do not.

Consider the qualities which enlisted men believe important in leaders. The first is competence and ability. Competence is based on learning. The good leader has learned his job thoroughly. His men can trust him to know what he is doing. He knows not only what he learned in his training courses, but he has kept up to date. If he is an artilleryman, he knows how the Germans use artillery and what guns they have. The rule is a simple one: *know your stuff*.

Second to competence is the officers' interest in the soldier as a man, a demonstrated interest that gives the soldier confidence that, when he stands hardship or is in trouble, the hardship is a necessary part of the job and his troubles give his officer concern. Every man can by practice improve his skill in human understanding and increase his repertoire of actions that demonstrate interest in others. The rule here is less simple. It is: *know your men and show it.* Know their names, their history, their weaknesses, their good points, their morale. Begin by studying their qualification cards.

Decisiveness is a skill harder to acquire. But it can with attention be cultivated. When you have a hard choice, remember you do not usually have to make a snap judgment. Careful consideration—weighing the merits of alternate courses—is not indecision. Your men will respect your judgment even more if you reserve decision until you are in possession of all the facts necessary for a wise choice. Do not set up a "council of war" to pass on things by vote; *you are the leader.* But seek advice when you need it, and do not hesitate to call on your subordinates for counsel if they are qualified to give it. *But*

383

choose your course before you give your orders.

Probably only experience, together with genuine interest in other men, makes a good teacher. But there are many rules for good teaching that may help. One of them is: Remember that men learn to do by doing. Lectures are only the embroidery on training. It is actual performance that does the work.

Another suggestion to the leader is: Remember, when men do not understand you, *that is your fault.* You must talk their language—plain language. If you cannot express yourself clearly, it may be because you do not understand the subject well yourself. Think things through carefully before you try to explain.

A leader then, to be worthy in the eyes of his men would do well to follow these commands:

1. Be competent.
2. Be loyal to your men as well as to your country and Army.
3. Know your men, understand them, love them, be proud of them.
4. Accept responsibility and give clear, decisive orders.
5. Teach your men by putting them through the necessary action.
6. Give only necessary orders, but—
7. Get things done.
8. Be fair.
9. Work hard.
10. Remember that a leader is a symbol. Men need to respect and trust you—don't let them down.

XVII: MOBS AND PANIC

THE ARMY MUST BE PREPARED to deal with mobs and panics. Civilian crowds may hamper military operations; military units suddenly broken into a disorderly rout may spell the loss of a battle or a whole campaign.

Native people, streaming with their belongings over the one road out of combat territory, are suddenly machine-gunned from enemy planes. The result may be panic, paralyzing military traffic.

A weary crowd is waiting in a railroad station for transportation out of danger. Someone shouts "Time bomb!" Result: a shrieking, wild mob.

Service men are relaxing and drinking and dancing in precious off-duty hours. Suddenly the hot breath of flame shoots along the paper decorations. What happens? A wild dash for the exit and trampled bodies in the way. Panic.

Ordinarily mobs do not gather and orderly crowds do not turn into riotous mobs unless some situation arises for which their training and habits do not prepare them or unless some powerful emotion causes them to forget their training.

Thus the men of an Army unit in combat can usually be counted upon to act as all their drill, discipline, and training have prepared them to act. They advance and retreat according to command.

But even the best drilled unit and the most seasoned outfit is never absolutely proof against panic

385

and rout. Surprise, a hasty or excited action on the part of a leader, an unexpected danger—sometimes just an imagined threat from the enemy—may throw good soldiers into most disgraceful flight. Then the carefully organized military unit becomes a mob.

Mere numbers do not make a group of individuals into a crowd or a mob. A well-disciplined Army unit, no matter how large, while it is acting under orders, is never a mob, or even a crowd.

POWER OF THE MOB

Because men in a crowd or a mob sometimes do unreasonable things that even they cannot account for later, a great deal of nonsense has been said about the power of the mob—about the "mob mind," about "crowd psychology." Some men have the fear that when they become surrounded by a mob, they may lose their own ability to think and act independently, that they may be seized by a mysterious insanity.

Psychologists know that this is not so. Men in a mob act just as much in keeping with their past training and habits as they would if they were alone.

But part of this training which men get from earliest childhood is to follow the example of other individuals and also to respond to their gestures, facial expressions, and tones of voice, as well as to the spoken words of others.

The drill sergeant often sees a demonstration of the power of command given by example. He is putting recruits through the manual of arms and is following the manual himself to show them what to do. If he now gives a command without executing

386

it, some of the men may not obey it. They were in part following his example, not his words alone.

When a soldier misunderstands a command, he starts to execute it as he interpreted it. But suppose in the middle of a movement he becomes suddenly aware that the other men in the ranks are doing something very different. Immediately he corrects his action to do what the others are doing.

In the same way, the sight of a leader running or galloping to the rear in combat area may start a whole company heading after him on the double. His example can become as much a command or order as his words.

When the leader is not present to give orders, or when a leader for any reason is no longer trusted, men follow the example of their comrades. Their minds may then take the sight of other men running, or the sight of other men throwing away their rifles, as an order.

Mostly it's a good thing that men naturally follow the example of others. It makes the world run more smoothly. Yet the good principle has vicious results when mobs form or panic starts.

Why Mobs Form

Mobs form because some one event or condition has brought people together and captured the attention of every person in the crowd. Usually the mob is angry about something and its angry excitement makes it ready for action. Panic based on fear is something else.

A crowd which is excited and absorbed in looking at, listening to, or talking about the same event, readily becomes a mob when some simple line of action is proposed. It does not then take skill in leadership to sway a mob to action. Nor need the leader be possessed of any wisdom in the course of action proposed. All that he must have is an ability to get attention—as he may, if he is big, noisy, ugly or standing on a box.

Besides a common focus of attention, *emotion* is characteristic of all mobs. Mobs act as a unit primarily because their members are all swayed by the same emotion. They all have similar attitudes, beliefs and wishes that underlie the emotion.

Since a mob is driven by a powerful emotion, it is necessarily crazy to do something. It wants action. So it only takes a cry of "Lynch him!" or "Burn it!" to set the mob in motion.

Yet, it is not often that the emotion which stirs a crowd to mob action is created on the spot. Sometimes the driver of a car who has injured or killed a child is attacked at once by men who were peaceful pedestrians five minutes earlier. Occasionally a thief is roughly treated by the crowd that captures him. But usually the mob has been stirred long before by the news of some horrible happening, like a murder or a rape, and it was this news that led to the gathering of a crowd in the first place.

Mob action involving soldiers sometimes begins in some drinking place. If a quarrel starts between individual soldiers of different friendly armies, or between a soldier and a marine or sailor, it may readily spread to others who happen to be on the spot. The lines will almost certainly be drawn on the basis of uniform, and the resulting free-for-all will have very little to do with the justice of the original quarrel.

It is the shared attitudes which form the basis for this kind of mob action.

After a mob has been drawn together by shared anger or fear and common attitudes, and with a common object of attention, then it will almost inevitably follow the *example* of the one or several men who make the first move.

Mostly, when you get into a crowd, you *join* it. You do just what other people do. You all stand looking at the parade, you all hurry along to the ball game, you all cheer, boo, and clap together. So, in a crowd, the example of others is more powerful than under any other circumstances. It is easy to be different if you are one of three, hard to be different if you are one out of a hundred.

The sight of others seizing stones, or starting for an attack, so grips the men watching them, that they think of no other course of action. And once the action is begun, then that mere fact causes most men to follow the lead of the others. Action fills the mind, driving out the thought of other possibilities.

Mobs are, therefore, uncritical. The exciting presence of other men and the sight of their action drives doubts and questions from the mind. All the training of most men leads them to believe that what lots of other people do is proper—is right. Thus a mob is really stupid, because it provides no opportunity for dissenting voices to be raised and heard. When nearly everyone has his attention fixed on the event or on the actions of a leader, dissent rarely arises, is seldom expressed when it does arise, is almost never heard if it is expressed.

Mobs are not wicked. Being uncritical, they lack consciences. There is, in the mob, simply no occasion—no time—for thinking of rules and laws and morals. For the time being, the whole universe is narrowed down merely to action, violence, and relief for emotion.

PANIC

Soldiers do not often form mobs. Mob action among soldiers usually occurs only when they are away from the usual reminders and circumstances of discipline—when they are on leave and mingling with men from other organizations, without leadership.

But panic can occur in the best-drilled, thoroughly seasoned troops. It can occur in the midst of combat. Some of the greatest routs in history have been cases of panic.

The panicked group is much like a mob, but it acts from fear, not anger. Its attention is focused on the object of fear. Its thought and its talk is of danger and disaster. Its aim is escape. Action becomes definite and mob-like only when obstacles to escape are encountered.

Men and women in a crowded dance hall, threatened by sudden fire, have only one thought—escape. If they are not hindered, they will flee and do no violence. But if the doors are blocked, they will push frantically, claw, throw others down and let them get trampled to death.

Soldiers on leave are no more proof against panic than is a civilian. Under command, however, the well-disciplined soldier has fixed habits of obedience and fixed habits of behavior proper to effective military action. He will usually act according to these habits despite terrifying distractions of enemy attack.

So long as a regiment encounters only situations like those for which it has been trained, panic does not occur.

But even a well-disciplined regiment can disintegrate into a panicky crowd when it meets a situation for which it has never been prepared.

WHAT STARTS PANIC

It doesn't take much to touch off a panic among troops who are "panic-ripe." Then a single cry of "Gas!" or "Run!" or "We're cut off!" may start a mad flight.

The enemy, aware of this fact, plays upon it whenever possible. In the first AEF, agents were planted among the American troops to yell "Gas!" when times of confusion made them think the cry might start a panic. It became necessary to work out a code warning for the actual presence of gas—a code known only to trusted men. "New York" would mean gas one day, "Minneapolis" the next. The men were instructed not to cry "Gas!"

Dive bombers and shrieking bombs are used in part to misdirect the attention of the soldiers, to frighten more than to kill. Actually the dive bomber does surprisingly little damage to trained troops who know what to do when such planes attack. But with them the enemy hopes not only to inflict casualties. He also hopes that with the terrifying noise—it is blood curdling but it's just a loud and physically harmless noise—panic may be started.

But trifling things can also serve to start a panic. Historic cases of panic among soldiers have been described by Captain C. T. Lanham in The *Infantry Journal*. "A word, a gesture, even a shadow," he said, were enough to "transform men into stampeding cattle."

In 1866, a dust cloud was enough to start the cry, "The German cavalry is charging!" among exhausted and frightened Austrian troops. The dust cloud was raised by a herd of frightened pigs.

In 1918, a runner handed a message to a battalion commander. The major read it and called to his adjutant, "Come on, let's beat it." The two started toward the rear at a dead run. The entire battalion was instantly in wild flight behind them. The message was only an order to report to headquarters.

In 1904, a shadow in the dark turned a well-trained, rested, Russian rifle brigade into a fighting, milling mob of men and animals. Shortly after dusk, in the vague shadowy twilight, several Russian soldiers from the rifle brigade went into a near-by rice field to relieve themselves. One of these men, while in an awkward position, saw something. He leapt up and shouted, "The Japanese are coming!" That was enough. What did he see? Probably just some projection of his own frightened, jittery imagination. The Japanese weren't coming.

PANIC RIPENESS

Anything that makes men tense, on edge, jittery, and over-sensitive to slight noises, half hidden sights, or sudden movements will make them easy victims of panic.

392

For this reason prolonged anxiety makes men panic-ripe. So does over-fatigue, too much beer or liquor or a hangover. So does lack of proper food, especially a deficiency of B vitamins. And so does exhaustion from lack of sleep. Prolonged exposure to the noise and alarm of modern battle may produce the jumpy state of mind from which panic arises.

One main cause of panic is *lack of training*. Training must cover practice in defense and retreat as well as in attack, if panic is to be avoided—if the retreat is not to turn into rout. Troops trained only in methods of attack, may, when forced into quick retreat and separated from their leaders turn into a typical mob. The example of other men then calls the turn, instead of orders or the habits practiced in training and maneuvers.

The sight of one or several men running to the rear, the sight of others throwing away their gear or weapons, may cause a general scramble and the discarding of arms. When two units become mixed during a forced retreat, the confusion of command and the confusion of example—some going one way, and some another—readily breed panic.

Whenever men are placed in a new situation for which they have not been trained, they do not know what to do. And that is no time to think things out. They need orders, will accept direction from a private who speaks with confidence and implies by his assurance that he knows what is best. If commands are not given or not heard, example provides the command. And if that example is the wrong one, if some one man or some small group breaks and runs for it, then the rest are very likely to follow.

Bad morale is another cause of panic. The Russian rifle brigade of 1904 terrified by one scared soldier seeing things in the twilight, was already torn by internal strife, dissension and petty feuds among its officers. *Esprit de corps* was nonexistent. Another unit encamped in the same region had high morale. Its colonel was loved and respected and the other officers were competent and coöperative. This unit was able, simply by presenting a calm and unperturbed front, to halt the panic in the rifle brigade.

Rumor sometimes plays an important part in readying men for panic. During the invasion of Abyssinia by Italy in 1896, rumors, combined with poor morale and mutual distrust among the soldiers and among officers who betrayed their fright before their men, served to prepare the way for a disastrous panic that reduced an army of 15,000 men to 3,500.

The terrain was rough and cut into deep, parallel ravines, separated by steep ridges. One unit advancing through one of these defiles was attacked by wildly shouting native troops. The supporting artillery was unable to get the range and almost at the first brush the Italian infantrymen discarded their rifles and raced away in disorder.

The most important contributing cause of this disaster seems to have been the circulation of wild tales about the cruelty of the native Abyssinians in torturing their prisoners—bloody stories filled with anatomical detail.

Poor leadership can make the ground ready for panic, impairing the confidence in command necessary to hold troops to the performance of duty. Contradictory or ambiguous orders make troops ripe for

394

panic. So does apparent stupidity or vacillation in officers. Or prolonged waits under tension. Or frequent false alarms. Or long retreats. Or unexplained retreats on the heels of victory. Anything the soldier thinks is evidence of poor organization increases the possibility of panic.

The death of a leader in whom confidence has been too much centered also makes the grieving men more ready for panic.

Insecurity, whether actual or only in the mind, sets the stage for panic. An enemy threat, real or imagined, to the flank of a unit or to its communications and supply, will do this unless men are thoroughly trained to know these things may happen and do not necessarily mean defeat. Surprise by the enemy will also do it. Especially surprise by new and unexpected weapons. Defeat, high casualties, disorderly retreat through ranks of unburied dead. Being lost in a woods or at night. Ignorance of the position of the enemy. All these may cause it.

Doubt, worry, anxiety. Loss of faith. Panic feeds on them.

An army that is puzzled, discouraged, worn out, uninformed, and lost is like a forest that is so dry that any spark will start a forest fire. There you have conditions that were never practiced in maneuvers, conditions out of which panic can grow.

How to Stop a Panic

Once panic has begun, the only way to halt it is to capture attention and then provide positive, clear commands. Leaders must act with decision, firmness and courage. If no officer is present, any self-pos-

395

sessed man can assume leadership and give the scared men what they need—clear confident direction.

The leaders' example of confidence in themselves and in their men must compete with the examples of those who are running away in terror. Unconcerned calm and routine attention to duty is effective, if it can but once get full attention. One officer got attention in the First World War by standing up on a stump and laughing loudly and pointing at panic-stricken men who came running by him following others.

But the best way to stop a panic is never to have it at all. Train all men thoroughly so that they have confidence—in themselves, their leaders, their weapons. Train their leaders and select the best of them. Let good leaders build up good morale. Avoid hunger, thirst, fatigue, and boredom as much as it is possible to do in war, and all the conditions that lead to nervous tension and complaint. If you cannot avoid them—and no war is a bed of roses—fight them with morale. Fight the feeling of insecurity. Tell the men all they need to know. Let them know all possible information about the enemy—where he is, what he is like, how he attacks, what weapons he is using.

Last, but not least, build up faith. Be sure the men know why they are fighting, why it is a good cause. Let them be sure that their officers are with them all the way. Faith in an ideal, plus faith in your leaders, plus faith in the other fellows in your unit, can win a victory against superior forces.

XVIII: DIFFERENCES AMONG RACES AND PEOPLES

MODERN TOTAL WAR has placed a new responsibility on the shoulders of the soldier. Once his only task was to destroy the enemy. But now psychological warfare requires him to play a new rôle—he must help to win allies for Uncle Sam in many strange lands.

In the Solomons, in China, in North Africa it matters a great deal whether the native people, as well as the soldiers of Allies, like Americans or resent them. To these people, the soldier is America's representative. If he offends them, it will be America and Americans who seem offensive—not just the soldier himself.

An American soldier entering a Moslem church with his shoes on could counteract all the friendly counsels of generals and diplomats in a palace in Algiers.

The American who gets to be like an own son to an Irish mother has forged a link between peoples that no German propaganda could weaken.

There are no infallible recipes for making friends the world around. But there are two basic rules for all soldiers in the manual of psychological arms:

(1) Mind your own manners.

(2) Understand and respect the manners of strangers, especially of strangers who might help both you and the cause for which you are fighting.

How Nations Differ

Men differ from one another in their natural inborn characteristics and in the habits of thought and conduct which they have been acquiring ever since they started as babies to get an education in living.

The acquired differences are particularly important to the American who wants to make friends and obtain cooperation and help from natives in the lands where he is fighting.

Nature settles the questions as to whether you will have two noses or one, two eyes or one, and it has a lot to do with whether you are bright or stupid, although environment—education, learning—helps a lot there too. But it is the way you are brought up that pretty much settles the questions of whether you speak English or Chinese, whether you can read or write, whether you are a Catholic, a Jew, a Baptist or a Moslem, whether you like baseball, trigonometry or poetry, whether you eat rice or spaghetti or corn on the cob.

No one knows exactly which is most important, your heredity or your environment in determining what you are—*nature vs. nurture,* the argument is called. Actually you never can get nature entirely separated from nurture for study. You may like poetry because your mother taught you to like it. Or you may like it because you were not very strong as a child and became a book-worm instead of playing with the other boys. It doesn't really matter which is which—nature or nurture—because the important thing is that grown men change their habits of thought and action only with great difficulty, although they can if the need is great.

The average American soldier when he goes abroad to Great Britain, Norway, France, North Africa, Burma, China, Australia, the Solomon Islands, or to whatever distant land this global war may take him, will meet people who think and look and act in ways very different from the men and women in Omaha, Nebraska, Atlanta, Georgia, or San Francisco, California. The soldier needs to know how these new people differ from the postmaster and the druggist and the school teachers at home. He needs, too, to know how these differences have come about, what they mean, and especially what he himself ought to think about them.

There are only three possible kinds of differences between the many peoples of different nations. And only the third is really important. Even that becomes less important when the soldier understands about it.

(1) First, there are *native physical differences.* These are sometimes very conspicuous, and so attract attention first. Some men have black skins, some brown, some yellow, and some white. Most Japs are short. Negroes have kinky hair. Chinese and Japs, besides having yellow skins, have an extra fold in the upper eye-lid, a fold which makes them look slant-eyed.

None of these differences is, however, without exception. The races in the course of history have gotten themselves all mixed up. Many Norwegians are not blond. Certainly not every German is. A Jap is more likely than a Chinese to have wavy hair, a beard and short legs but a sentry had better not try to decide between them just by their looks.

399

Distinguishing between friend and foe among strange peoples is made more difficult because of the fact that, until we get used to strange people, we are inclined to think all of them look alike. It is not until we become better acquainted that we notice the small differences that might distinguish them. It is hard to tell friendly natives from those who may be hostile. It may be very hard to tell a Jap infiltrated through American lines from some of the natives he tries to resemble.

Looks, of course, are not important in determining the character of people. The dislike which most people feel at first for persons of other races is based on the belief that other races are different in character and temperament as well as in looks. Are they?

(2) Well, there might be *native psychological differences* between races, and many people believe that such fundamental unchangeable differences do actually exist.

They think, for instance, that some races are less *intelligent* than others, that they have inferior capacity for learning rapidly and accurately, that they would always do poorly on the Army's General Classification Test.

But that is not true. The southern Europeans in the U.S. Army in the First World War did much worse than the northern Europeans and the Americans in the Army intelligence tests, but that was because the southern Europeans in the Army were poor immigrants who had not had much schooling. There were and are plenty of bright Spaniards, Greeks, and Italians. Their countries have produced many of the brilliant men of history.

400

Every time a psychologist has set out to study inherited racial differences in intelligence he has not found that any existed, and there have been many long and thorough studies of this kind made. The racial differences turn out to depend on the educational advantages of the particular groups of persons tested. There is presumably some inheritance in genius, some effect of nature in addition to nurture—identical twins tend to be alike even when they have been separated at birth and given different foster parents and different amounts of schooling; but such differences do not run by nations. The nations are too mixed up in their populations. Differences between individuals in any nation are so very great that any differences that might exist between nations become so small by comparison that you cannot find them.

Some people think that there are native differences in *emotionality,* that the British are stolid and diffident, that the Italians are excitable and voluble. There are, of course, those differences, but it is not at all clear that they are native, inherited traits. They are probably learned habits of conduct. You get to gesturing with your hands when you talk if everybody else does too, and especially if your parents do it. You learn to talk rapidly if other people do, and if they interrupt when you don't talk fast. You learn to suppress evidence of emotion if your parents and all their friends are quiet and restrained and raise their eyebrows when you cry out or exclaim before others. You may even learn to hide your feelings by expressing opposite ones—laughing when you are grieving, as the Japanese do.

Anyhow it is not the trait of emotionality that creates serious misunderstanding between peoples of different nations, and so it does not much matter to the soldier abroad whether emotionality is learned or native—whether it is a distinguishing characteristic among strange peoples.

(3) What really matters in this war are the *learned traits,* the habits of thought, the national customs, the things that people of another country believe without ever asking themselves why.

A Moslem never eats with his left hand. Silly, is it? You yourself do not reach into a meat pie, grab a fistful and eat it with your fingers. That might look silly to some people, too. But fingers were made before forks, and 400 years ago the King of England was eating meat with his fingers.

An otherwise kindly Chinese peasant may beat the daylights out of his tired horse because it refuses to do his will. An American might protest such cruelty. In the United States he might even telephone the Society for the Prevention of Cruelty to Animals. But an American does not have this sort of sympathy for rats or mosquitoes. Your conscience about animals is whatever it is because it was so formed by your parents or other older people when you were very young.

A Moslem takes off his shoes and keeps on his hat when he enters a church. You take off your hat, but you keep your shoes on. Both of you are expressing reverence. The Moslem's act is more cleanly. Yours is only a symbol.

A Chinese peasant fears a camera. It is for him an "evil eye." An American farmer fears the night air as unwholesome—or at least he did not long ago.

A German youth hates the democracies. But this, too, is a habit of thought he has learned, and it takes only one generation of education to change such habits in the youth of a nation. Not so many of the older Germans have believed as fanatically in the Nazi doctrine. They got their own beliefs earlier before Hitler and his helpers began to spread the Nazi propaganda.

So it is the beliefs and habits of thought that make up the most important national differences. And the well equipped soldier needs to know all he can about them. He wants to know how friendly people are in the habit of thinking and acting. And it will pay him too to study the ways of his enemies.

Many American lives might have been saved earlier in this war if the soldiers had understood the Japanese way of thinking about surrender and taking prisoners. Americans, attempting to save Japs who had had to jump into the water from sinking transports, were killed in their act of mercy. They did not understand that many Japs would rather die than be rescued under such circumstances.

RACE PREJUDICE

It is also extremely important for the American soldier to understand clearly some of his own peculiar habits of thinking and acting.

It will help him, for example, to understand the basis of the race prejudice that is all too common among many Americans as well as among Germans and many other peoples.

The reason for race prejudice can be traced back

403

to a natural need for security. Everyone wants to feel secure. And he feels most secure in familiar surroundings with people he knows. For this reason it is natural for us to resent it when strangers come among us, get jobs, and settle down to make themselves at home. We do not understand the "foreigners," and deep down beneath the surface we are afraid of them. This resentment happens unless we have become used to strangers by travel or by living among them as friends. On the surface, it is usual for men to belittle the stranger, to make fun of his ways. When the unconscious fear of strangers is very great, men will even gang up on them.

In ganging up on foreigners, a group or a nation gets an unthinking new sense of its own strength, solidarity and security. Hitler was trying this trick when he undertook to turn Germans against Jews. They were labelled outsiders and foreigners, and the German people, insecure since their defeat in the last war, found strength and confidence—some of them —in persecuting the Jews.

Color of skin is often the basis for prejudice because it so clearly is a badge of difference between peoples—a mark that sets one people apart as different, as not "one of us." American whites have been prejudiced, not only against black skins, but also against yellow and against the copper skin of the American Indian. The United States excluded both Japs and Chinese from immigration when our western states became afraid of their cheap labor. And the old German Kaiser invented the slogan, "The Yellow Peril," when he wished to unite Europe against the Asiatics.

Sometimes the prejudice against the Negroes flares up in the Army. It is not a problem, however, in a camp where it is well understood that a soldier in United States uniform is a *soldier,* not a white or Negro, Christian or Jew, rich man or poor, but a soldier and as such worthy of respect.

And not everyone feels race prejudice. There are plenty of white men who are constantly meeting and working with black, brown, and yellow men of education, culture, brains and ability. These white men know that skin color is not a sign of inferiority or superiority, and they tend to forget about it, or at least to regard it as unimportant. These white men are numerous in Europe, South America, Asia, and Africa, where the races are mixed up in business and politics.

In the United States, we are more used to seeing large numbers of men with dark skins who are un-educated. We do not often meet the scholars among the Chinese, Negroes, and other dark-skinned peo-ples. The two oceans have in the past prevented most of us from becoming acquainted with the more able and successful men of Africa and Asia. And so we keep our prejudices. Nowadays, with the great American enthusiasm for the bravery of our Chinese allies, this prejudice is a little less, but strong.

Now, however, the American soldier is going among people who do not share his prejudices. The unprejudiced white men may find it hard to under-stand it if he shows antagonism toward other Amer-icans or our Allies on account of their color, just as the American may be surprised at these more lib-eral attitudes.

405

If, however, the American soldier understands the basis for his own feelings as well as those of the men he meets, he can avoid friction and embarrassment to America.

The strange people will still seem strange to him because they have strange customs and novel habits of thought. But he will be on the right track when he realizes that the differences are superficial; that other races, while different from his own, are not necessarily inferior. He will know that he cannot tell just from a man's color whether that man will bind up his wounds, guide him to a hospital when he is lost, feed him if he is hungry, or help him repel enemy invaders.

The soldier who is going to represent America fairly and wisely among the peoples of North Africa or in China or the South Pacific should think these matters over. It will help him to remember that skin color in itself means nothing about the intelligence, wisdom, honesty, bravery or kindliness of man. If he studies carefully the people of other races whom he meets, he can satisfy himself that this is true.

And he must come to understand and learn to respect their manners. Only then will he realize that national differences in manners and customs are mostly due to differences of tradition, climate and religion.

CLIMATE MAKES MANNERS

Do clothes make the man?

No, but clothes like skin color favor national prejudice because they are national badges. They distinguish the people of one nation from those of another. They favor prejudice until you get accustomed to the differences. Then they don't matter. Then you think about the man inside the clothes —or inside the skin if he hasn't many clothes.

All sorts of differences in clothing help to set one people off from another—the strange dress of the people of India, the gerd of the Libyan nomad, the sombrero of the Mexican peon, and the all-the-year-round thick woolens that the people of Ulster wear.

Most of these national peculiarities in dress depend upon climate. The American soldier in Ulster could do very well with woolies in summer, and he does do very well with practically nothing in New Guinea. But, until he learns the reason for special clothes and for no clothes, the strangers seem queer to him, perhaps even a little crazy.

Another way in which climate affects manners is the siesta. In towns in the South Pacific area, everything closes up tightly for a few hours in the middle of the day. At first the American soldier thinks this is a silly, indolent custom. What would happen, he thinks, if Detroit shut down from twelve to four every afternoon? Why, you can't even buy a smoke in the early afternoon in New Caledonia. But, after he has lived six months in this climate he changes his mind. Human beings need to rest when it is very hot and to save their activities for the cooler parts of the day. The New Caledonians are not being so lazy as they are using common sense.

Still another effect of climate on national habits and character comes about because climate in many tropical regions makes food plentiful and easy to get.

New Caledonia has cobalt, iron, and nickel mines, but it is hard to get the natives to work in them. Coconuts and fruits are abundant. Shelter is easy to arrange. Why work, when life is so easy?

The American soldier naturally feels contempt for such a lazy attitude toward life. He comes from a land where living is more difficult, where hard work is necessary to secure shelter and food, a land of steam-heat and hot-dog stands, a land where industry produces power, property, and a host of fancy and often handy gadgets. But there is no use in his being contemptuous. Perhaps the New Caledonian, lucky to live in a land of plenty, has never had to worry about work or steam heat and doesn't have much use for the gadgets. And he has been that way for a long time, and there is some sense in it.

Religion and Manners

Religion makes just as many strange differences as climate.

The Moslem bows toward Mecca and prostrates himself in prayer five times a day. The reason he eats only with his right hand, is because of religious law. He avoids dogs as unclean, will not touch pork or anything cooked in lard, abstains from alcohol, refuses to expose his body. Is it a crazy religion? Not at all. Catholics, Jews, Episcopalians and all the other sects so well known in America also have their special customs and forbidden behavior. Many of us feel that we must eat fish on Friday or abstain from pork, or we dislike horse meat, object to divorces, require women to wear hats in church. Live and let live is the rule for religious differences.

To the Hindu, the cow is a sacred animal. Even a sick cow covered with sores as it wanders about the streets of Calcutta cannot be killed and must be reverenced. Because the Hindu believes that the souls of men enter the bodies of animals, Hindus rarely kill animals, even for food, and hence seldom eat meat. And then in India there is the caste system, that system of prejudice against groups within a race. A high-caste Brahman dare not defile himself by even touching a low-caste Hindu or getting within his shadow. Much less would he eat with him.

These, too, are things to understand and accept. The caste system is not the ideal of democracy. Sick cows in the streets of Chicago would be mercifully killed by the Board of Health. But American soldiers are out to win the war. Fortunately, they don't have to reform the world. They are just ambassadors, not missionaries.

The Chinese peasant is cruel to horses and dogs. No matter how kindly he may be toward other men, and he usually is, it is not in his code of ethics to be kind to animals. In his whole life no one has ever even suggested to him that he do anything but get all possible work out of a horse, and he often has to do this or go hungry himself. Americans do not like to see animals maltreated but that is simply the way Americans have been educated. Chinese can learn by education to be kind to animals. But the American soldier had better not interfere between the Chinese farmer and his horse. It is better to have the friendship of the man than the animal.

Especially does religion determine the attitude of men toward women.

In a Moslem household the women reserve the sight of their faces and their conversation to the men of the household. They live in a separate part of the house. If a strange man enters the house, he calls out so that they can put on their veils or retire. No Moslem ever touches a woman not of his own household, not even to help her in difficulty. He would be ridiculed if he did, and his action would be resented by the woman's own men. When other men dine with a Moslem, the women, with their faces covered, appear silently to serve the food.

Not all women of the Orient are thus subject to men. In Burma they enjoy great independence, resent domination, are influential and respected.

But in Japan there is a special rule of obedience for women. A woman obeys her father in everything until she marries, then her husband. If she is widowed, she must obey her eldest son.

How to Win Friends in Foreign Lands

Every American soldier in a foreign land becomes an American diplomat. He has his role to play in making strange people into America's friends. Here are some rules he will find helpful.

(1) Try first of all to *understand* strange customs, habits and ways of thinking. There are real reasons back of all of them just as there are real reasons back of our own. Some of them depend on climate, some on religion, some on very old traditions. Some are sensible. For some the reason is obvious. For others the reason cannot be seen, though there almost certainly is one. Try to find it.

(2) *Respect* these customs and habits of thought,

even when you can't understand them and even when they seem unpleasant or effeminate or crazy. They seem as natural to the people who have them as yours do to you. Foreign peoples cannot seem any more queer to you than you do to them, unless they are wiser than you, have had more experience in the ways in which peoples differ from one another.

(3) When you cannot respect foreign countries, then *suppress your disapproval*. Some of these customs have existed for many centuries. No one likes to have a stranger correct his virtues—or what he and his ancestors have always thought were virtues.

(4) When you can respect foreign customs, *show it*. You can win many friends for America in this simple way.

(5) When you associate with foreign people, try to *adopt their manners*. Do not ask them to adopt yours. Theirs may be more important to them than yours to you. Eat only with your right hand if you eat with a Moslem and take off your shoes if you go into a Moslem church.

(6) *Suppress your own peculiarities* as far as possible, when they are contrary to the custom of the land. Remember that some acts which are all right in America may hurt feelings or even be insulting abroad. Don't follow American customs before foreigners when they contradict the foreigner's rules.

(7) When the foreign customs are none of your business, then *mind only your own business*. Don't stare open-mouthed at a prostrate Arab in prayer. Ignore him. That is the custom.

(8) *Be friendly*. After all, the only way to make

other men like you is to like them. You won't like them right away, perhaps, because no one is immediately fond of strangers. But from the start, act as though you liked them. You will find *some* things to like about people everywhere. Your friendliness, if it is genuine, will usually bring out friendliness in them.

(9) *And take people as they come.* Like them for what they are, not for the way they happen to measure up to your own standards—what you expected of them. Of all the billions of men and women in this world, each one is different from every other one. You are different, too. Each stranger you meet will surprise you, interest you, thrill you or puzzle you. Each is a challenge to you to show the best that is in *you.*

XIX: RUMOR

HAVE YOU HEARD that one of the Japanese pilots brought down at Pearl Harbor had a loaf of fresh bread from a Honolulu bakery in his pocket?

Did you know that, when they sank a German submarine off Cape Cod, they picked up the body of a German sailor who had in his hat a two-day-old theater stub from a New York theater?

You know, there was a fellow in Tony's barber shop tonight and he has a brother in Camp Mix. He says that the colored and white soldiers have gotten into so many fights there that the troops are all forbidden to have firearms when they are off duty.

These are rumors. Unfounded? Yes. Stupid? Yes. Repeated and believed? Unfortunately, yes.

A pilot would not be carrying a loaf of bread in his pocket even if he had got hold of one. If a body were recovered from a sunken submarine, it would be most unlikely that the hat would still be with it or the stub still in the hat. No soldiers off duty are ever allowed to carry firearms.

But it doesn't matter that these stories do not make sense. It doesn't matter that they have been told over and over about different peoples and places through many years and many wars. The stories are still being told by many and being believed by some.

Rumor is the most primitive way of spreading stories—by passing them on from mouth to mouth.

It is just as inefficient, inaccurate, and unaccountable as it is primitive.

Civilized countries in normal times have better sources of news than rumor. They have the radio and the newspapers. But in times of stress and confusion rumor emerges and becomes rife, still further increasing the confusion. At such times you may find two different kinds of news in competition: the press and radio *vs*. the grapevine.

Especially do rumors spread when war requires secrecy on many important matters. Then the press and radio are censored. The customary sources of news no longer give out enough information. Since the people cannot learn through legitimate channels all that they would like to learn or are anxious to learn, they pick up "news" wherever they can get it and when this happens, rumor thrives.

It thrives everywhere—in the Army as well as among civilians. Military leaders have to guard against rumor, because it disrupts carefully prepared plans and may even lead to loss of morale, and even to panic and defeat.

It was a rumor that helped to start the great Indian Mutiny in 1857. In those days the soldiers, with muzzle-loading rifles, had to bite a greased patch of paper from the end of each cartridge in order to release a charge of powder, which was then poured into the muzzle of the gun before the bullet was rammed home. That mutiny was really all ready to begin, and rumors got started about this grease. The Moslems heard that it was pig grease—lard—and that they had been defiled by putting grease from an "unclean" animal in their mouths. The Hindus heard

that it was cow grease and that they had lost caste
by putting grease from a sacred animal in their
mouths. These rumors spread like wild-fire, each
within its appropriate group. The British tried in
vain to correct them, to let the men grease their own
powder-papers with butter, but it was too late. Rumor
had touched off the magazine. The mutiny was on.

WHY RUMORS SPREAD

Rumors are repeated even by those who do not
believe the tales. There is a fascination about them.
The reason is that the cleverly designed rumor gives
expression to something deep in the hearts of the
victims—the fears, suspicions, forbidden hopes, or
day-dreams which they hesitate to voice directly.

If a soldier doesn't like his commanding officer
because he thinks him too hard or unfair, he won't
take any direct action. He won't offer to fight him,
or tell him what he thinks of him. In wartime he
probably wouldn't even say out loud to others what
he thinks of the Old Man.

But suppose the soldier hears a rumor that the
commander he hates or fears has been reprimanded
by the general and is likely to be relieved of his command. What will happen? Why, the soldier will pass
the rumor on. He doesn't feel guilty. He isn't responsible for the story. It is just something people
are saying. But in listening to it and telling it, he
gets some satisfaction. He hopes it is true. It relieves
his pent-up feelings.

It is the same way in civilian life, or anywhere that
men or women meet and exchange a few words of
idle chatter.

A rumor that a certain draft board is crooked or unfair will spread among men who secretly resent the draft or are suspicious of the way it is being administered. Such stories are circulated more by young men who are scared of being drafted or by older men who are afraid they will be turned down than by any others.

Workers gathered in groups at lunch time will often be passing on a yarn about some unfair treatment of labor. Bankers at a club will often be passing on rumors about the wasting of money in the war.

Pessimistic rumors about defeat and disaster show that the people who repeat them are worried and anxious. Optimistic rumors about record production or peace soon coming point to complacency or confidence—and often to overconfidence.

So, if a commanding officer can keep track of the rumors that are going the rounds among his men, he will learn a great deal about their current fears and hopes. He will have a sort of barometer that registers the rises and falls of their morale.

For this purpose, he would need to find out the answers to just three questions:

(1) Among whom are rumors current? It makes a difference which groups of men are spreading these tales.

(2) What are the rumors about? Here lies the clue to what many of his men are thinking, what they fear, what they hope.

(3) What emotions do the rumors express? Do they betray depression and discouragement, or are they cheerful? Do they reveal resentment and conflict?

Sometimes rumors are told as if they were fact, but often the one who passes it on will say that it is just rumor: "Here's what I heard, but I don't know whether it is true or not. . . ." "You know, I don't really believe it but all over town they are saying that. . . ."

Such words free the man who tells the rumor from any feelings of responsibility, lets him tell it without any qualms of conscience. It also gives him a chance to improve it a little by adding a detail or two to make it a better story.

That is the way the German sailor on the submarine gets equipped with a ticket stub from a local theater. The name of the show or the theater is different depending on whether the story is retold in Baltimore, Norfolk, or Miami.

A rumor travels far, and grows as it moves when people want to believe it, or when they get some satisfaction out of hearing and telling it. You are glad to repeat the story that verifies your suspicions, voices your own alarms, amuses you by giving you a laugh at the expense of someone you don't like any too well.

So it might almost be said that it is public opinion which originates rumors, that the hardy rumors are those that fit in with the suspicions and fears everyone is sharing with everyone else. But rumors may also create public opinion.

An alarming rumor will rouse or increase the fears that serve to push the rumor on. Thus rumors grow from rumors. And fears from fears.

Everyone has seen the way this works. One man cheers. Three more join him. Then there are four, and that gets a dozen cheering, then fifty.

417

Psychologists are able, with modern polling methods like those used to predict elections, to watch rumors spread from place to place and even to measure the speed with which they travel. When a rumor starts in New York, interviewers in Boston, Chicago, New Orleans, Miami, Seattle, and other cities all over the country can be notified to listen for that rumor. As it is picked up, the channels through which it spreads may be revealed.

RUMOR MAY BE TRUTH

A rumor is not always a lie, not always a malicious story. Especially in time of war, the grapevine is sometimes the only way by which certain facts are circulated.

Eyewitnesses may, by rumor, spread accounts that cannot be published because of military necessity. A ship is sunk off the coast. Those living along the shore see the happening; they aid in the rescue of the torpedoed sailors. You don't see a thing like that without mentioning it to your friends. But the newspapers don't say a word about it, because they must avoid giving information to the enemy. You, on the other hand, keep talking. You only tell your friends, of course, but they tell only their friends. And in just that way the news spreads by rumor.

Personal knowledge of a military event may be less direct and still lead to the spreading of fact as rumor. A naval vessel is attacked by the enemy. The wounded sailors are sent back to the United States for hospital treatment. Relatives are notified. Often the relatives of several wounded men are acquainted and hear of each other's bad news. Then the items are pieced together and the rumor starts that the ship has been damaged. Soon, according to the rumor—which always grows to be a better story—the ship has been sunk.

Or the rumor may be only a shrewd guess based on a few known facts, and yet turn out to be true.

Troops waiting in camp or embarking at a port are concerned about their destination. They make many guesses and many rumors float around camp—unless discipline concerning rumors is excellent and the troops just don't talk. An overheard remark, a guess based on the nature of the equipment, is repeated as fact—it may, indeed, be fact.

Because men grow to like their own stories, have pride in them and resent any doubts about them, their answers to doubters become more positive or more detailed, increasing the plausibility of the rumor. At this stage the rumor is generally attributed to an "authoritative source." It may become known as a statement by a "high-ranking officer" or of "someone at GHQ."

But although rumors sometimes contain fact or are based on fact, they can never be relied upon. Often they are entirely fictitious and are deliberately started by those who want to help the enemy as part of the war of words.

Uses of Rumor in War

The Germans have long used rumor in psychological warfare. It is very effective because it comes to the hearer without appearing to be propaganda. It comes self-propelled, as all rumors do. What starts as a short-wave broadcast in Germany, or as a story planted by a German agent, perhaps in a newspaper of a neutral country, is presently being told by Americans about Americans in America. Its German origin is completely lost. The hearer cannot ask for evidence because the teller never claims to have evidence. He is repeating only what he heard, and belief is easier than disbelief, especially if hope or fear supports the rumor.

These are the ways in which rumor is used in the war of words.

(1) *For disruption.* Rumor can be made to play havoc with morale.

The Germans helped to disrupt French morale in this manner. They alternated optimistic rumors with pessimistic. In the confusion of the German attack most of the French kept shifting between elation and despair. Soon they no longer knew what to believe, ending up in utter uncertainty and more confusion.

Propagandists also start rumors to create distrust among allies, or to increase disunity within a country. Necessary coöperation can be ruined merely by the rise of plausible suspicions. Rumor never proves anything. It does its work if it creates distrust.

(2) *As a smoke screen.* Rumor can hide the truth.

The technique is to tell so many secrets that the true secret cannot be detected among all the conflicting reports. The Germans are past masters at this art of letting many conflicting "inside stories" slip out of Germany into the countries they wish to confuse.

(3) *For discrediting news sources.* This is a special technique.

During the second year of the war, the British
420

tried several times to bomb the chief railroad station in Berlin. They failed, but the Germans planted "unconfirmed reports" that the British had succeeded. When these rumors came back to England, the British took them as confirmations of their success and broadcast them. Then the German Ministry of Propaganda took American newspaper men to the scene to prove that the British statements were not true, thus discrediting the broadcast.

(4) *As bait*. Rumor may be used to learn the truth.

The Japanese may try to start rumors about American losses in a naval engagement. They do not know what the losses were and they wish to know. The rumors may spread, affecting American morale. If the American government, to bolster morale, then broadcasts the truth, the Japanese have the information they wanted.

Kinds of Rumors

Rumors differ according to whether desire or fear or hate gives them force. Here are the three most common kinds.

(1) *The pipe-dream rumor* depends on wishful thinking. There is pleasure in believing and repeating what you hope is true.

Three common pipe-dream rumors in February of 1942 were these:

"The Japs do not have enough oil and war supplies to last six months."

"There will soon be a revolution in both Germany and Italy."

"Lloyds of London and Wall Street are betting 10 to 1 that the war will be over by fall."

(2) *The bogey rumor* is the opposite of the pipe-dream. It expresses a fear, not a wish. Examples of this for early 1942 are:

"The Germans have a new secret weapon against which there is no defense."

"The entire Pacific coast is completely devoid of antiaircraft defenses."

(3) *The wedge-driving rumor,* perhaps the most dangerous of all, is the rumor that attempts to create hostility and distrust between allies, or between particular groups within a country. It, too, depends on an emotion, hostility. People repeat it because they dislike a nation or a group. Some early 1942 examples of it are:

"Churchill blackmailed Roosevelt into provoking war with Japan."

"The British never fight with their own troops, only with their colonials and troops from their allied nations."

"Gasoline rationing is necessary because so much is being used in joy-riding by the British who get it through lend-lease agreement."

The Office of War Information has published a list of the targets at which the 1942 crop of wedge-driving rumors—the "hate rumors"—were aimed. They were: Army administration, business, Catholics, defense workers, draft boards, English, farmers, Jews, labor, Negroes, profiteers, rationing boards, Red Cross (blood donor service), Russia and unions.

EFFECTS OF RUMORS

Some rumors appear freely in the press and radio. They are frankly reported as rumors and usually do little harm. They do not get exaggerated by repetition.

Others are covert and secret, being repeated *sub rosa* and often growing to fantastic proportions. These are dangerous. The teller, having no responsibility, is free to let his wishes, fears, and hostilities work.

Most rumors can be accepted passively. They are insidious but slowly undermine confidence.

Other rumors, however, incite action. They are the panic rumors that come as reports of military defeat or of the approach of enemy troops. With them the danger is real, palpable, and immediate, for the listener tends to do something about them suddenly and violently. He packs a few of his most cherished possessions in a wheelbarrow, collects his family, and starts trudging out of town away from the enemy. Then he himself becomes a rumor, and the rumor becomes a fact, for people see him going and decide to go too.

Presently the procession along the road is the most potent rumor of all, a visual symbol that needs no words. Everyone seeks to join it. Panic is on.

WHAT MAKES RUMOR WORK

Rumors thrive on fertile soil. What soil is fertile?

A community, a city, or an army moved by common emotions is fertile soil. And war is a circumstance that produces this state. Then men share the hope of victory, the fear of defeat, and hostility against both the enemy and all others who threaten them with failure. A rumor that gives expression to these emotions is easy to tell, easy to hear.

423

Lack of information about important things favors rumor. People demand information about what concerns them most. The greater their concern, the more information they require. When news is scarce and interest high, newspapers have to string out their accounts of trivial events in order to satisfy the public appetite. Then it is that rumor spreads easily. People want news, and they lack the factual information that would contradict and stop a false rumor.

Rumor is encouraged by *discontent, frustration, boredom* and *idleness.* That is why rumor spreads so easily in small communities, like prisons and hospitals—and sometimes in camps. Men really need to be active, and idleness puts them under tension. Gossip and rumor provide release for this tension—a certain amount of release, although it is not very satisfying. Every leader of troops can fight rumor and boredom by keeping his men busy, even though they are trained and ready for action and forced to wait through the months until a new fighting front can be established. If you are an enlisted man, welcome work. It's better for you.

Expectation fosters rumor. Men are eager for news, eager for action, eager to hear of victories, eager to be off to the war. If no one feeds them facts, they will take half-facts as better than nothing. Men readily believe what previous events or experiences have prepared them to believe; they discount stories contrary to what they expect.

HARDY RUMORS

Surprisingly enough, the rumor you hear today as if it were fresh news may be a veteran of many wars dressed up in modern uniform. It was told in 1918, it may have been told in 1861 or even in 1776. Here is one such in the 1942 version:

"An American prisoner in Japan writes home that all is well. At the end of his letter he asks that his family save the stamp on the letter for his collection. So the family soak the stamp off, and beneath it they find the message: 'They have cut out my tongue.'"

Rumors persist in this way because the human needs, the fears and hopes and hatred that the rumor satisfies, are very much the same from generation to generation.

The persistent rumor in 1915, that Russian troops had been seen in England, lived because the British wished it to be true. Its cousin in 1942, the rumor in Russia that the British were landing forces to defend Russia, may crop up again and again for the same reason.

Other reasons why rumors become perennials, cropping up year after year, and in war after war, are because they are timely, natural, easy to remember, easy to repeat, plausible but not too plausible to be impressive, and unverifiable.

To survive for posterity, rumor, like other more reputable forms of literature, must have qualities that command attention. It must have punch, it must be striking, with maybe a wry and unexpected twist like the slogan, "England will fight to the last Frenchman." It is helped tremendously by humor, for everyone notices, remembers, and repeats a good story.

"The British could not use the American tanks that they got because Americans make tanks without reverse gear." It is natural for an American to chuckle over a rumor like that, remember it, and repeat it, because it is obviously funny—it is only subtly malicious.

Censorship and Rumor

Censorship, since it blocks important news, favors rumor. In France, at the time of its invasion when censorship was strict, all sorts of demoralizing rumors were current. In Great Britain, where the censorship has been fairly lenient, rumor has been neither widespread nor demoralizing.

The censor is, of course, between the devil and the deep blue sea. If he lets too much be told, the enemy benefits unduly. If he stops too much news, he demoralizes his own people. Somewhere between these extremes he must make his choice.

For instance, the American authorities do not release for the news statements about the places at which ships are torpedoed. They wish to prevent the Germans' learning of the success and whereabouts of their own submarines. But in the spring of 1942 a ship was torpedoed off the coast of Shangri-La, let us say, and the dead and wounded were brought into one of the smaller coastal ports. There were hundreds of witnesses, but the news was suppressed from the papers. So the false rumors began to fly:

"15,000 troops were lost off Shangri-La."

"The whole region of Shangri-La is under martial law and great numbers of bodies are being washed ashore."

"The bodies of two hundred nurses have been washed up off Shangri-La."

426

"All the hospitals and hotels in Shangri-La are filled with wounded and dying."

"All cold storage space in Shangri-La is filled with corpses."

"All the troops washing up at Shangri-La are Negroes."

"The shores near Shangri-La have been lined with undertakers for days."

RUMORMONGERS

What kind of a man spreads rumors? Does everybody spread them? If not, who does?

Everybody likes to repeat a story, a humorous story, a story which is apt and catchy or is remarkable because it makes a huge unexpected assertion. Many people repeat such stories without believing them, expressing disbelief or laughing them off. That is a fairly healthy kind of rumormongering.

But there are, nevertheless, differences among people in the credence that they give to unverifiable rumors, in the readiness with which they repeat them. Psychologists do not have the complete answer to this question, but there is good evidence that the most persistent rumormongers are persons who feel emotionally insecure, who are not well adjusted to life. Such persons fear and hate most readily, trying to offset their fears with hopes; and fear, hate, and hope are the ingredients of the soil in which rumors thrive.

It is also true that these less secure people lack and need prestige. Repeating a rumor gives prestige to the repeater. News always seems to be the property of the teller. Potentates used to kill the bearers of bad news, as if the messengers were responsible for this news. Everyone knows what fun it is to be the person to spring a surprise or to tell a great secret. Some people are never the center of attention except when telling a secret—perhaps a secret that isn't true.

How to Control Rumor

Officers or officials, who must try to control rumor among their men or in dealing with civilian populations, will find these rules, based on scientific observation, helpful.

(1) Insure good faith in official communications. If the public loses confidence in the reliability of the communiqués of the armed forces, and of the press and radio, then rumors begin to spread fast.

(2) Develop faith in leaders. People can stand censorship and lack of news when they feel sure that they are not being told falsehoods and that what is held back is held back for good reason. That applies to all leaders from the President to the humblest schoolteacher, from the general to the corporal.

(3) Present as many facts as possible. Let the press and radio give as full and circumstantial news as they can without giving too much aid to the enemy. Let the armed forces do the same. Men want facts. When they can't get facts, they take rumor.

(4) Keep men and women busy. Prevent idleness and monotony. Empty minds are easily filled with untruths and worries. Idle hands make busy tongues.

(5) Fight rumormongering. Campaign against rumor. Expose it as enemy propaganda. Discredit specific rumors as inaccurate and false. Caricature rumormongers.

428

A camp or a factory may keep a Rumor Board. That is a bulletin board on which apparently false rumors are posted. After a while the exhibit becomes ridiculous, because the board has on it so many rumors that contradict each other, so many already disproved by publication of the truth.

There is also the Rumor Clinic, one of which has been operating in Massachusetts. The Clinic collects all the rumors it can get hold of from interested citizens, from persons who monger their rumors to the Clinic, from men like bartenders who hear lots of idle talk. Then it investigates them, publishes them, refutes or corrects them, and incidentally, by showing that rumors are usually false, ridicules them.

A company commander could have his own rumor clinic, along with a rumor board. He can encourage his men to form the habit of asking, in the words experienced American soldiers have used for many years, "What latrine did you hear that one in?"

But the best way to scotch rumors is to oust them from mind. Keep your troops busy. Keep busy yourself. Since nobody can keep the great public busy, there have to be these rumor clinics and campaigns. But the right things will happen oftener if the soldier is too busy with his job for wishing, worrying and passing guesses along.

XX: PSYCHOLOGICAL WARFARE

DEATH CAN BE INFLICTED upon the bodies of the enemy, destruction upon property, but defeat is a conquest of the mind.

Some military men think of war mainly in terms of actual military action—advancing or retreating troops, bombing raids over enemy territory, naval battles. Yet success in most military actions depends ultimately upon psychological factors. Not only are the chances of success in an attack upon an enemy position greatly increased when the enemy's soldiers suffer from low morale; the final victory means that the enemy soldiers are defeated because they have to give up, and that the enemy nation is defeated because its people at last submit their wills to the will of the conqueror.

The Russian soldiers defending Stalingrad withstood fierce German assaults from siege guns and systematic Stuka bombing for three months and never surrendered. The German army had already overcome with much less effort other cities with military defenses just as good. But at Stalingrad, all the bombings, the artillery fire, the assaults failed because they could not break the fighting spirit of the defenders nor induce them to surrender.

And the Dutch lost their country but not their independence. They did not submit.

In total war economic, military and psychological action are all used to bring about submission in the enemy. Economic action deprives the enemy of vital materials. Military action destroys his armies by killing, capturing or scattering the soldiers, smashing or capturing the guns, tanks, planes, trucks, and supplies. But it is successful psychological action that in the end deprives the enemy of his will to resist, and can spoil the individual soldier as a fighting machine by removing the one thing that makes him fight, the hope of success. The soldier without hope is like a tank without gas.

When you come right down to it, all warfare—military and economic too—is psychological warfare. Since willingness to surrender is a state of mind, all these different means are used to bring about a change of mind, to convert *determination to resist* into *willingness to accept defeat.*

The chief tool of psychological warfare—the one that is most peculiarly psychological—is propaganda. It involves the strategy and tactics of changing opinion in a nation, in a group within a nation, or even in specific enemy troops. The troops can be bombarded by loud-speakers in the front line or by leaflets dropped by planes behind the front.

With the strategy of psychological warfare the average soldier has little to do directly, for it is in the hands of specialized services. It goes on, whether he knows about it or not, softening up the enemy. And it may be one of the main reasons why he finds enemy troops surrendering so easily, or the people of an occupied country so docile or even friendly.

But any soldier may himself be the subject of propaganda. His best defense is to know about propaganda, about what is going on, about how the total

431

war is being won. If he is to be more than a cog in the war machine, he wants to know why the enemy reacts as he does. And American soldiers want to know *why* about such things.

If you have picked up a leaflet, scattered by the enemy behind your lines, you ought to be able to give it a critical once over, and to protect yourself by understanding just what it is the enemy is trying to do to you.

Since propaganda tries to change opinion, the people who plan propaganda have to know all about the opinions they are trying to change. You can't be intelligent about changing anything unless you know what it is you are trying to change.

If it's a whole nation or a part of a country that is to be propagandized, then the propaganda staff has got to find out about public opinion in that country in order to go ahead. If it's only an enemy division that is to be subject to attack, then the staff has to know a lot about that particular division. Are its soldiers getting fed up with the war? Are they beginning to give up hope? Do they know they are surrounded? Did Italian soldiers in Africa know what was happening to their divisions in Russia? Do Japs in the Aleutians get news of the Solomons?

So enemy opinion and morale have to be discovered first. Then propaganda can start working.

POLLING FOR OPINION

If you want to know what people want, you can ask them. That is what an election is. The people are polled, and the results show who they want for President, or senator or mayor.

432

And if you want to know what people think, you can ask them that too. You could ask *every person* in the United States whether he believed that our main attack should be directed first at Germany or at Japan, whether he thought that the voting age should be lowered to eighteen like the draft age. You could, but you wouldn't find out about it that way because it would be too much trouble and expense.

Instead you'd take a *sample*. If you want to know the purity of water in a reservoir or the heating capacity of a carload of coal, you don't examine all the water or all the coal. You take a sample.

If you want to know how many men of every different height there are in the Army, you could wait until all the statistics are in and counted by machines, but you don't have to. You can take a sample. But then you must be careful to get a fair sample— to choose men from different parts of the country, from cities and from the country, from well-to-do families who always have plenty of the right foods and from poor families who don't, and you choose the right numbers of men of each kind to make the sample fair. But, if you choose wisely, then the sample will tell you what you want to know.

If you want to know what the people of the United States are thinking about some problem connected with the war during the first week in January, you can find that out too if you take a sample— a *fair sample*—and have skilled interviewers ask them carefully worded questions. That will tell you. The method works again and again. It can predict the results of elections—if the sample is fair—except

433

when the opinion happens to be very evenly divided.

In the democratic countries these principles have been used in public opinion polls, which determine how people are feeling about questions of social or political importance—and nowadays particularly about the conduct and the progress of the war. Interviewers are trained to ask questions without implying that one answer or another is preferable or popular.

You have to choose the fair sample carefully and intelligently. It must include both men and women, in about equal numbers. It must include rich and poor, so chosen that the different incomes in the sample have about the same frequencies as do incomes in the country at large. Religion is important only when the issue affects religion or the church. Age is important when radicalism and conservatism are touched by the question, for old people are more conservative than young. Business occupation doesn't generally matter, unless the question is related to business or income. Such things as height, weight, and hair color can nearly always be neglected entirely—unless you are trying to find out such a thing as how many people like fat men. Then you'd have to interview thin people, medium people, and fat people, all three.

The results of such polls are analyzed and, in the democratic countries, published in the newspapers. They tell how the country is feeling.

The things thus found out are important for the men in Washington to know. Even in war the United States remains a democracy. The President, Congress, and the armed forces all need to know what the country thinks about the war, about the lend-lease arrangements, and about the taxes that buy the materièl.

Of course, the enemy knows all this too—if it's in the newspapers. But experience shows that, in a democracy, it is better to let everyone know how everyone else feels, even though the enemy finds out too, than it is to hush the truth up. The totalitarian countries don't believe that this statement is true, but then they don't believe in democracy either.

You don't have to have a very big sample if it is wisely selected. You can—believe it or not—predict an election among 50,000,000 voters pretty well from 10,000 careful interviews. That's taking only one person in 5,000. As a matter of fact, 3,000 interviews will give a pretty good idea of how opinion is runing among the 130,000,000 inhabitants of the United States.

The method of polling samples is not, however, limited only to these huge populations. You can use it on much smaller groups. For instance, a sample of the U.S. Army has recently been polled in order to find out what the new soldiers think about Army life, and also what soldiers do with their after-duty hours. Soldiers have also been asked to say what they think makes a good leader, what inspires loyalty in them to a leader, what hinders loyalty. They may not all be right in their opinions, but it helps the leaders to know what the soldiers are thinking about them and about leadership.

And you don't have to ask these questions of all the soldiers. You take a sample, from a variety of camps, and certainly from various outfits which have different leaders. And then you know—pretty accurately.

Spying and Listening

Not all polling is public. The Nazis, who must keep themselves informed about public opinion in Germany, use what is really a spy system. They cannot ask direct questions because Germans are trained to reply to political and social questions in the "right" way, whatever their real opinions. But the Nazi party workers ask indirect questions, listen to overheard conversations, observe the actions of the people. They report to their leaders, who report to their district leaders, who report in turn to the regional leaders, who, after putting everything together, report to the German Ministry of Propaganda.

This is valuable information for the German government, but you're right: it isn't printed in the newspapers.

In Great Britain they do a great deal of interviewing to check on public opinion, and the interviewers are also instructed to keep listening. They listen to conversations they hear on the street, in the streetcars, in places of amusement. They overhear whatever they do overhear, and their results are tabulated and published. It is a kind of eavesdropping, but it is not the German system. It is not elaborately done, the government is not directly concerned with it, and the results are published. Espionage agents or foreign military attaches can also get some information about public opinion without having available any of this sort of machinery.

You can get information about opinion by finding

436

out which expressed opinions are popular. One way is to see what the newspapers are saying in their editorials and then look up the sizes of their circulations. Editors generally manage to express the opinions their readers want. If they don't those readers stop reading and the circulation drops, unless other readers start buying the paper because they like its views.

You can see which radio commentators are popular and what opinions they support. You can study the applause at movie theaters when the newsreels show statesmen and generals. You can see how many persons go to mass meetings held for particular purposes. People don't often go to meetings hoping to get their opinions changed. They go hoping to hear arguments for what they already believe.

The Japs are reported to have used the applause method to find out how the Chinese in occupied China felt about the occupation. They interrupted a film to show a picture of Dr. Sun Yat-Sen, China's George Washington. The audience hesitated; then applauded. Then they showed a picture of Generalissimo Chiang Kai-Shek. There was a thunderous ovation. Then they showed the Chinese puppet governor, whom they themselves had placed in power. The audience booed, and the Japs had the answer to their question.

Most of these techniques can be used by a wise leader to determine opinion and morale in his outfit. The leader does not have to snoop, but when he begins to hear grumbling or to hear of grumbling, he will take notice and try to find out whether it is representative of his whole unit. Applause or boos

437

at a camp show may tell him a lot. If he really wants to find out about how his men are feeling, he talks to them—not all of them, but a fair sample of them. There may be times when he ought to conduct a poll of opinion—not about a military decision, but at least on how to spend the company fund.

Being interested in what other people think is not undemocratic, even though you have to do some eavesdropping. It's the essence of democracy. And the wise leader, being a man who wants to help his men be successful, needs to know what the men are thinking and how they feel.

PROPAGANDA

The truth is the best propaganda. Propaganda does not have to be dishonest or lying. Hitler said that a lie will be believed if it is big enough, and it may be at first. But the big lies don't stand up. Eventually the truth catches them and unmasks them.

Yet even the truth has to be interpreted, has to have its bearing on obscure larger issues shown.

That's propaganda. It states a fact and also interprets it. It is trying to change opinion.

The goal of propaganda is always *a change in state of mind*. In psychological warfare the goal is the undermining of enemy morale, the persuading of the enemy that his cause is hopeless and that he will be better off if he gives up. The propaganda may be directed at the whole enemy people, but it may also be directed merely at the other side of the front lines. It may be leaflets dropped on an enemy division, telling him that he is surrounded, pointing out to him the evidence that he is really surrounded, reminding him of the kindly treatment he will get as a prisoner of war.

Propaganda works on feelings that are already present in the enemy. No use to argue to a victorious column while it presses into new territory that final defeat for it is sure and that surrender would be better. But when enemy morale is low, propaganda can make it lower—wise, effective propaganda can. Doubt, insecurity and frustration are the fertile soil for psychological warfare.

Good propaganda always starts from a *fact,* an event. There has been a victory. You cite that victory and then interpret its significance to the enemy. Or there has been an air raid on a harbor or an unusual spell of cold weather with lots of snow at the front. The fact is known to the enemy, and forms a good start for propaganda. If you are attacking the whole enemy country, then the basis of the attack must be some important event that is believed by everyone to be true as well as important. Only weak propaganda starts with an unknown event or a lie and then enlarges upon it.

Starting the propaganda off with an important fact gets attention for it and also gives it the flavor of truth. Even falsehood may seem true when closely connected with the truth. A jury may believe everything a witness says if he goes into minute detail and most of the details are obviously true. You don't expect a rotten apple among all the good.

Since propaganda takes this advantage of facts, it must be *timely.* There is no use in telling the enemy what good chow you have until you know he is short of food. Then it's a pity to miss a chance of

439

reminding him what he would have to eat as a prisoner. You can't build on his defeat until he has had a defeat. Then you should go right to it and worry him a little more.

Good timing is essential. Save your propaganda until the target shows. Then let go with your psychological fire.

If you aren't prompt, you may miss the boat—with propaganda. The first interpretation is nearly always the longest lived. Watch for an opportunity and then use it at once. Especially does that rule hold for large scale radio propaganda. If we get our version of an important battle on the air first, the enemy's version may never catch up with it—or be believed when it does come along.

Good propaganda *never forgets its audience.* You can't persuade unless you know what kind of minds, what set of opinions, you are talking to. That's why a nation cannot be propagandized unless its state of public opinion is known. What you are saying must seem important to the listeners—important enough for them to risk their lives to listen. And important enough for them to repeat to their friends and neighbors. That is how propaganda gets around, mostly, by being passed on.

A group of people with different desires and different feelings make a poor propaganda target. No one argument appeals to them all. But soldiers generally form a good target. They are closely united by similar experiences, almost sure to feel the same fears, frustrations, and doubts at the same time.

In order to start good propaganda you have to find out how the enemy is feeling. At the front that is

440

generally done by questioning prisoners. The intelligence service may help in other ways.

For propaganda directed at an enemy nation, the information about what is going on inside the nation is obtained from neutral travellers who have come out, from eavesdropping on the enemy local radio broadcasts, and sometimes also from prisoners. Often a prisoner will talk about what happened when he was recently on furlough, although he stays quite silent about what is going on at the front.

Timely information about the enemy people is particularly important for *black propaganda*. This type of propaganda is new in this war. Radio broadcasting developed it.

Black propaganda consists of radio broadcasts beamed to the enemy, but pretending to come from within the enemy's own territory. Sometimes it pretends to criticize the enemy government or his conduct of the war. And it makes all sorts of suggestions that persons in the enemy nation might, often for selfish reasons, be disposed to carry out, once they are put in mind of them. Sometimes the suggestions are in negative form, suggestions not to do something. Everybody realizes that the admonition, "Johnny, don't put beans in your nose!" is likely to end by Johnny's putting the beans just exactly where he was told not to.

Suppose a scrap dealer in London picks up a broadcast which really originates in German-occupied territory, saying that British scrap dealers are holding on to their scrap because they think the price is going to rise. The broadcast enlarges on the need of the British government for scrap and urges the dealers to sell at once for patriotic reasons. Well, the genuine patriot will sell, if he has not done so already. But the selfish man—and how many of them there are—will think: "But why should I sell when the others do not?" And so he holds on to the precious scrap when it really is not true that many others have been holding on to it.

The suggestions would not work, of course, if it were known that the broadcast really originated with the Germans. It has to seem to the hearer to arise in his own country.

Combat Propaganda

Combat troops—at least in the German, Russian, and Japanese armies—are accompanied by propaganda units. They use public address systems, installed in field headquarters or in mobile units, to talk directly to the enemy soldiers. They also broadcast behind the enemy lines, and drop leaflets behind them.

It was such a German unit that broadcast to the French soldiers in June, 1940, the "news" that a French Armistice commission was going to meet with German authorities to sign an armistice. The broadcast had a devastating effect on French morale. The French troops in the front line reasoned: "Why hold the line and be shot today, when the war will be over tomorrow?" Resistance crumbled.

During the Polish campaign German propaganda units encouraged fraternization between the French and German troops on the Maginot line. They wanted the French to think that this was a "phony" war—until Poland was out of the way. So they bellowed friendly greetings over the lines with their loud speakers, and even sometimes warned the French that a German shell was coming over.

Dropping leaflets or newspapers behind the lines is a common form of propaganda. The enemy opposes this kind of attack by prescribing severe penalties for keeping or reading the material dropped.

In the First World War the American forces used the following device for getting enemy soldiers to break the rules by keeping the leaflets dropped. Each leaflet carried a coupon which provided safe passage across the lines for a soldier who would surrender. Then, in addition, it described the rations of the U. S. Army and promised the same food to its prisoners. Many German soldiers, tired and hungry, kept and used the coupons.

It has been suggested that a leaflet might carry coupons which could be exchanged by soldiers after capture for beer, cigarettes, or similar luxuries.

The Russians publish a newspaper for the benefit of the German soldiers. They call it *The Truth* and drop it behind the German lines. By April 1942 there had been 250 issues of this paper, and 15,000,000 copies had been distributed. That made 15,000,000 bloodless shots at German soldiers, and some of them took effect. German prisoners taken by the Russians were found to have read many issues of *The Truth* and so to have learned the Russian point of view toward the war.

The Japanese drop leaflets over Chungking and other parts of China. This propaganda urges the Chinese to join with the Japanese in "throwing off the yoke of Britain and America." They also dropped

443

a number of similar leaflets on our troops in Bataan.

British bombers drop thousands of tiny newspapers all over Germany and German-occupied countries. These papers have four pages, each eight inches square, are folded up to the size of a cigarette and are printed in several different languages. They have illustrations and carry the latest news—the real news of the United Nations, the news which cannot pass the German censor.

Victory for Psychological Warfare

There is a formula for victory in psychological warfare. It applies to whole nations and to small groups, to civilians and to troops. It is the formula for breaking the will to resist, for creating surrender. In war you can kill men, coerce them, or change their minds. Psychological warfare aims to change their minds.

Here are the four steps in this kind of victory. They do not have to happen in quick succession. If you catch the enemy at any one point you can perhaps help him on to the next. The order may change, but this is the most effective one.

(1) The enemy must be weary. He must be sick and tired and discouraged. Sick of being separated from his loved ones. Tired of cold and short rations, of grief and blood, of maiming and privation, of desolation and the destruction of war.

And the civilians at home can be sick and tired too. Tired of working long hours, tired of being bombed. Tired of going without enough food. Tired of the privations and horrors of total war.

This first step—getting the enemy war weary—

depends on the military and economic arms. There has to be blockade and defeat. People do not get sick of success and plunder and plenty.

(2) The second step in psychological warfare is to turn disillusionment into despair, to convince the weary enemy that victory is impossible. Here propaganda can help the military. Every defeat serves this purpose, but a defeat of the enemy skillfully interpreted to him serves the purpose better. Show that he lost the battle because he did not have enough ammunition, and that he is never going to have enough ammunition when the munitions factories are being bombed so heavily at home.

(3) The third step is to promise something better. Show him a way out. The cornered beast fights to the death unless he sees a way of escape. To the troops in the enemy line, offer good rations and the comforts accorded to prisoners of war. And to them, as well as to the entire enemy nation, offer a fair peace, a peace that is better than what they have, than what they can any longer expect. Woodrow Wilson's Fourteen Points did much to shorten the First World War. They were a blueprint for a fair peace. Now we have the Atlantic Charter, with still further specifications possible later.

This is wholly the job of propaganda. Military offense cannot accomplish it, although the Army can conduct the propaganda at the front.

(4) After the creation of despair, after the promise of something better, there is left still one further step for psychological warfare. The enemy must be led to fix the blame on his own leaders. The soldier who surrenders when he could have fought on must

445

have some excuse, and he will find it if his discipline is broken down by his conviction that his own leaders are responsible for his unnecessary predicament. That last step may come of itself, but propaganda can help it.

THE PSYCHOLOGICAL DEFENSIVE

The defense against psychological warfare is sophistication, knowing all about it. You have got to know what the enemy is up to. You have got to know what propaganda is, how warfare is conducted by it, what the enemy is trying to do to you. Then you will not be duped.

Don't trust the enemy. If you hear a broadcast, get hold of a leaflet, are told a rumor, *inquire into its source*. Be suspicious if you can't tell who started the ideas. Trust the enemy only when he is fighting you. If he starts giving you advice "for your own good," you may know for sure that it is really for *his* own good.

Remember that broadcasts and leaflets don't necessarily come from the sources from which they claim to come. And rumor never states its source except in vague terms.

Be critical. Even though a story starts off with what you know to be true, don't trust the interpretation that is tacked on to the truth. Think it through. Distinguish between facts that can be verified and alleged facts that can't. Distinguish between facts and interpretations. Don't be a sucker. Use your head.

And so *don't accept the first interpretation* you hear about the reason a battle was won or lost, or

446

the reason there isn't any more coffee. Wait. The first story is the best propaganda, because it has no other story to overcome, but it is not necessarily the best for you to believe. There may be another story along in a few days that will make the basic fact in the story look very different. Don't snap at the bait. Wait for a worm without a hook in it.

But, in general, don't trust the enemy. *Don't trust the enemy.* If he turns friendly, fear him—or better, understand that he's up to no good. If you are captured, tell him your name, rank, and number, and nothing else. Just because he seems friendly and well-meaning, don't spill things you think are unimportant. You can't know what is important to him. The little details of the life in your outfit or back in the States may be just what he wants to know. If he has been a tourist in your own home town, don't be led into exchanging reminiscences of your old haunts. And don't tell how your folks at home are getting on, no matter how sympathetic he is about them. He needs to know or he would not spend time talking about such things.

Trust only your own leaders. They're for you. Trust them, and be wise.

Index

In order to make it useful to psychologists as well as laymen, this index includes many technical terms not used in the text.

Accommodation, 31-3, 36f., 43
Acuity, auditory, 118f.
 visual, 24-6
Adaptation, bodily position, 160
 bodily rotation, 157-9
 dark, 60-70
 light, 66f.
Adjustment, aggression, 316
 aggression against comrades,
  325-32
 Army life, 343-5
 civilian, 343-5
 compensation, 358f.
 cooperation, 345-7
 death, 348f.
 defeat, 312-21
 defense mechanism, 356-60
 discipline, 345-7
 escape mechanism, 359f.
 failure, 318-21
 fear, 347-9
 food, 333f.
 frustration, 313-21
 healthy mind, 350, 363-5
 hysteria, 319f.
 identification, 360
 individualism, 345-7
 mental breaks, 350-4, 363-5
 mental conflict, 360-5
 mental defense, 356-60
 mental fatigue, 354
 mental symptoms, 354-6, 363-5
 neurosis, 127f., 318-21, 350-4,
  363-5
 projection, 357-9
 psychic illness, 318-21
 sick-call, 359f.
 transferred feeling, 360
 war shock, 353-6, 363-5

Aggression, against comrades,
  325-32
 frustration, 316
Air-sickness, avoidance, 163
 causes, 161-3
Alcohol, aviation, 279
 coordination, 279f.
 depressant, 276f.
 efficiency, 276-80
 intoxication, 277-80
 judgment, 277
 limits, 277-80
 sensitivity, 276f.
Altitude, cold, 272
 low oxygen, 273-5
 mental effects, 273-5
Anger, conditions, 322
 control, 323f.
 effects, 321-5
 mobs, 386-9
 spread, 324f.
Anoxia, 273-5
Anxiety, see Fear
Aptitude, clerical, 193f.
 definition, 178f.
 mechanical, 193
 tests, 192-4
Aviation, alcohol, 279
 cold, 272
 deafness, 121-3, 129f.
 effects of altitude, 273-5
 fatigue, 293
 landing, 53f.
 learning, 224f.

Balancing, 151-4, 159f.
Beats, acoustic, 128f.
Benzedrine, effects, 283
Binocular parallax, 48-51

448

Blinking, 39
Boredom, chronic fatigue, 261f.
  day-dreaming, 261
  intelligence, 261
  work, 260-2
  See also Fatigue
Brain injury, 353
Bravery, see Fear

Caffeine, effects, 282f.
Camouflage, 76-9, 85-110
  color, 107f.
  color blindness, 108-10
  contours, 94-6
  contrast, 88-90
  counter-camouflage, 104-7
  dazzle painting, 94f.
  filters, 106f.
  infra-red, 103f.
  lighting, 26f.
  lights, 88
  movement, 100-3
  new objects, 105f.
  odors, 149f.
  paint, 103f., 106f.
  photography, 103-7
  principles, 88-104
  regular patterns, 96-8
  shadows, 91-4, 106
  size, 88
  sound, 138f.
  stereoscopy, 104f.
  texture, 90f.
  uniqueness, 98-100, 102
Censorship, rumor, 426f.
Chemical sense, 143
Classification, of jobs, see Jobs
  of men, see Selection
Climate, customs, 406-8
  mental attitudes, 407f.
Cochlea, 120f.
Coffee, effects, 282f.
Cold, clothing, 271f.
  effects, 269-73
Color, 79-85
  circle, 82-4
  mixture, 81-4
  retinal sensitivity, 63

Color blindness, 107-113
  camouflage, 108-10
  frequency, 108f.
  kinds, 109
  tests, 111-3
Communication, auditory, 129-33
  telephone, 133
  testing, 132
Compensation, 358f.
Compass, sun or stars, 171f.
  use, 169
Conditioning, see Learning
Cones, retina, 60-5
Conflict, mental, 360-5
Contours, camouflage, 91-6
Contrast, visual, 72f.
Convergence, eyes, 44f.
Coordination, eyes and muscles,
  55-7
Counter-camouflage, see Camou-
  flage
Courage, see Fear
Criticism, rules, 332

Dazzle painting, 94f.
Deafness, 121-5
  airplane, 121-3, 129f.
  faked, 125
  gun-fire, 123-5
  neurotic, 125
Decibels, 117f.
Defeat, adjustment, 312-21
Defense, psychological warfare,
  446f.
Defense mechanisms, 356-60
Desires, 285-9
Direction indicators, 169-72
Direction sense, clues, 164-7
  maps, 168, 172f.
  orientation, 165-72
Discipline, leadership, 367-72
  panic, 390-3
  personal adjustment, 345-7
Dizziness, 157-9
Drill, 202, 207f.
Drives, 285-9
Driving aptitude, 180

449

Ear, cochlea, 120f.
  hearing, 119-21
  otolith organs, 155f., 159-61
  rotation sense, 154-61
  semicircular canals, 164-61
  See also Hearing
Efficiency, alcohol, 276-80
  altitude, 273-5
  benzedrine, 283
  body temperature, 269-71
  caffeine, 282f.
  carrying loads, 249
  coffee, 282f.
  cold, 269-73
  heat, 269-71
  job analysis, 247-9
  learning, 237-43
  low oxygen, 273-5
  mechanical work, 248f.
  need, 244-6
  planning work, 248f.
  sleep, 262-7
  tea, 282f.
  tobacco, 280-2
  work standardization, 249
  See also Boredom, Fatigue, Sleep
Emotion, adjustment, 18f.
  See also Anger, Fear, Mobs,
    Panic
Eye, cones, 60-5
  fatigue, 34-9, 251-3
  focussing, 31-3, 36f., 43
  lens, 31-3, 36, 43
  mechanism, 30-7, 60-3
  muscles, 32, 35-7
  pupil, 60f.
  retina, 32-4
  rods, 60-5
  See also Sight

Fatigue, chronic, 261f.
  comfort, 252-5
  continuous work, 251, 257-9
  eyes, 251-3
  flying, 293
  illumination, 259
  mental, 354
  mental strain, 255f.

Fatigue, *continued*
  morale, 293
  noise, 253, 260
  physiology, 250f., 255
  poor work, 256-9
  rate, 257-9
  relaxation, 257-9
  rest, 257-9
  rifle sighting, 252f.
  small muscles, 251f.
  tired feeling, 256
  ventilation, 260
  visual, 34-9
  See also Boredom, Efficiency,
    Sleep
Fear, action, 300
  adjustment, 347-9
  avoidance, 300f.
  causes, 298f.
  companionship, 300
  effects, 318-21
  foolhardiness, 304f.
  humor, 303f.
  idealism, 305f.
  knowledge, 301
  morale, 295f.
  occasions, 296-300
  panic, 392f.
  prayer, 304
  prolonged, 302f.
  rumor, 415-7
  statistics, 301
Fighting, reasons for, 306-12
Filters, camouflage, 106f.
Finding the way, 169-72
Flying, *see* Aviation
Flying fatigue, 293
Foolhardiness, 304f.
Frost-bite, 273f.
Frustration, effects, 313-21
  rumor, 424

Gases, *see* War gases
G.C.T., 187-92
General Classification Test, 187-92
  Army grades, 188f.
  distribution of grades, 190
  schooling, 191f.

Getting lost, 164-74
Glare, 28-30, 73
Gun-fire, hearing, 123-5

Habit, *see* Learning, Teaching, Training
Harmonics, 114f.
Healthy mind, 350, 363-5
Hearing, alcohol, 276f.
  beats, 128f.
  deafness, 121-5
  ear-plugs, 124f.
  effects of noise, 126-8
  gun-fire, 123-5
  harmonics, 114f.
  limits, 116-8
  localization of objects, 133-8
  loudness, 114, 117
  masking, 129f.
  mechanism, 119-21
  pitch, 114-7
  quality, 114f.
  rules, 139-41
  sensitivity, 118f.
  sound camouflage, 138f.
  thresholds, 117-9
  timbre, 114f.
  See also Ear, Sound
Heat, effects, 269-71
Homosexuality, 340f.
Hue, 81-4
Hunger, food, 333f.
  morale, 293f.
  sex, 334f.
Hysteria, 319f., 363-5

Identification, 360
Illumination, fatigue, 259
Incentives, 285-9
Individual differences, 178-82
Insanity, *see* Adjustment
Instruction, *see* Teaching
Intelligence, *see* General Classification Test
Interest, aptitude, 179f.
Interviews, leadership, 379f.
  selection, 186f., 196f.

Jobs, analysis, 197-9, 247-9
  aptitude tests, 192-4
  Army, 175f., 183f.
  critical, 182f.
  efficiency, 247-9
  family tree, 184, 198f.
  relationships, 182-4, 198f.
  trade tests, 194f.
  See also Selection

Lacrimator gases, 147
Leadership, commands, 369-72
  discipline, 367-72
  dissension, 328-31
  good leaders, 369-82
  individual differences, 182
  learning, 382-4
  morale, 315f.
  obedience, 367-72
  panic, 394-6
  qualities, 381-4
  rules, 384
  selection, 379-82
  soldier complaints, 377-9
  soldier opinions, 372-5
  soldier's role, 375-7
  tests, 381
Learning, alcohol, 277
  association, 206-8, 223
  attention, 204, 213f.
  conditioning, 206-8
  discipline, 367-72
  distractions, 213f.
  drill, 202, 206-8
  fatigue, 221
  habit formation, 200-2
  incentive, 204-6, 215f.
  insight, 203f., 211, 215f., 220-2
  interest, 215f., 228-30, 240f.
  memorizing, 222f.
  memory systems, 222f.
  mistakes, 208-11
  motivation, 204-6, 240f.
  nature, 210f.
  overlearning, 212
  participation, 228f., 241f.
  plateaus, 223-6
  practice, 211f., 228

Learning, *continued*
  reading, 216-20
  relaxation, 212f.
  repetition, 222f.
  reward, 204-6
  shortcuts, 206-8
  solving problems, 220-2
  trial and error, 237
  unlearning, 202f.
  See also Teaching, Training
Lens, eye, 31-3, 36, 43
Light, nature, 79-81
Loudness, 114, 117

Maladjustment, *see* Adjustment
Maps, 168, 172f.
Masking, auditory, 129f.
Masturbation, 339f.
Mechanical aptitude test, 193
Memorizing, *see* Learning
Memory, *see* Learning
Memory systems, 222f.
Mental conflict, 360-5
Mental illness, 350-6, 363-5
Mobs, anger, 387-9
  causes, 386-90
  example, 386-9
  imitation, 386-9
  uncritical, 389f.
Morale, assessment, 290-2
  combat, 295f.
  criticism, 331f.
  defeat, 312-21
  discomfort, 294
  dissension, 325-30
  drives, 285-9
  family background, 289f.
  fatigue, 293
  fear, 295f., 347-9
  health, 289
  healthy mind, 350, 363-5
  hunger, 293f.
  incentives, 285-9
  loyalty, 307, 310
  motivation, 285-9
  needs, 285-9
  neurosis, 127f., 318-21, 350-4,
    363-5

Morale, *continued*
  opinions, 437f.
  panic, 394
  personal adjustment, 343-65
  punishment, 328
  rumor, 415-7, 419f., 423f., 428f.
  self-confidence, 289f.
  vitamins, 294
  work, 290
  zest, 292-6
  See also Adjustment, Anger, Fear
    Mobs, Motivation, Panic, Sex
Motivation, blame, 287
  commendation, 287
  competition, 288
  fighting, 306-12
  ideology, 310-12
  incentives, 285-9
  meeting defeat, 312-21
  military, 18f.
  morale, 286-9
  personal adjustment, 343-65
  pride, 288
  rumor, 415-7
  sex, 334-42
  social, 287f.
  See also Adjustment, Anger,
    Fear, Morale
Motor mechanics, G.C.T., 190
Movement, camouflage, 100-3
  perception of, 55-7

National differences, acquired,402f.
  animals, 409
  climate, 406-8
  cultural, 402f., 406-10
  emotionality, 401
  inherited, 398-401
  intelligence, 400f.
  native, 398-401
  nurture, 398-403
  physical, 399f.
  psychological, 400-2
  religion, 408-10
  rules of conduct, 410-2
Needs, 285-9
Neurosis, 127f., 318-21, 350-6,
    363-5

452

Night vision, 60-75
  fatigue, 74
  health, 73f.
  observation, 68-75
  preparation, 65-7
  red light, 67
  vitamins, 73f.
Noise, distraction, 126
  emotional effects, 126-8
  neurosis, 127f.
  stimulator, 128
  work, 260
  See also Hearing
Nystagmus, 158f.

Observation, night, 68-75
  rules, 37-9
Odor, *see* Smell
Officer candidates, G.C.T., 189
Officers, *see* Leadership
Opinions, *see* Public opinion
Orientation, 151-74
Otolith organs, 155f., 159-61
Oxygen, low, *see* Altitude

Paint, camouflage, 103f., 106f.
Panic, avoidance, 395f.
  causes, 390-5
  fear, 392f.
  lack of training, 393
  leadership, 394-6
  morale, 394
  rumor, 394
  troops, 389-95
Pep pills, 283
Perception, alcohol, 276f.
  direction, 169-72
  military use, 21f.
  objects, 76-9, 85-8
  position, 154-61
  recognition, 76-9, 85-8
  speed of, 179
  visual depth, 26f., 41-8
  visual distance, 39-54
Personality, interviews, 196f.
  preferences, 196f.
  selection, 195-7
  tests, 195f.

Personality, *continued*
  See also Adjustment
Perspective, 42
Photography, camouflage, 103-7
Pitch, 114-7
Placement, of men, *see* Selection
Plateaus, learning, 223-6
Polling, *see* Public opinion
Position sense, air-sickness, 161-3
  balance, 151-4, 159f.
  eye-movements, 158
  mechanism, 154-61
  vertical perception, 151-4
Projection, 357-9
Propaganda, 17f.
  audience, 440f.
  black, 441f.
  broadcasting, 442
  combat, 442-4
  factual basis, 439
  leaflets, 443f.
  newspapers, 443f.
  purpose, 438f.
  techniques, 439-46
  timing, 439f.
  truth, 438
  See also Psychological warfare,
    Public opinion
Psychological warfare, 16-18
  defense, 446f.
  mental surrender, 430f.
  victory formula, 444-6
  See also Propaganda, Public
    opinion
Psychology, combat, 11-23
  individual differences, 19f.
  military, 11-23
Public opinion, applause, 437
  interviewing, 436
  listening, 436
  mass observation, 436
  military unit, 437f.
  newspapers, 436f.
  polling, 432-6
  radio audiences, 437
  sampling, 433-5
  See also Propaganda, Psycho-
    logical warfare

Qualification card, 185
Quarrels, morale, 325f.

Races, inherited differences,
    398-401
  intelligence, 400f.
  physical differences, 399f.
  prejudice, 403-6
  psychological differences, 400-2
  skin color, 404
  See also National differences
Radio mechanics, G.C.T., 190f.
Rage, see Anger
Range-finding, contour break, 51-3
  stereoscopic, 48-55
  use of star, 54f.
Reaction time, 179
Reading, organization, 217-20
  rapid, 216-20
  visual, 218
  See also Learning, Study,
    Training
Recognition, night, 71f.
  odors, 143-6
  visual, 76-9, 85-8
Religion, fear, 304
  national differences, 408-10
  women, 409f.
Retina, 32-4
  cones, 60-5
  rods, 60-5
Retinal disparity, 48-51
Rods, retina, 60-5
Rotation, after-effects, 157f.
  perception, 154-61
Rumor, bait, 421
  bogey, 422
  boredom, 424
  causes, 414-8
  censorship, 426f.
  conditions, 423f.
  control, 428f.
  discrediting, 420f.
  disruption, 420
  effects, 422f.
  expectation, 424
  fear, 415-7
  frustration, 424

Rumor, *continued*
  kinds, 421f.
  lack of information, 424
  mongering, 427f.
  motives, 415-7
  panic, 394
  perennial, 424-6
  persistent, 424f.
  pipe-dream, 421
  smoke screen, 420
  spread, 415-8
  true, 418f.
  uncritical, 413
  use in war, 419-21
  wedge-driving, 422

Saturation, color, 81
Scotopic vision, 60-70
Scout duty, 164-74
Sea-sickness, see Air-sickness
Selection, aptitude tests, 192-4
  educated men, 181f.
  General Classification Test,
    187-92
  individual differences, 178-82
  interviews, 186f., 196f.
  leaders, 379-82
  methods, 186-99
  personality, 195-7
  placement, 176-8
  preferences, 196f.
  qualification card, 185
  trade tests, 194f.
  See also Jobs
Semicircular canals, 154-61
Sensation, see Direction sense,
    Hearing, Perception, Position
    sense, Sight, Smell
Sex, control, 341f.
  derived needs, 336-8, 341f.
  fantasy, 338
  food, 334f.
  homosexuality, 340f.
  instruction, 335f.
  masturbation, 339f.
  promiscuity, 336f.
  substitutes, 336-8, 341f.

Sight, acuity, 24-6
    aerial perspective, 42
    aid to action, 57-9
    airplane landing, 53f.
    binocular, 44-8
    brain function, 34
    camouflage, 76-9, 85-107
    color, 79-85
    color blindness, 107-113
    contrast, 72f.
    convergence and distance, 44f.
    dazzle, 29f.
    eye mechanism, 30-4
    fatigue, 34-9
    glare, 28-30
    interposition, 42
    light and shade, 26f.
    military use, 24-113
    monocular, 41-4
    motion and distance, 42f.
    night vision, 60-75
    observation, 37-9
    perceiving speed, 55-7
    perspective, 42
    range-finding, 48-55
    retinal disparity, 48-51
    scotopia, 60-70
    shadows and depth, 43
    sharpness, 24-6
    size and distance, 41f.
    stereoscopy, 45-51
    See also Eye
Sleep, daily rhythm, 262, 267
    day-workers, 267
    deprivation, 262-6
    keeping awake, 262-4
    need, 266f.
    night-workers, 267
    restoration, 265-7
    See also Fatigue
Smell, camouflage, 149f.
    chemical sense, 143
    fatigue, 149f.
    masking, 150
    mixture, 150
    names, 143f.
    new odors, 145
    qualities, 143f.

Smell, continued
    recognition, 143-6
    sensitivity, 146
    taste, 142f.
    war gases, 146-9
Smoking, effects, 280-2
Social facilitation, 287f.
Sound, camouflage, 138f.
    direction-finders, 137f.
    distance, 119
    frequency, 114-8
    localization, 133-8
    nature, 115
    See also Hearing
Spectrum, 80f.
Speech, communication, 129-33
Speed, perception of, 55-7
Spinning, perception, 154-61
Stars, telling directions, 171f.
Static sense, see Position sense
Stereoscopy, 45-51
    counter-camouflage, 104f.
Sternutators, 147
Study, distractions, 213f.
    habits, 213f.
    methods, 213-23
    solving problems, 220-2
    See also Learning, Reading,
        Training
Suggestion, mobs, 387-9
    panic, 391-3

Tank mechanics, G.C.T., 190-2
Taste, 142f.
Tea, effects, 282f.
Teaching, Army requirements,
        227f.
    individual, 229, 234-7
    insight, 229f.
    instructor, 229-34
    massed individual, 234-7
    models, 232-4
    non-essentials, 229f., 237-9, 241
    rifle fire, 235f.
    standardization, 239f.
    student instructors, 234-7
    visual aids, 232-4
    wholesale methods, 230-4

Telestereoscopy, 48-51
Temperature, effects, 269-73
Texture, camouflage, 90f.
Thresholds, hearing, 117-9
Timbre, 114f.
Tobacco, effects, 280-2
Tones, *see* Hearing
Total war, 16-18
Trade tests, 194f.
Training, combat, 245f.
    efficiency, 237-43
    plateaus, 223-6
    reading, 216-20
    speed, 208-13, 240-3
    standardization, 239f.
    See also Learning, Teaching

Ventilation, efficiency, 271
    fatigue, 260
Ventriloquism, 133f.
Vesicants, 147
Vestibular sense, *see* Position sense
Victory, psychological warfare,
    444-6
Vision, *see* Sight
Vitamins, morale, 294
    night vision, 73f.

War gases, 146-9
    sentry rules, 148f.
    table, 147
War shock, 353-6, 363-5
Women, national differences, 409f.
Work, *see* Efficiency
Worry, *see* Adjustment

Made in the USA
Middletown, DE
28 August 2024

59947999R00273